SELF-IMPROVEMENT
THROUGH
SELF-HYPNOSIS

How to use self-hypnosis as a tool to tap the immense
power of the subconscious and attain your goals.

By the same author

MODERN SCIENTIFIC HYPNOSIS

SELF-IMPROVEMENT THROUGH
SELF-HYPNOSIS

A complete programme to help you shape your own destiny.

by

R.N. SHROUT

THORSONS PUBLISHING GROUP
Wellingborough, Northamptonshire
-
Rochester, Vermont

First published June 1985
Second Impression October 1985
Third Impression July 1986

British Library Cataloguing in Publication Data

Self-improvement through self-hypnosis: a
  complete programme to help you shape your
  own destiny.
  1. Success   2. Autogenic training
  I. Title
  158'.1   BF637.S8

ISBN 0-7225-0987-1

Printed and bound in Great Britain

Dedication

This book is dedicated to Dr Charles W. Brooks, who gave unselfishly of his time during my adolescence in Decatur, Illinois (USA), to instruct me in an affirmative philosophy of life and to teach me by precept and example that 'Our treasure ships come in over calm seas.'

— Richard N. Shrout

I do not believe that we can put into anyone ideas which are not in him already. As a rule there is in everyone all sorts of good ideas, ready like tinder. But much of this tinder catches fire, or catches it successfully, only when it meets some flame or spark from the outside, i.e. from some other person. Often, too, our own light goes out, and is rekindled by some experience we go through with a fellow man. Thus we have each of us cause to think with deep gratitude of those who have lighted the flame within us. If we had before us those who have thus been a blessing to us, and could tell them how it came about, they would be amazed to learn what passed over from their life to ours.

— Albert Schweitzer, *Memoirs of Childhood and Youth*

Contents

Introduction

What will this book do for you? Everything — if you apply it! Self-improvement and inspirational books are becoming increasingly popular with the public. As Abraham Maslow pointed out in *Toward A Psychology Of Being*, there is a great difference between 'deficit motivation' and 'growth motivation'. When the struggle for the basic necessities of life is of paramount importance, there is neither time nor interest in education, leisure-time activities, or any self-actualizing programmes. Most citizens enjoy an unprecedented standard of living compared with their forebears and can turn now to the 'luxury' of various kinds of self-improvement.

In this age of extreme scientific technology, the average person tends to feel far more inadequate than a primitive man who is only confronted by the mysteries of nature. Instead of making us feel wiser and more powerful, the mysterious complexities of technology often confuse us and make us realize our basic powerlessness. The modern person's desire for personal power is reflected in types of TV entertainment which feature beings with extra-terrestrial or magical powers who can make things float in the air, read minds or disappear at will. This sort of wish-fulfilment fantasy is a pacifier for purposeless people, but serious people seek practical ways truly to better themselves.

With so many self-help books being published today, the existence of this one would not be justified unless it made a unique contribution and met a special need. There are two constant 'enemies' of successful achievement: emptiness and idleness. The 'empty' person is one without purpose, without a goal, and without necessary knowledge. The 'idle' person is one who has no plan, no blueprint to follow. Inaction or misguided activities characterize such people. They may give the appearance of keeping busy, but in reality they make no progress towards any predetermined goal.

Self-improvement books fail in their purpose if they do not meet the needs of these two kinds of people. Many books are filled with platitudes instead of helpful information and seem to be the product of hack writers who have little desire to render a genuine service. To say 'have faith' or 'be enthusiastic' without explaining how to do so is worthless. A serious flaw in such books is a *lack of plan* for the reader to follow. This book will give you both the knowledge and the plan you need to shape your personal earthly destiny.

This book is a scientific and practical one. At the risk of being misunderstood, I believe that a metaphysical orientation to the subject of hypnosis is often a hindrance rather than a help. I believe that the complex neurological and biochemical mechanisms by which ideas and mental images profoundly affect our bodies and our minds — and by extension affect all else — are beautiful object-lessons which indicate a Creator who has planned for our well-being with infinite wisdom. However, it is not at all necessary for others to agree with me, for the laws of God in nature work indiscriminately to the believer and non-believer alike. To insist on acceptance of metaphysical and spiritual presuppositions in the matter either of self-hypnosis or self-improvement is to unnecessarily handicap some people in their search for success and happiness. For this reason, this book has been written for the widest possible appeal and acceptance among readers who may prefer a somewhat more materialistic approach to the subconscious, regardless of their religious orientation or lack of it.

For those who have a meaningful religious philosophy of life, or for those particularly interested in seeking one, religious and metaphysical matters are dealt with in a special appendix at the end of the book.

To all those who seek to use their minds constructively, this book is sent forth with my sincerest best wishes.

Part One

The Person You Decide to Be

The title of this section was chosen with great care. The beginning of any successful self-improvement programme is to decide exactly the kind of person you wish to become. Many people have vague goals which reflect wishful dreaming rather than a clearly thought-out decision. It will do you little good to dream about the person you want to be unless you *decide* to become precisely that person.

Many people find it hard to make decisions of any kind. This is because they are ignorant of the available choices, or they are intimidated by the confusing number of alternatives, or because they are ignorant of the possibility that a decision can be made at all!

This is particularly true when it comes to serious attempts at self-improvement. If people are ignorant of the many ways in which self-improvement is possible, or inhibited when faced with too many choices, they remain frozen in indecision. More seriously, they do not realize the importance of making their own decisions in the matter. They mistakenly labour under the delusion that life is what it is by reason of heredity and environment alone. They feel that due to their parents, their upbringing, or their present circumstances of life, they have no alternative to the way they live. It simply does not occur to them that they have any decision in the matter. They do not know they can take charge of life by making the right kind of decisions.

The improvement of oneself is obviously a worthy goal in which most people are willing to express a mild interest, yet few people do serious thinking about it. It is only those sincere people who decide as well as dream who ever attain their goals.

Three characteristics of idle and empty dreamers who never decide to improve themselves are *failure, boredom and drabness*. Their need may lead them to enrol in certain classes, read books or join study groups *if it is convenient* to do so, but without decision and firm resolve it is impossible for them ever to approximate to their dreamy goals.

Their lives are characterized by failure in that, failing to change themselves, they fail to change anything of consequence in their lives. Bound by habitual indecision, they are doomed to suffer habitual failures. Lacking either the knowledge or the willingness to make life-changing decisions, they become so accustomed to failure that they come to accept it as a permanent fixture. Failure and indecision guarantee a miserable *status quo*.

Lack of decision to change means that things will stay the same, and the sameness of things breeds boredom. When there is an unwillingness to make the kinds of decisions that could really change things, then this habitual reluctance ensures that dismal boredom will continue.

A life of boring failure becomes drab, colourless, dull. It is precisely because of this lack of colour, flair or sparkle that many people awaken to the need for self-improvement. However, if they fail to realize that the very drabness, boredom and failure they experience is the result of a simple indecision to change, then it is unlikely that they will make any decision at all.

Dreaming about self-improvement is futile unless it leads to decision. And that decision is not merely 'to change', but to change in specific and particular ways. In the most literal sense, it is essential that you must decide (in sufficient detail) the kind of person you wish to become. The purpose of this book is to help you decide with sufficient clarity to initiate and implement a programme of self-improvement that cannot fail.

Thus it is that you must *decide* the person you are going to become. The following pages are designed to help you do just that. Study them thoughtfully. The truths contained in them will lead you to contemplate, meditate, and constructively dream about the person you can become through the application of these principles. But before you make one real step in the direction of your goal, you must decide and determine within yourself that you will not be denied that goal.

Self-Improvement through Self-Hypnosis

A number of studies analysing the reasons behind job and career failures indicate that by far the main cause lies in the realm of personality defects rather than the lack of knowledge or job skills. In stable economic times, the inability to get along with others is behind most job firings, resignations and demotions. Therefore, for economic and vocational reasons alone, we should be vitally interested in following an effective self-improvement programme.

The school drop-out is a matter of concern to the government as well as to parents. The sixteen-year-old who leaves school is often characterized by personality inadequacy as well as academic inadequacy. It is the inability to adapt to authority, adjust to frustration, or co-operate with peers that in turn leads to the learning problems — which in turn feed the personality frustrations. There are many college students who become drop-outs because of personality problems which are completely unrelated to their scholastic abilities or disabilities. The person who drops out of educational opportunities frequently compounds his or her problem because the life-long sense of failure and incompleteness from the interrupted education contributes to his or her feelings of inadequacy over the years. Education is really a life-long process, and when we allow our personality problems to impede our progress, we are creating failures which will worsen our personalities. For the sake of our continued growth and acquisition of helpful knowledge, we should place a high priority on self-improvement programmes.

Marital discord and many divorces are rooted solely in the personality problems of one or both partners. The money troubles, mental cruelties, in-law problems, etc., are superficial rationalizations indicative of the incompatibilities of inadequate personalities. Immature and neurotic people are always incompatible in relationships which require sacrifice, compromise and responsibility. The unhappiness of such unions is often unfairly perpetuated in the lives of their children, whose personalities are crippled as they are inexorably drawn into a cycle of tragic misery. The Bible says that sometimes the sins of the parents are visited upon the children even unto the fourth and fifth generations. Parental ignorance and personality defects naturally tend to be inflicted on their helpless and impressionable children. One of the greatest problems affecting Western civilization is the breakdown of the home and family, with its dire effects upon future generations who lack the loving nurture of well-balanced adults. A widespread utilization of an effective self-improvement programme needs no further justification.

This brief sketch of the scope of personality problems is given merely to expand the too narrow view that, although serious to the person involved, such problems are relatively unimportant to others. Every personality problem influences countless other lives through the interpersonal relationships inherent in a civilized world, and is projected into an ever-widening society through the family, school, business and social contacts of the individual. Social disintegration and individual personality disintegration are inextricably entwined and the delineation between cause and effect becomes blurred in the miasma of collective as well as individual misery. The seriousness of personality problems should not be underestimated and the importance of correcting these deficiencies cannot be overestimated.

In the so-called 'me generation' of the 1960s, 'self-improvement programmes' were looked upon as luxuries, escapes from boredom, or self-centred exercises in self-indulgence. But true self-improvement programmes are now becoming a matter of increasing interest to people in the modern world. The proliferation of adult education courses, self-help books and public speaking courses attest to the need and desire of many people to work seriously at improving themselves, not only to make themselves better people, but to make the world a better place.

The improvement of skills, the attainment of knowledge and cultural enrichment all comprise worthy objectives in and of themselves, but the greatest need for improvement lies in the direction of building healthy, well-balanced personalities. It takes a great deal of sincerity to seek to change oneself in any real sense of the word.

One's natural defensiveness makes change painful and threatening, and there are cynics who think all 'self-improvement' is compounded of delusion and hypocrisy. It could well be argued that this sort of scepticism is either a defensive rationalization or an imputation of bitterness towards sincere folk who seek to help themselves to a better life adjustment. Probably every person in moments of honest self-contemplation experiences 'moments of truth' too painful or too intimate to share with others. These insights are certainly repressed or ignored by most people, but there are individuals who, driven by either determination or desperation, are genuinely willing to improve themselves by any method or means. Self-improvement is not an illusion, but a real possibility attainable by a planned programme utilizing many methods. Hypnotherapeutic guidance and planned self-hypnosis are the most powerful and effective tools in a serious self-improvement programme.

There seem to be two basic components in conscious personality development: self-knowledge and self-discipline. To neglect either of them is to guarantee failure in advance, regardless of the method. The superficiality of many self-help books ensures their ineffectiveness, because the emphasis is on 'fast, easy and sure-fire'. These adjectives can apply only when the techniques of self-discipline are imposed over a foundation of self-knowledge.

Various psychological testing methods have been devised which in the hands of testing psychologists can add immeasureably to the scope and depth of one's self-knowledge. A thorough testing of abilities and interests on an objective basis and an exploration of personal psychodynamics through projective tests can provide a blueprint for programmed self-improvement. Such psychological evaluations, in written form, are well worth the nominal expenditure to those in earnest in their quest for self-knowledge. Hypnoanalysis is a most potent aid in delving deeply into the causative and contributory factors behind many personality problems, but unless the problem is extremely serious, neither it nor formal testing is necessary in a simple self-help programme.

Will-power alone is an inadequate force for most people in changing their lives. Self-discipline predicated solely on will-power is generally a frustrating disappointment for the majority of people. Even when prepared with a schema for their efforts and motivated by sincere desires, the burden of achievement through will-power alone is too much for them. People with personality problems of any significance naturally lack the strength of character to discipline their admittedly inadequate behaviour patterns continually. It is to this inherent hopelessness (the inadequacy of will-power) in the problem of self-improvement that hypnosis brings a significant measure of encouragement.

Emile Coué formulated his 'laws of suggestion' in the 1920s, and little has been discovered since then to modify or add to them. The basic tenet was that the imagination is stronger than the will and that whenever the two are in conflict, the imagination invariably wins! For example, if one's imagination pictures fattening foods as desirable, then will-power will fail to keep one on a diet. Only when the imagination pictures the forbidden foods as representing literal fat or as being totally artificial and disease-producing, is the will-power effective at all in avoiding them. The principles Coué discovered are clear: imagination is stronger than the will, and only when the two are in agreement can there be any successful outcome.

Inferiority feelings, timidity, and other personality defects are rooted in, and perpetuated by, the power of imagination. For that reason alone, such problems cannot be countered effectively by will-power alone. Will-power is a function of the conscious mind, and it is always at the mercy of the subconscious. It is upon this elementary truth that the techniques of hypnotherapy and self-hypnosis are founded, and because of their utilization and manipulation of the force of imagination upon the subconscious, they are the most effective means of implementing one's will-power. Self-hypnosis thereby deserves supreme consideration in any effective programme of self-improvement.

One's habits represent either the most efficient structuring of time and the expenditure of energy, or a form of bondage to maladaptive conditioned responses which continually increase the level of frustration. People with personality problems habitually act and react in ways which offend or irk other people, whose natural response to the offensive and irksome habits serves as a rebuff to such persons. This undesirable response of hostility or indifference on the part of others to the annoying habit patterns is the cause of much unhappiness to those who suffer the bondage of their own defective personality habits. Their habitual ways of interacting with others constantly produces irritation, resentments and misunderstandings. The friction-producing habit may be anything from a physical mannerism to a mental attitude of superiority or bigotry. A large number of people are totally insensitive to the ill feeling generated by their own peculiar patterns of thought and behaviour. They do not see their faults, rudeness, intolerance, impatience and general unsociability. When their faults are discovered and defined, many sincerely motivated people are still unable to change.

Clear identification of the problem and insight into its causes do not always provide the ways and means to improvement. Self-hypnosis offers a way to mobilize the imagination in the achievement of goals (most people perceive this as a 'strengthening of will-power') and maintain motivation at an optimum level during the self-improvement programme.

Simply stated, a reconditioning of one's emotional responses can be achieved through self-hypnosis. Negative reactions of inferiority, shyness, timidity, etc., can be replaced with positive virtues of confidence, courage, cheerfulness, tolerance, kindness, etc. This is achieved relatively simply through self-hypnosis and should not be thought of in the grossly misunderstood context of mere 'symptom substitution', for the theoretical framework which justifies the method follows current behaviour therapy and learning theory. Such negative reactions, although habitual in practice and in the nature of conditioned reflexes, are by no means to be considered as unchangeable or permanent traits. Their alteration is compatible with the laws of learning theory which affect behaviour, and consistent with the testimony of innumerable people who have in fact found self-improvement through self-hypnosis exceptionally effective.

The Miracle that Is You

There are two concepts about mankind that seem opposed at first glance, and yet are both necessary for group or individual progress. One is the concept of *brotherhood* based on an intellectual appreciation of the underlying *unity* of the human race. The other concept is that of *individuality* which is based on an intellectual appreciation of the incredible diversity within the human family.

Brotherhood and individuality are our emotionally coloured values which are based on scientific facts about the unity of the human race and the uniqueness of each human being. They are not mere sentimental beliefs; they are founded upon incontrovertible fact.

A study of anthropology reveals that mankind represents a unity amid the diversity of climates and cultures. In spite of the barriers of language and different societies, race and religion, humans show themselves to be basically the same throughout the world. From savagery to civilization and from totems to technologies, man demonstrates himself to be similar to other men throughout the centuries. Improvements in travel and communications have resulted in an increasing awareness on the part of civilized man that he cannot successfully support any claims to superiority over others just because of superficial differences. The unity of the human race is an indisputable fact of science. In spite of the horrible demonstrations throughout history of that classic phrase 'man's inhumanity to man', the fact remains that all men are brothers both in their goodness and in their evil. No person is subhuman; it is just that human nature can sometimes become a dirty, degraded and disagreeable thing. Our human nature seems compounded of a mixture of animal nature along with special dimensions of the devilish and the angelic. In both its glories of lofty accomplishment as well as in its defilement and villainy, the human race reflects a unity that ought to be an embarrassment to the prejudiced beholder.

From the intellectual acceptance of this scientific fact of human unity, an ethical consequence has evolved: a sense of brotherhood. It is both a natural and a moral truth that all of us are indeed 'brothers and sisters under the skin'. Because the unity of the human race is indisputable, the logical correlate of human brotherhood is also indisputable.

The acceptance of this concept of brotherhood is absolutely essential to either group or individual progress, for it is only when brotherhood is accepted that our exploitation and aggressiveness is realized to be eventually self-defeating, and the advantages and possibilities of co-operative goodwill become more compellingly attractive.

The second great concept about humanity which is also necessary for progress is that of individuality. It is this concept which must be thoroughly understood and wholeheartedly accepted before you can make real progress in a planned programme of self-improvement. Just as the tragedies of prejudice and bigotry exist when people do not realize the unity and brotherhood of the human race, so also an ignorance of the individuality and uniqueness of every human being results in the tragedy of defeated, negative and wasted lives. Self-improvement is an unattainable ideal until you know beyond a shadow of a doubt that you are *unique*, for that uniqueness is your hope of unlimited potential.

Everyone is alike — and everyone is different! Although apparently a contradiction, both propositions are scientifically true and philosophically valid. It is this dual truth which provides the fuel and the fire for those who are serious in a determined desire to change themselves and become what they want to be.

Sadly, the vast majority of the human race is content with the *status quo*, the sameness of things. As long as they feel comfortable in conformity, their lives will reflect the same purposelessness, drabness, unhappiness and failure.

Such people have learned the lesson of unity and brotherhood well, but it has made them not only more civilized but also more complacent. Unbalanced by a commitment to the complementary truths of uniqueness and individuality, it has caused them to measure themselves only by the standards of others. It has inhibited them from becoming different, even in good ways, from the herd of other nice but complacent folks.

The unity and brotherhood of the race is your heritage — but your individuality and uniqueness is your destiny!

For a good part of your life you have been reminded that you are just like others (no better and no worse), and this has been good to the extent that it has cultivated within you a sense of brotherhood. It has had a civilizing, socializing, humanizing influence on you. However, unless you remain a bigot who believes in the superiority of 'your' people, you don't need any more emphasis on unity and brotherhood. You've heard it enough.

It is to be hoped that now you will permit your individuality to be characterized by a high-level differentiation (uniqueness) rather than by a low-level differentiation (sameness). The Bible says: 'If the light that is in thee be darkness, how great is that darkness!' This could be paraphrased here as: 'If your uniqueness is manifested only by a sameness, how mediocre is your individuality!'

Some people are so neurotic and insecure that their only goal in life is to scramble up to the level of common mediocrity where they can feel secure in sameness and conformity to the average person. This sort of person may need sympathetic counselling or perhaps some form of psychotherapy — in short, a therapeutic rather than a self-improvement programme. If you need professional help in your life adjustment, then by all means get it. But if you want to rise above average, then help yourself. The observation that 'the average man is considerably below average' is probably too cynical, but your aim in a serious self-improvement programme should be to aim as high as you possibly can, certainly far above 'average'.

It is a fact that people are unique as they are, and in terms of their potential to become better. Because your uniqueness as a human being is the basis for your unrealized potential, you must be absolutely persuaded that you are indeed a very special person in your own right. To prepare for a serious self-improvement programme in which you desire to be above average in most respects and definitely superior in others, you must have a clear understanding of your unique individuality and the tremendous potential inherent in that fact.

Physical Individuality

It is obvious that racial and national groups have physical characteristics that distinguish them from other races, nationalities and ethnic groups. It is equally true that certain group identities carry such distinctive appearances that one is often able to guess the larger group to which an individual belongs. In spite of this, it is true nonetheless that each person in the world is physically distinct from every other in many ways.

When one looks beyond the surface similarities of members of a group, it becomes obvious that each individual is physically different from others within his own group, just as he is distinct from those outside of it. It is a rare person who hasn't enthusiastically greeted someone in a crowd only to be chagrined at finding out the person was a total stranger who bore only a superficial resemblance to a friend. Even when people have so-called 'doubles' or 'look-alikes', the similarity is really only very superficial. When the person moves or speaks, the illusion is broken and the dissimilarities stand out in sharp contrast.

It is interesting to note that early attempts to formulate a system of criminal identification were based on a series of body measurements (such as the length of certain fingers, the nose, upper lip, ear, etc.) in the hope that such a combination of measurements would be distinctive enough to provide an infallible identification. (It is possible that many people have the same measurement between the first two knuckles of the second finger on the left hand, but when combined with the length of the nose, the mouth, the shin bone, etc., the odds increase against the probability that two people would be found with identical measurements in every respect.) No doubt this would have been adequate if enough anatomical features were measured with equal accuracy by the different people who made them. It was a cumbersome method, however, a fact which detracted from its basic ingenuity. For that reason, fingerprint identification soon replaced the anthropological measurements as an apparently infallible method of distinguishing between individuals worldwide.

It is a good reminder sometimes to examine your hand and realize that the little lines on any *one* of your fingertips is not duplicated on any other finger of anyone else in the entire world! This is a commonplace reminder of your physical uniqueness among your fellow humans.

The uniqueness of a fingerprint is being used to build self-esteem in kindergarten children in the USA through the 'I. M. Thumbody' programmes. The children are taught how name tags are used at certain adult functions. They know that they are identified by their names, but other children may have the same name. It is explained that even if everyone had the same name, each one would still be an individual, a 'somebody' important. They are given a name tag with the slogan 'I. M. Thumbody' above their thumbprints and their names. The I. M. Thumbody (I Am Somebody) programme thus emphasizes each child's unique personal identity. (To identify missing children better, many police departments in the United States offer parents a voluntary fingerprinting service for children. This is made more appealing to the children by giving them 'I. M. Thumbody Award' certificates.)

It's also believed that 'voice prints' (the visual recording of electrical stimuli of the human voice) may be unique for each individual. The patterns that can be seen of the retina of the eye when viewed through special instruments are also believed to be infallible identification data. Forensic scientists are constantly discovering new ways of cataloguing individual differences in body fluid samples such as blood, saliva or semen through electronic microscopy of enzymes, chromosomes, etc. Compared to techniques which will be developed in the future, our present methods are relatively crude, but it is clear that there are innumerable differences between individuals which are almost incomprehensible.

Look again at the tiny lines on your fingertip. Realize that they show you to be different from every human being on the face of the earth — living or dead, or yet to be born. You are indeed unique!

Less measurable but no less important are the differences between individuals in their perceptions of the external world. We seldom think of it, but it is clear that no two people can stand in exactly the same place at the same time. Photographs taken at the same time by two people looking at the same object will not be identical, because the perspective is naturally always slightly different. Because no two people can be in the same spot at the same moment, no two people can ever see exactly the same thing at the same time! Each person perceives things from his or her point in space and time, and that is unique to each person at any given moment. Thus we can truly say that each person has a unique perception of the environment.

Temperamental Individuality
In all probability, no two people ever have exactly the same subjective experiences. This is hard for some to grasp because it is a basic assumption that 'everyone knows' how it feels to love, hate, be angry or jealous, etc., but it is far from provable that any two people actually ever feel the same emotions in the same ways. Everyone has had a headache, but no two people have ever experienced the same headache. No one can ever experience another person's pain. We know what an apple tastes like, but we can never know what other people taste when they taste an apple, even the same apple! The same obviously applies to every sensation or emotion.

It was a desire to emphasize the unity and brotherhood of the race, not the uniqueness of the individual, which caused Shakespeare in the *Merchant of Venice* to have Shylock say:

'I am a Jew. Hath not a Jew eyes? Hath not a Jew hands, organs, dimensions, senses, affections, passions? Fed with the same food, hurt with the same weapons, subject to the same diseases, healed by the same means, warmed and cooled by the same winter and summer as a Christian is? If you prick us do we not bleed? If you tickle us do we not laugh? If you poison us do we not die? And if you wrong us shall we not revenge? If we are like you in the rest, we will resemble you in that.'

Shylock is indeed one of the most unattractive characters in all literature, but this passage is not, as some would have it, an example of anti-Semitism. On the contrary, its purpose is to show that everyone shares alike in the human condition, including the negative emotion of revenge. It could as easily have read: 'Hath not an Eskimo (or any other category you could name) eyes? Etc.' It says nothing about the uniqueness of any individual's emotions.

In spite of the fact that all human beings have identical needs and drives and react to life in rather conforming and predictable ways, it would seem certain also that in the apparent similarities there would exist infinite varieties as well. Although there is nothing more universal than pain, a little reflection indicates that no people ever experience the same pain. Neither do they experience the same hates and loves. *Your subjective life has always been, and will continue to be, as unique as your fingerprints!*

'Positional psychology' is the school of thought which emphasizes that the order in which children are born within the family structure has a profound influence on their personality development. That is to say, the parents' expectations and treatment of the oldest child cannot be identical with their handling of the youngest one, and so forth. This leads to the startling conclusion that each child experiences a different environment within the same family!

Furthermore, within each family unit there exists not only a relationship between two people (the parents) but also between two generations (the parents and the children). If you take time to consider it thoughtfully, you will realize that no two children actually have the same environment in any significant way. Parents are sincere when they say 'We treat all the kids alike,' but they are voicing an obvious psychological absurdity.

I myself have an older brother, and the above truths were brought dramatically in focus during a recent family reunion. We found ourselves discussing certain aspects of our childhood together, but the longer we talked, the more puzzled we became. We could not seem to agree on anything pertaining to our childhood together! It was as if we had lived in different houses in different towns. We couldn't agree on what kind of town it was, what kind of neighbours we had, the kind of people our grandparents were, and so on. In fact, we scarcely agreed on anything at all! We looked at each other in astonishment, wondering why we couldn't recall or describe our own mutual childhood experiences.

We figured it out. You see, there has always been a six-year difference in our ages, and although I once childishly believed

I would someday grow up fast enough that we would be the same age, I soon learned it could never be. No matter how old I get, he will always be six years older. As we compared notes on the various events while living with our parents, my brother saw through the eyes of a twelve-year-old the 'same' things I was recalling through the eyes of a six-year-old, and so on throughout all our reminiscences. For this reason alone, we have always lived in different worlds, so to speak. (We are quite unlike, something for which we both profess to be profoundly grateful!)

Because of its position in the family and the fact that it necessarily views the environment from a different level of maturation, each child in a family is distinctly individual. Each child also differs in its need for demonstrations of affection, its feelings of security, its reactions to stress, and in a thousand other ways. It is a wise parent or teacher who is alert to these unique patterns of personality needs and development within any group of children.

A husband and wife who live in ideal compatibility, intimately sharing bed and board and all else with a high degree of 'togetherness', cannot really experience the same environment. (That is to say, the 'same' environment they seem to share is quite 'distinct' in the way it is perceived by each of them.) If you are observant, you'll notice that people who live together do not even eat the same diet. To be sure, the groceries are bought, cooked and served routinely, by an almost unchanging ritual. However, they do not eat the same sized portions, perhaps one always skips a certain vegetable, one salts the food while the other peppers it, each drinks a different beverage, and so forth.

If married couples do not even eat the same diet, it should be little wonder they do not think the same thoughts. To be sure, being exposed to the same stimuli at home, it is natural at times their thoughts will so coincide that they will be inclined to think they are communicating with telepathy. ('Why, isn't that amazing! I was just going to say the same thing!') However, there will also be innumerable times when communication between them breaks down entirely, even though each makes a real effort to be understood and to be understanding.

When the Creator made the human race, 'male and female created He them'. Accompanying the obvious physical distinctions there is a fantastically complex biochemical system which not only distinguishes between the sexes in function, but also creates emotional differences which are further differentiated by the roles and expectations of society into classifications of behaviour we usually think of as attributes of 'femininity' and 'masculinity'.

When I married, I chose a charming bride of a different nationality and language. In the serious discussions during our courtship and engagement, we could not ignore the fact that in all our future discussions one of us would be speaking in an acquired language. What might have become a problem in our relationship was headed off early when my wife expressed her fear that our language difference might be a persistent barrier to understanding. I replied with humour and conviction that we should just agree to attribute any differences and difficulties of our life together to the basic fact that I was a man and she was a woman, and that alone would be a perfectly adequate explanation for any misunderstandings which might arise, and that distinction was a common ingredient in every couple's marriage. We enjoy what we consider to be an ideal marriage, I might add, having discovered that love speaks a language of its own! Whenever I hear a husband remark: 'That's just like a woman!' or a wife say: 'Isn't that just like a man?' I am tempted to reply: 'What else would you prefer to be married to?' I confess I usually yield to that temptation.

Yes, there certainly is a difference between men and women, and in spite of those who advocate a unisex society, there always will be. It's hard to imagine anyone whose basic life assumptions would be shaken by that fact. The only normal reaction to that simple truth is the humorous 'Viva la difference!' It is mentioned here only because it is a factor that makes you a unique individual.

Character Differences

Your background, experiences and training are really quite different from everyone else's, and this gives you a unique character. One's morals, ethics and values are the result of highly individual life experiences and thought which could not possibly have been duplicated by any other human being.

Although the expression of these inner values may be conventional and codified in ways common to many others, still it is the inner processes and the intensity that led to them which add up to form your character. The degree and quality of the goodness and badness, the honesty and the deceit, the principles and the opportunism which comprise your character are truly yours and yours alone!

A Unique Heredity

There is a genetic basis for your unique individuality that is easily understood from a scientific point of view. The concept of Individuality is not based on questionable theory, but on undeniable scientific fact. It is important that you have an intellectual as well as an emotional conviction that you are indeed a unique individual who is utterly distinct from every other person who is living or dead, or yet to be born!

This unique individuality began, not at the age of twenty-one or at puberty, or even at the hour of birth, but *at the moment you were conceived*! Upon the union of egg and sperm in a split second of time, the infinite complexities which comprise the undreamed-of potentials of your personality were brought into being.

The belief in genetic determinism, which was a basic presupposition to Darwin and Freud, has never been popular with the public. The expansion of social welfare programmes was predicated on the assumption that the environment was the determining factor in personality development. The public has often felt that to overemphasize the importance of heredity might tend to detract from the worthy programmes of social reform. Also, the doctrine of genetic determinism has been abused by those who have distorted it for racial or political aggrandizement (such as Hitler's `Aryan super-race' nonsense), causing it to be extremely distasteful to all sensitive people.

The science of genetics and heredity does not offer justification for any group's pretentions to superiority, and should never be used as an excuse to circumvent environmental changes in the interest of human welfare. The fact is that neither heredity nor environment are the sole determinants of personality and behaviour; rather it is a synthesis of both, plus the subjective reaction to that combination, which gives us the best understanding of human nature.

However, it is a fact that the *uniqueness that is you* is based upon the hereditary combination you received from your parental ancestry at the very instant of conception. Hereditary characteristics are transmitted through genes and chromosomes. Genes are protein molecules containing a most vital constituent known as DNA. There are countless types of genes, each with a specific function. Genes can reproduce themselves with fantastic rapidity. By the time a baby is born, it has an established 26 trillion cells, with the same genes in each cell. The total number of genes is unknown, but present estimates range from 40,000 to 60,000 or more genes in the 23 *pairs* of chromosomes that go into *every* human cell. These chromosomes are strings of genes and there are 46 (23 from the father and 23 from the mother) in every human cell.

The male sperm and the female egg alike contain genes which are the exact replicas of those which were received from their parental ancestors at the time of the man's and woman's own conception. When a man produces sperms, there is a process by which for every two sperms, his 23 pairs of chromosomes sort out into two groups, with only one chromosome of each pair going in each group, around which a single sperm then takes shape. Thus, every sperm contains 23 *single* chromosomes. A similar process takes place in the female so that each egg carries only 23 single chromosomes. Each male sperm carries only half of the father's chromosomes, and each egg of the mother carries only half of hers. A woman produces only one egg a month for about thirty years, but a man is constantly producing sperms.

Thus, one sperm might get a combination of chromosomes quite different from every other sperm. It is therefore possible for a man to produce sperms with 16,777,216 different chromosome combinations. The same number of combinations could exist in any given egg. Together the sperms and eggs of any couple could produce *any* of about 300 million million (300,000,000,000,000) different chromosome combinations.

In the act of intercourse, the male propels into the female 50-500 million sperms, which are so small millions could be packed onto a pinhead. In a single ejaculation there are enough sperms to impregnate every fertile woman in the world! (Not all fertile women in the world are fertile at the same time.) The point is that *only one of the sperms fertilizes the egg.*

The numbers are mind-boggling. Thus, it is easily seen that, genetically speaking, each person born into this world is *truly unique* in every sense of the word.

A Walking Miracle

The human body is incredibly complex in both its design and function. Every cell holds unfathomed secrets beyond our dreams. Scientists have hardly begun to understand the intricacies of the bio-electro-chemical process which maintain and direct physical and mental life. The mechanisms by which every gland and system functions within the organism (including the processes of thought) require a continuing sequence of miraculous sub-microscopic events.

You are a walking, breathing miracle. Even as you read this page, your eyes scanning the words, your brain interpreting the printed symbols into their thought-equivalents by drawing upon your past education and experience which is somehow coded in certain brain cells, a trillion miracles are simultaneously occurring within you. These simultaneous miracles, taking place every millisecond of your life, go on continuously every second, minute, hour, day, week, month and year of your entire lifetime — *without your conscious knowledge*!

Contemplation of these tremendous truths will lead you to a new awareness of the *miracle that is you*! Never again will you feel unimportant or insignificant. Nature has packaged within you, through countless ancestors, the miraculous mechanisms which maintain and direct your life. In each cell of your body exist incomprehensible mysteries and undreamed-of potentials. You are not a mere lump of clay mass-produced on a cosmic assembly line. You are a unique product of the human race and you should be aware of it and rejoice in it. Realizing this to be an incontrovertible fact, you will find a new enjoyment in daily life, and your dreams of tomorrow should know no limits once you are firmly convinced of your uniqueness and individuality!

With the two concepts of brotherhood and individuality clearly understood and firmly fixed in your consciousness, you should be able to recognize both your unity and your uniqueness *in relation to others*. This, plus an expanding awareness of the miracle-like basis of every moment of your life, should condition your mind for greater insight into yourself so you can prepare scientifically for self-improvement of the highest quality.

The ability and the potential of deciding your future success, health and happiness is within your power! The very fact that you are reading this book in the present is undoubtedly the result of your past, but it can become a pivotal point as you plan the future. You have reached a new stage in the cause-and-effect chain that heretofore has made your life what it now is. You can decisively introduce new causes to produce new effects for the future!

If you can understand what you are reading, you certainly have the mentality to define and decide your future. If you had the motivation to obtain this book, you also should have the motivation to put your plan into action. This book will help you do that, but you must be confident of your ability to put the plan into action once it is clear in your mind.

The Self You Know

'Know Thyself!' has been the philosophers' advice to people for many centuries. They apparently supposed that mere self-knowledge would lead to happiness. Psychotherapy is designed to give people insights into their personalities and problems. There is an assumption most of us have that if we only knew ourselves, our problems would vanish. Unfortunately, this does not always seem to be so. It is an indispensable part of the formula, but something still is missing. Many people who have undergone extensive psychoanalysis have reported that they worry much less about their problems, but the problems are still there. Even accounting for the 'false insights' (which are really convincing falsehoods the patient unconsciously devises as a way of maintaining his defences to decoy the therapist and himself away from the real truth), there is still reason to question whether intellectual understanding alone goes very far towards achieving any kind of lasting adjustment.

To know oneself is not easy. If it were, everyone would do it. In fact, in a certain sense, it is impossible to know oneself completely. Exactly what 'self' are we in fact ever capable of knowing? To truly know the 'self' in the ontological sense is probably impossible, even though this 'self' or 'soul' is real in the sense that it exists. The nature of the true self (the ontological self or soul) is beyond our real knowledge. We may believe in it and philosophize about it, but our lack of knowledge prevents us from saying anything for certain about it. This problem was recognized by Biblical writers who usually used the word 'heart' to refer to the ontological self. It not only remained undefined, but it was recognized as being essentially beyond the capabilities of human knowledge to describe properly. If a reference may be made to the ancient wisdom of the Old Testament prophets, the observation of Jeremiah is of interest in this regard:

> The heart is deceitful above all things,
> and desperately wicked: Who can know it?
>   (Jeremiah 17:9)

The verse goes on to teach us that only God can know the heart, the ontological self or soul. For this reason, the main thrust of Biblical teaching is that we should never judge another person's soul or heart. Only God has the knowledge to do that. We cannot even judge or know our own heart, for the duplicity and defensiveness of the inner self (whatever it really is) seems to make it inaccessible to conscious analysis. Psychoanalysts call this duplicity and defensiveness 'unconscious ego defence mechanisms', and theologians call it 'original sin' or the 'Adamic nature'. Perhaps we can save ourselves a great deal of time by accepting the assertion that the ontological or metaphysical self or soul is, *in the very nature of things*, unknowable.

There is a 'self' we can know, however, and thus if we are willing to be practical and confine our inquiry to that which is knowable, we can make great strides in our study of self-improvement. 'Know thyself' becomes a possibility if we limit our inquiry to this 'self'.

The self we can know is called the 'phenomenological self'. This is merely the self which we perceive, or to be more exact, the 'selves' we perceive. We all have a self-concept, which is really our own opinion of ourselves. There are psychological tests which claim to measure this self-concept in several ways, such as: physical self, moral and ethical self, family self, social self and personal self. In other words, there are facets to the many-sided phenomenological self which are knowable. The overall self-concept can be broken down into these minor categories in which we conceive of ourselves. All these ways in which you perceive yourself in relationship to your various environments (as you have come to experience them) add up to your self-concept.

To illustrate, if you were asked to describe yourself, you probably would not respond with mere statistical information about your birthplace and date of birth, your height and weight, colour of hair and eyes, and a description of the clothes you are wearing. If you did, the information would sound exactly like the 'missing persons' reports or the 'wanted' posters for criminals which the police circulate. This kind of physical data may be of great help when authorities are searching for a particular body, but it is not the kind of information which reveals anything about yourself.

That simply isn't the kind of answer you give someone who says 'Tell me about yourself.' You realize that the person isn't interested in that kind of description. No matter how much of that type of information you give, it simply doesn't answer 'Tell me about yourself.' It is a meaningful question which requires a more meaningful answer.

When you are asked to describe yourself, or when you think of an answer to the question 'Who am I?', you probably respond somewhat as follows: 'I am a man/woman, white/black/oriental/ hispanic, and I am *x* years old. I am from the lower/middle/upper class. I am single/married/divorced/widowed, and I am well-educated/or have a limited education, etc.' However, you would soon sense that this doesn't answer the question either.

You would feel dissatisfied to be described so meagrely with such cold facts; you would begin to add adjectives to describe yourself better. It is important to note that the adjectives you use to describe yourself are, in fact, value judgements on your part.

For example, you would tend to say things like this: 'I am a *good* husband/wife/son/daughter, a *bad* golfer, a *sharp* businessperson, a *lousy* housekeeper, a *poor* carpenter, a *faithful* churchmember, an *honest* citizen, etc.' In other words, you have to make value judgements in describing yourself — even to yourself!

The sum total of these various facets of yourself in relationship to different aspects of your environment, *as you perceive and evaluate them*, is what is known as your 'phenomenological self'. It is this 'self' alone which is knowable. 'Perceptual psychology' is a school of thought which teaches that all our behaviour is a reflection of those things we believe will preserve, defend, maintain or enhance our phenomenological selves.

Whatever we may perceive our phenomenological selves to be, it is certain that we always tend to do those things which we feel will preserve, defend, maintain or enhance this self-concept. The reverse is also true: the things we *don't* do are left undone because we feel that doing them would *not* preserve, defend, maintain or enhance our self-concept! Everything we do or don't do is done or not done because, at all costs, we must preserve, defend, maintain or enhance the way we see ourselves!

We say that 'self-preservation is the first law of life' but this is true only in a limited sense for humans. We all know of instances where people are not governed by simple self-preservation, and this is just as true in examples of noble self-sacrifice as it is in tragic cases of self-destruction. Psychologically speaking, it is not 'self-preservation' which governs human behaviour; it is rather the 'preservation of the self-concept' which does!

It is plain that behaviour isn't changed simply by telling people what they should do. Good advice doesn't change anyone's behaviour. (There has been enough preaching and advice-giving to reform the world, but the world still isn't reformed.) To change behaviour, you must first know what a person's self-concept is. It is certain that unless the self-concept is changed, the behaviour won't change, because the behaviour must always serve to preserve, defend, maintain or enhance that particular self-concept.

'I've told you and told you, and still you do it! If I've told you once, I've told you a thousand times, and still you do it! How many times do I have to tell you?' How often we've heard that! How often have we said that? It is indeed a waste of breath to think that simply telling people will change their conduct. The most incorrigible people have had plenty of 'telling' and it still hasn't done them any good.

A few probation officers decided that some delinquent children were maladjusted because they couldn't read properly for their age levels. Special remedial reading classes were formed and the juvenile delinquents were enrolled. However, there were many drop-outs and repeat offenders among them. The experts soon discovered the reason. A big tough teenager has his own self-concept. His behaviour tends to preserve, defend, maintain or enhance that self-concept. His actions and attitudes reflect how he sees himself, not how others see him. When others expected him to learn to read by standing in front of the class and reading that 'The big red hen went cluck, cluck, cluck,' the big trouble-maker decided it was 'sissy stuff'. Before he would do that, he'd run away, steal a car, or do something else which *would* preserve, defend, maintain or enhance *his* self-concept.

The teachers, wise in the ways of perceptual psychology, devised a different type of reading material in the form of comic books where stories began: 'Shots were fired. Bang, bang, bang! The man fell down. His blood went drip, drip, drip!' The big tough trouble-makers then decided it might be worthwhile to learn to read after all. The programme was successful, quickly leading to a higher class of reading material.

There was a civic uproar when some adults learned what the youngsters were being taught to read. The content was made less violent. ('The motor bike went zoom, zoom, zoom!') When learning to read was made less threatening to the delinquents' self-concept, they readily took to it. Soon their success in reading, and the discovery that interesting things could be found in the world of books, brought about subtle changes in their self-concepts. From then on, reading became a skill which could preserve, defend, maintain and enhance their ever-improving self-concepts.

When I once interviewed a female homosexual who had been referred to the Hypnotherapy Clinic by a court agency for behavioural treatment, the ensuing conversation revealed how much one's actions depend on how one perceives oneself, and how everyone behaves in ways which tend to preserve, defend, maintain or enhance the phenomenological self.

Seated across from me was a prospective client who had been referred for a consultation prior to possible hypnotherapy. I had been told a young girl in her twenties would be coming in, after having just been released from gaol for a 'crime against nature' with a minor girl. (This was in the days before the modern liberal tolerance for homosexuality in general.) The girl looked like a man — a very tough man. Her appearance, speech and mannerisms projected a strong aura of aggressive masculinity. Although she seemed hostile about the idea of treatment, she was willing to be frank during the consultation.

'Tell me about yourself,' I began pleasantly.

'Well, I'm a lesbian,' she answered bluntly, her eyes narrowing.

'I'm sure there's more you can tell me about yourself than that,' I replied with a friendly chuckle.

She thought seriously for a moment and then replied with good humour, 'What else is there to say? I'm a lesbian!'

It is a pity when one's perception of self has been narrowed down to only one aspect, and especially sad when that one aspect is socially disapproved. This girl could not talk easily about her education, home, family, friends, hopes, ambitions, work, past, present or future, without every aspect being permeated and overshadowed by her perception of her homosexuality. This one fact was the sum and substance of the way she viewed her 'selves' in relation to her environments. On a psychological questionnaire which measured self-concept, her only high positive scores were her 'physical self' and her 'social self' — precisely the two areas in which nearly everyone else would have rated her the lowest!

Her physical and social self-concepts being as they were, it was understandable that her behaviours were what they were. Everything in her life had to preserve, defend, maintain or enhance her own concept of herself. There could be little change in her behaviours until some changes were effected in her self-concept.

Another time I interviewed a client who wanted to be treated for obesity. She was indeed grossly overweight, a grotesque caricature of an average person. When asked to tell a little about herself, she replied: 'What's there to tell? I'm fat!' The only thing she could tell about herself was that which was perfectly obvious to any observer, namely her incredible fatness. Nothing of her family, her husband, children or anything else was even worth mentioning, *in her estimation*. She later made the comment that she 'detested big people', and that she had been 'big' all her life; she seemed surprised when it was pointed out to her that such statements were really tantamount to saying she had detested herself for many years, indeed, 'all her life'.

It is a mistake to believe that self-concept is formed by behaviour; The opposite is true. Self-concept determines behaviour.

It is not only misfits whose lives are governed by their self-concept — it is true of each of us. The answer you give to the question 'Tell me about yourself' gives, in part, the self-concept you possess and the behaviours you adopt to preserve, defend, maintain or enhance that concept. It should be clear by now that your self-improvement programme must begin with your self-concept. You must understand exactly what it is and how it can be changed. That's what this book is about.

It is well to keep in mind that you alone are the interpreter of your 'self'. It is you alone who really attach value judgements to those perceptions which you made in the first place! Other people's concept of you has nothing to do with your self-concept. It is *your* concept of yourself. A negative self-concept is not inflicted on you by others; it is self-generated. It is your own perceptions, your own evaluations, that comprise your phenomenological self. It was formed in your mind and *it exists solely in your mind*. It is self-created and self-defined. Only you can change it. And you can.

Plan Your Self

'Know yourself' is not nearly as good advice as 'Plan yourself.' The phenomenological self, the self you know and recognize as being *you*, can be changed. Your 'self' is not a static thing; it is dynamic and ever-changing. Unfortunately, it can tend to become more preserved, defended, maintained and 'enhanced' by your behaviours which are designed to do just that — to maintain the *status quo*. It often attains an apparent permanency or solidification by the lifestyle we choose. However, since we know it can become worse, we also know it can become better. We can't change it simply by an exertion of will. We must have a plan that will work.

The self-concept can be changed because it consists of the way you perceive your interaction with the various facets of your environment. Therefore, it can be changed by manipulating one or more of these three factors: (1) the environment; (2) your ways of interacting; and (3) your perceptions, both of the environment and of yourself.

Environment can be manipulated to change our self-concept only when more opportunities for success experiences can be built into the structure of our lives. Success experiences build a positive self-concept, and that is the reason early successful experiences are so important for us to have. If the educational system is interested in building sound mental and emotional health in growing children, then every effort should be made to build success experiences into the structure to which every child is subjected by law. Some people are fond of saying that we learn from our failures, but this is not really so. We learn and grow only by our perceived successes.

My early school experiences with arithmetic were frustrating. I was made to feel nervous, insecure, inadequate and dumb. It was predominantly a failure experience for me. What did I learn from my failure? I 'learned' that simple arithmetic was hard and higher mathematics was impossible. It was not until many years later when I was exposed to a more understanding teacher that I realized there is really nothing particularly hard about the subject at all. As a youngster I had perceived myself as *poor* at maths; I naturally governed my future conduct by doing those things which preserved, defended, maintained or enhanced my phenomenological self by avoiding those things which threatened it. Maths was hard for me because I had been taught it was hard for me; I did poorly because I had no confidence in my ability to comprehend what I imagined was surely an incomprehensible subject. The brighter side of my life was, of course, that I also perceived myself as successful in other endeavours, which I naturally cultivated because those activities were compatible with my self-concept — that is, they tended to preserve, defend, maintain and enhance my perceived self as good at other things besides maths. Failure begets failure; success breeds success. All we ever learn from our failures is an avoidance reaction, a fearfulness which tends to be demoralizing, paralysing and inhibitory. Success, on the other hand, builds us up, gives us confidence and inspires us to higher achievement. If you want to improve yourself, meditate more on the successful experiences of your life and see what you can learn from them.

Your *interaction* with your environment can be changed even when the environment itself cannot. The principle 'Act the way you want to feel, and you will soon feel the way you act' is based on sound psychology. Most people who try it give up too soon, however. In his book *Conditioned Reflex Therapy*, Andrew Salter lists the principles of action which he claims build mental health, supposedly based on Pavlovian principles relating to cortical inhibition and excitation. It is basically an encouragement to be emotionally honest and give expression to honestly felt emotions. He believes in standing up for your rights, including 'telling people off' if they deserve it, being as independent as possible, observing social conventions but always asserting yourself. Salter admits he is known as the psychologist who gets people in fights in restaurants, and that one of his patients characterized his therapy as 'freedom through bitchery'. Nonetheless, his thesis is fascinating, and the principles are sound. You can change your ways of acting and reacting, if you choose to do so.

Let us suppose you don't want to get angry so often. Do not deny your anger, but identify what makes you angry. If you tend to think 'He makes me angry,' that isn't helpful because it reinforces the belief that others can make you angry. If you accept the idea that other people literally can 'make' you angry, there isn't much you can do. You have given someone else the power to make you react in certain ways. You must be more precise in identifying the source of your angry responses by thinking: 'When he does such-and-such, I allow myself to feel angry about it.' Then you have correctly identified the problem — your reaction when certain things are done or said in your presence. You make yourself angry.

Sometimes you may say that a member of the opposite sex 'turns me on'. The fact may be that the other person doesn't even know you exist! Nobody can 'turn you on' in reality. What you really mean is that when the other person acts in certain ways, you allow yourself to feel 'turned on' to that person, regardless of the intention. Properly identifying the reason for your emotion, you can realize the reaction is caused by you, not the other person. You should never say that anyone or anything 'makes' you feel or react in a certain way, because it simply isn't true.

Your *perceptions* of your environment and yourself can certainly change if you work at it. You perceive yourself today in relationship to your past, which is logical because you could not normally perceive it in relationship to anything else — anything else, that is, except *a plan you have in your mind*. If you decide exactly what you want your phenomenological self to be, you can imagine it in relationship to the various aspects of your environment and then visualize it in a way that will affect your subconscious mind.

Decision, imagination and visualization are your steps in changing yourself. The perceptions which most profoundly affect our lives are those which reach our subconscious and then work from the inside out, as it were. For this reason, we are influenced more by subliminal perceptions than by arguments or advice. We are constantly perceiving things unconsciously and it is these perceptions which feed and mould our subconscious minds. Suggestions perceived in a hypnotic state are of this nature and for this reason are so powerful.

Self-hypnosis is nature's tool for re-engineering human personality according to plan, because self-hypnosis works in and through the subconscious.

The Subconscious Mind

If you speak of 'the subconscious' to a psychiatrist, he will most likely correct your terminology by assuring you the correct term is 'unconscious'. Because hypnotists tend to use the popular term 'subconscious', it is therefore helpful to define what is meant by it.

There is a difference between the unconscious and the subconscious. Obviously, *un*conscious means that which is *not* conscious and *sub*conscious means that which is *below* or *under* consciousness. Both terms have an interesting history.

The concept of the unconscious was popularized among German writers by Sigmund Freud, and among Swiss, German and French writers by Carl Jung. Although agreeing in important ways, both Freud and Jung each gave a specific meaning to the way they used the term 'unconscious'.

The Freudian model of the mind includes three components: the Ego, the Superego and the Id. The Ego is the more conscious 'I' or the 'self' of the person. The Ego is conscious of the world and of itself (that is, it is mostly self-conscious) and is the part of the psyche which 'tests reality'. The Ego develops when the child becomes aware of the difference between 'self' and things which are 'not-self'. The Superego is the 'conscience', made up of the internalized taboos, prohibitions and moral restraints imposed by parents and society. These parental and societal inhibitions are instilled in childhood and remain largely unconscious. The Id is the sum total of the primitive drives and urges of one's nature. The Id is completely unconscious. Its energy is called 'libido' and is governed by the 'pleasure principle'. These three concepts, Ego, Superego and Id, form the structure of the psyche, according to Freud. To simplify and summarize: the Id says, 'Do it now!'; the Ego says, 'Not now. This is not the appropriate time and place to do it'; and the Superego says, 'Don't do it at all — ever! It's evil and wrong to do it under any circumstances.'

Freud taught that the Id was never conscious; it always was and will remain totally unconscious. Most of the Superego is unconscious; a tiny bit is conscious. The Ego is mostly conscious, some of it is 'preconscious', but a large part of it still functions entirely on an unconscious basis. The unconscious part of the Ego is filled with contents that have been repressed from consciousness because they were too threatening or unacceptable to the Ego or Superego. It is important to understand that to Freudians, repression is not simply forgetting. In ordinary forgetting, we usually remember what it is we have forgotten: 'What is that phone number?' However, in repression, we not only have forgotten, but we have forgotten that we have forgotten; we have no awareness of ever having known it!

Experiences which once were conscious but now are imperfectly repressed are said to lie in a borderline area between consciousness and unconsciousness known as the 'preconscious'. A memory is preconscious when we can say: 'It's on the tip of my tongue . . .' Things in the preconscious were once conscious and now are below consciousness but still are recoverable.

In general, what Freudians call the preconscious is what most hypnotists call the subconscious.

Freud's vision of the mind was somewhat like an island in the sea: most of it is beneath the surface. Jung had a different view of the same analogy. To him, there was also a 'collective unconscious', symbolized by the sea which surrounds the island. To Jung, just as we have inherited a body which is the product of evolution, so we have inherited an evolved mind which is the collective unconscious, distinct from the personal unconscious. In this race-mind are certain motifs which he called 'archetypes'. The archetypes of the collective unconscious are in themselves formless, but have taken form in fairly stereotyped ways throughout mankind's history in the symbolisms of myths, legends, religions, dreams and even psychotic hallucinations. These archetypes (such as the Self, the Good Mother, the Witch, the Wizard, the Mysterious Helping Companion, Rebirth, etc.), have a profound impact for both good and evil. It is possible for one to become engulfed in these archetypal contents of the collective unconscious, identifying personally with them instead of realizing that they are a collective phenomena, and thus becoming 'inflated' or possessed and obsessed by them to the point of individual personality disintegration. Like Freud, Jung believed the individual unconscious was like the submerged part of an island, but also surrounded by the sea of the collective unconscious.

Before Freud elaborated his concept of the Id, Georg Groddeck wrote his *Book of the It*, in which he conceptualized the unconscious as an autonomous, playful, self-directed force which was sometimes helpful, sometimes harmful in its activities.

It was Pierre Janet who originated the term 'subconscious', a claim Freud did not dispute. Pierre Janet worked at the Salpêtrière in Paris where he used the term 'subconscious' in elaborating his theories of psychopathology based on his extensive work with hypnosis.

In England and the United States, through the writings of Myers and Prince, the terms 'subliminal' (meaning below the threshold of consciousness) and 'co-conscious' (referring to the autonomous functioning of secondary personalities) were introduced. The English and French terminologies were nearly synonymous, but the German influence of the Freudian terminology largely prevailed in the medical and academic worlds. It is due to this influence of the Freudian model of the mind that many psychiatrists and psychologists consider the use of the term 'subconscious' by hypnotists to be inaccurate and unscholarly.

When we speak of the 'subconscious', we are legitimately using a term which followed Pierre Janet's great discoveries in hypnotism at the Salpêtrière asylum. The insights of Groddeck's 'It' and Freud's 'preconscious', along with modern computer analogies, have been added to our modern concept of the subconscious.

The subconscious of which today's hypnotists speak is the repository of forgotten memories, the source of the psyche's energy, the health-maintaining servo-mechanism, and the programmable bio-computer by which man can understand the mind, heal it and direct it into its highest accomplishments.

(The hypnological understanding of the subconscious is clearly and thoroughly discussed in the chapter titled 'Four Paths to the Subconscious' in my book *Hypnosis For The Modern Mind*.)

The subconscious is not inventive — it works with automatic and unquestioning accuracy upon the plans and concepts which are fed into it. It is completely un-self-conscious; it does not know what it is, or even that it exists — it just knows how to do its work. It only knows how to do what it does; it never knows or cares why. It does not search for truth; it accepts all input data as though true. It cannot predict anything because it does not know anything outside its own experience. The subconscious mind does many things which your conscious mind, and indeed the sum of all the conscious minds in the world, cannot do. It is infinitely complex and beyond the full comprehension of the conscious mind. All we can do is learn to utilize its great powers intelligently.

Part Two

The Power You Decide to Use

In attempting to 'Know Thyself', one can only know the sum total of the habits that go to make up the 'self', plus one's subjective reactions. This self-in-relation-to-the-environment, and one's feelings about it, is what is referred to as the 'phenomenological self'. (You will soon learn how to know your phenomenological self.)

But there is another 'self to be considered. It is the *potential self* or the *future self* you will design and actually develop through the programme suggested in this book. Because you are reading this book, it is assumed that it is this self you are most interested in.

Self-improvement is not merely a reworking or an overhaul of the present phenomenological self. It is the attainment of a carefully planned *future self* or *potential self* in which the desired self-improvement would be considered an accomplished fact.

This *potential self* or *future self* is developed according to the same principles of psychology by which the present self has been developed. Your potential self or future self will take form over the coming weeks, months and years. It will be formed either accidentally (that is, without conscious design) or it will be carefully planned and programmed *by you*.

The self-you-will-become will be the result of either the random experiences of your daily future life, or it will be the effect of other people upon your mind, or it will be achieved by you yourself according to the plan you develop by serious and conscientious application of the principles given you in this book.

In one case you abdicate responsibility for the formation of your future self, leaving it to the uncertainties of whatever the tomorrows may bring you in terms of your environment and the people and circumstances which may randomly cross your path. Just as your present self is the result of the past, so your *future self* will be the result of the past and present and the future.

If you wish to assume responsibility for your own *future self* and not leave it to chance or external circumstances, then you must begin now to make your plans and learn to put them into practice. There are some things in the future that will be entirely beyond the control of anyone, just as there are things in the present which are beyond the effective control of the individual, but there is one aspect of the future that anyone can control if he or she so desires.

If one has the desire and the know-how, one can control the formation of the *future self!* By thoughtful planning and assiduous application of all that this book teaches, this future self will be the *potential self* you desire.

The potential of the future is even more staggering to the imagination than the potential of the present. Of the many powerful potentials which you now possess, the most important one is the ability to influence consciously your yet undreamed-of future potentials.

Your presently unknown self and the constantly unfolding self of the future will be formed by the same forces by which you have become what you are now. These mechanisms of the subconscious are best understood in relation to the truths of hypnological science. You will now be introduced to the scientific rationale by which the purposeful shaping of your subconscious for success and personal satisfaction can be achieved.

The Suggested Self

The following material is rather technical and requires careful study. It was originally written under the title 'The Lies We Live By — And Their Conscious and Subconscious Correction'. It is intended as a rapprochement between rational psychotherapy and hypnotherapy, and the numbers at the end of some sentences refer to the source material presented in bibliographical form at the end of the book.

There are many theories in psychology as to why we behave as we do. Rather than representing opposing or contradictory points of view, they merely look at the same facts from different frames of reference. Although each psychological theory undoubtedly contains a great deal of truth, we are primarily concerned here with the usefulness or helpfulness of a theory or method. What is presented here is not intended in the least to establish a theory or prove the superiority of a psychotherapeutic method, but simply to reveal a pragmatic treatment principle we can apply to our purpose of self-improvement through self-hypnosis.

What is called 'Rational Psychotherapy' emphasizes the importance of a person's thoughts, ideas and perceptions in determining and influencing behaviour. We act in certain ways because we believe that our actions are indicated or justified by circumstances. For various reasons, we have come to believe that we ought to act in certain ways and we feel anxious or guilty if we don't.[10]

The simplest statement of this principle is found in Proverbs 23:7 of the Bible (Authorized version): 'As a man thinketh in his heart, so is he.' This has often been paraphrased as: 'It's not what you think you are — but what you think, you are!' Whatever else may be true of human behaviour, certainly that much is true. We act in certain ways simply because, believing as we do, we could not act otherwise. Mental and emotional health is not so much a matter of 'holding positive thoughts' as it is holding philosophical presuppositions which are conducive to personality integration, social adjustment, individual achievement and happiness.

Your 'behaviour pattern' is derived from your 'belief pattern', which in turn is derived from your value systems, intellectual processes and sensory perceptions.[22] This can naturally be traced back to earliest childhood and much could be made of the influence of parents, siblings and teachers, etc., but the fact remains that you have always behaved as you have because it somehow 'made sense' to you (however irrational in fact) according to your perception of the situation and the assumptions which guide you.

The well-adjusted person should be adjusted to reality, not merely to his own eccentricities. A firm belief system which is based upon erroneous presuppositions about self and the world cannot fail to result in behaviour that is to some extent maladaptive; that is, behaviour which has no survival or self-preservation value in either the physical or social sense, but rather the contrary. No amount of therapy or self-help programmes can have any lasting effect if such mistaken belief systems are left unchallenged and unchanged.

Human nature is such that people cannot guide their lives by presuppositions which seem absurd to them. However absurd the behaviour may be in fact, there is an attempt to rationalize it so it 'makes sense'.[12] One's erroneous presuppositions, based on mistaken or distorted perceptions, inevitably lead to maladaptive behaviour. One constantly makes minor adjustments to either one's behaviour or one's beliefs in order to keep them compatible with each other. Problems arise when this adjustment process is unaffected by reality, and is guided only by erroneous ideas about what is true, right or expected of one.

There is hope through rational psychotherapy because most people can be reasoned with, assuming, of course, that the therapist is rational and knows how to communicate properly.[23] With such help, a pattern of life which is inherently self-defeating can be changed for the better. Naturally, this rational approach is contraindicated with people who are intellectually inadequate or too emotionally aberrated to follow a rational discussion, but most people can be reasoned with. They are looking for answers and want someone to help them 'make sense' out of life. Everyone, whether normal or neurotic, can only change a mode of living when it is no longer justified by their value systems and philosophical assumptions. By means of rational psychotherapy they can definitely and permanently 'change their minds' and thereby adopt the needed basis for rational behaviour. Any neurotic, deviant and maladaptive behaviour can and should be attacked by the therapist as being irrational, that is, proceeding from false assumptions.

A patient became so infuriated with a psychiatrist that he refused to return, all because the psychiatrist constantly interjected 'that's silly' into the conversation. This was brusque and unsympathetic of the psychiatrist, and the patient was quite right to feel offended. When a symptom is gravely serious to a person, it is not proper to call it 'silly', regardless of how irrational it may be. Care must be taken not to minimize the importance of a person's feelings, which at least to him are never 'silly'. The reason why it is, in fact, a foolish and unnecessary response should be explained, however.

No maladaptive behaviour is silly in the light of its underlying belief and value system; on the contrary, it makes sense in terms of what is believed to be true about the self and its relationship to the believed-in world. However, if these underlying presuppositions are irrational, then so will be the behaviours which flow from them. Maladaptive behaviour could be called silly only if seen in the light of a more rational way of looking at life — and this is what a maladjusted person cannot do without help.

The technique of rational psychotherapy is based on the assumption that significant emotions and actions stem from the beliefs or basic assumptions a person consciously or unconsciously holds. Maladaptive, self-defeating, neurotic symptoms are either caused or maintained by illogical and irrational attitudes, and a vicious circle is put in motion whereby the wrong ideas and the actions tend perpetually to reinforce each other. A therapeutic or self-improvement programme based on this premise must bring to the person's conscious attention the irrational value systems that underlie and reinforce the maladjustment, interpret their origins in a lucid way which is acceptable to the person's intelligence, and then guide him or her into a more rational way of life. This means acting, thinking and feeling in an enlightened manner. The individual must see how important it is to stop maintaining these irrational beliefs by self-indoctrination with the nonsensical ideas he originally acquired. The person must be helped to substitute rational value judgements in their place and then by positive assertive behaviour to eliminate the old and reinforce the new.[28]

At this point, an examination of typical rational and irrational value systems and underlying beliefs is in order. The most basic and common life assumptions are listed in the following columns.[10] Those in column A are irrational, nonsensical, false and therefore can only lead to maladaptive and self-defeating behaviour. Those in column B are rational counterparts of those in column A. All of these assumptions are phrased in the first person in order to be more meaningful and personal, and also for reasons which will be explained later in regards to their application for self-hypnosis.

COLUMN A
Irrational idea 1
It is a dire necessity for me to be approved or loved by almost everyone for almost everything I do. It is most important what others think of me. It is better to depend on others than on myself.

COLUMN B
Rational idea 1
It is pleasant, but not necessary, for me to be approved or loved by most others. It is better to win my own respect than others' approval. It is more desirable to stand on my own feet than to depend mainly on others.

What's wrong with this?
In the first place, why should it be a 'dire necessity' for you to be approved or loved for everything? What terrible thing would happen if you didn't have this approval and love? No one else is loved and approved for everything, so why should you be? Secondly, to believe it's better to depend on others rather than on yourself is an attitude which will keep you forever dependent and immature.

Why is this a better idea?
First, because it distinguishes between what is pleasant and what is necessary — two entirely different things. Secondly, it places a healthy emphasis on true self-respect and makes you more mature and independent.

COLUMN A
Irrational idea 2
I should be thoroughly competent, adequate, talented and intelligent in all possible aspects. The main goal and purpose of life is achievement and success. I am worthless if I am incompetent.

COLUMN B
Rational idea 2
It is better for me to focus on doing rather than on doing well; to accept myself as an imperfect creature who has definite human limits and fallibilities, whether or not I am competent of achieving.

What's wrong with this?
We've all heard it said: 'If a thing is worth doing, it's worth doing well.' However, there are things which are worth doing whether you do them well or not! Certain recreational activities, cultural pursuits and growth experiences are worth doing at any level of competence. Few of us will become superstars at sports, music, art, etc., but these activities always reward us just for doing them. One's worth is not directly related to one's competence or mastery of anything.

Why is this a better idea?
Focus on 'doing well' often inhibits us from achieving, but if we focus on doing the thing itself, we may learn to do it well. It is part of being human to have limitations, so why not join the rest of the human race and stop the pretence of being a superhuman? Don't isolate yourself from growth experiences because you feel a need to surpass others; concentrate on participation and share in the benefits of worthwhile activities.

COLUMN A
Irrational idea 3
I should severely blame myself for my mistakes and wrongdoings. Punishing myself for my errors will help prevent future mistakes.

COLUMN B
Rational idea 3
I should acknowledge my mistakes and wrongdoings and use them as guides for self-improvement. Punishing myself for my mistakes will usually detract from and sabotage actions necessary to eliminate them.

What's wrong with this?
Self-blame and self-punishment are self-assumed responsibilities. No one expects such morbid introspection from you, and a martyr complex will only focus your mind more on the mistakes you are trying to

Why is this a better idea?
It's never a good idea to get stuck performing autopsies on unpleasant memories. It is a form of negative thinking to become obsessed with negative outcomes, and the autosuggestions in the subconscious tend to

avoid. Your experiences should provide you with necessary lessons for future improvement, but not an excuse to indulge a neurotic need for self-punishment.

precipitate the same errors over again. The wasted energy will misdirect your efforts for truly constructive actions.

COLUMN A
Irrational idea 4
I should blame others for their mistaken or sinful behaviour. I should get upset by others' errors and stupidities. I should spend considerable time and energy trying to reform others by roundly criticizing them and sharply pointing out the errors of their ways.

COLUMN B
Rational idea 4
People who make mistakes or act 'sinfully' are simply mistaken, and blaming them is neither just nor effective. Getting upset by others' errors and stupidities will help neither them nor myself. It is better to focus on correcting my own mistakes than on trying to reform others. I can help others best by serving as a good model of behaviour.

What's wrong with this?
Who appointed you the reformer of the world? It's a useless expenditure of energy to criticize and carp about things you don't like. If you think you should get upset with others' stupidities, you'll find there are enough stupid people in the world to engage your total attention and keep you in perpetual turmoil!

Why is this a better idea?
This is a better approach to life because it enables you to engage effectively in self-improvement, instead of (as Mark Twain once observed) 'going about inflicting unprovoked good on others' who don't appreciate it. Jesus said only the hypocrite concerns himself with the mote in his neighbour's eye. You'll help others more by devoting more time to improving yourself.

COLUMN A
Irrational idea 5
Because something once strongly affected my life, it should indefinitely affect it. Because I was once weak and helpless, I must always be. Because my parents or society raised me to accept certain traditions, I must always unthinkingly accept them.

COLUMN B
Rational idea 5
I should learn from my past experiences, but not be overly attached to or prejudiced by them. Even though I was once weak and helpless, I need not, as an adult, continue to be. I should thinkingly consider all alternative modes of present behaviour rather than act in a purely traditional or customary manner.

What's wrong with this?
The negative influences of the past don't need to be perpetual; you can change your life. The key word here is 'unthinkingly' — many traditions have outlived their usefulness. Whenever a person says he believes and acts the way his parents and grandparents did (as if that justified his lack of rational analysis), we can only be grateful that his ancestors were not criminals!

Why is this a better idea?
This is a better way to look at life because it places the responsibility where it belongs — on you. It may well be that you will end up living a rather traditional life, but it should be your free choice, based on a thoughtful consideration of your alternatives, not just followed out of ignorant custom.

COLUMN A
Irrational idea 6
It is terrible, horrible and catastrophic when things are not the way I would like them to be; they should be better than they are. Others should make life easier for me and help with life's

COLUMN B
Rational idea 6
It is unfortunate when things are not as I would have them be, and I should try to change conditions for the better; but when this is impossible, I had better be resigned to the way things

difficulties. I should not have to put off present pleasures for future gains.

are and stop telling myself how awful they are. It is nice when others help me with life's difficulties; but if they don't, I can confront those difficulties myself. If I do not put off some present pleasures for future gain, I will sabotage my own well-being.

What's wrong with this?
There's a tendency to over-dramatize every little thing in life and blow it out of proportion as if it had cosmic consequences. Nothing is truly a tragedy unless it creates widows and orphans. Save this dramatic description for events which cause tall buildings to crumble, not for the proportionately minor setbacks of life. You shouldn't expect others to help you any more than you help them, and you should help others without expecting anything in return. A present pleasure shouldn't be denied just because it's pleasurable, but if it jeopardizes some future gain, it is decidedly immature to opt for some relatively trivial, narcissistic satisfaction.

Why is this a better idea?
This is a better idea because it leads to more adaptive, independent conduct towards positive outcomes. It avoids negative autosuggestion and keeps your attention on attainable goals.

COLUMN A

Irrational idea 7

It is easier to avoid than to face life's difficulties and responsibilities. Inertia and inaction are necessary and/or pleasant. I should rebel against doing things, however necessary, if it is unpleasant to do them.

What's wrong with this?

Forced inactivity leads to boredom and unproductivity; why should chosen inactivity be any different? When a student said he hadn't done an assignment because he didn't feel like it, the professor replied: 'As you go through life, you'll be amazed at how many things in this world get done by people who don't particularly feel like doing them!' Furthermore, there are some necessary things in every task which are not especially pleasant to do; it is the finished accomplishment which brings satisfaction. The person who isn't cheerfully willing to do

COLUMN B

Rational idea 7

The so-called easier way is usually the much harder way in the long run, and the only way to solve difficult problems is to face them squarely. Inertia and inaction are generally unnecessary and relatively unpleasant; humans tend to be happiest when they are actively absorbed in creative pursuits. I should do necessary things, however unpleasant they may be, without complaining or rebelling.

Why is this a better idea?

It's a better philosophy of life because it is the mature way by which life's successful achievers approach their tasks. It's practically a credo for significant achievement.

the unpleasant but necessary things in life will never do much of anything worthwhile.

COLUMN A
Irrational idea 8
Much happiness is externally caused or forced on me by outside people and events. I have virtually no control over my emotions and cannot help feeling badly on many occasions.

COLUMN B
Rational idea 8
Most of my unhappiness is caused or sustained by the view I take of people and events rather than by the people and events themselves. I have enormous control over my emotions if I choose to work at controlling them by saying logical and un-self-defeating sentences to myself.

What's wrong with this?
This is what young people call a 'cop-out' and what diplomats would call a 'non-starter'. It's a whining 'poor-little-me' attitude which forever consigns you to the *status quo*.

Why is this a better idea?
It's better because it's the truth. It's better because it's an attitude that works. It's better because it liberates you from the error that you are victimized by external events, and it will enable you to start changing your life for the better.

COLUMN A
Irrational idea 9
If something is or may be dangerous or injurious, I should be terribly concerned about it. Worrying about a dire possibility will help ward it off.

COLUMN B
Rational idea 9
If something is or may be dangerous or injurious, I should face it and try to render it undangerous or uninjurious; and, when that isn't possible, focus on other things and stop telling myself

what a terrible situation I am in. Worrying over a dire possibility will rarely ward it off and often prevents me from effectively counteracting it.

What's wrong with this?
Simply being 'terribly concerned' and 'worrying' is a panic reaction which doesn't solve anything. Many people are like the old lady who said: 'Don't tell me worrying doesn't help. The things I worry about never happen!' Too many people either worry about things in the past which didn't happen, or things in the future which won't happen! It's a terrible waste of mind-power. Fretting is the commonest form of negative thinking; it blinds you to alternatives and solutions, and it paralyzes you from taking practical actions.

Why is this a better idea?
It's better because it's better! By now you should get the point.

The self-propagandizing whereby we reinforce our beliefs and value systems usually takes the form of self-verbalization (that is, mentally talking to oneself), which is really autosuggestion.[16] This role of suggestion, either originating in self or others, in establishing our inner beliefs (however false)[8] naturally leads to a consideration of the role hypnosis can play as an adjunct to rational psychotherapy. Since it is clear that suggestion (by oneself or others) plays a major role in establishing our inner beliefs (whether true or false),[8] it is natural to conclude that hypnosis could indeed facilitate rational psychotherapy.

The phenomenon of adult behaviour which is at the same time

irrational, maladaptive, and yet almost fixed and compulsive, is completely comprehensible only when viewed in a hypnological context. Clinical hypnotists are well aware of the fact that suggestions can be quite illogical and still be carried out. A hypnotized person accepts and acts upon suggestions which may be quite inconsistent with objective reality.[26,33] The subconscious mind evidently does not reason inductively.[25] To a limited extent it reasons in a deductive fashion, and thus 'logical' results will follow a completely illogical or false premise.

Thus, a patently false statement such as 'The room is getting colder. It is getting colder and colder. You can feel it getting colder,' *if accepted by the subconscious mind* (as in the case of a hypnotized subject whose conscious critical faculty is temporarily bypassed to some degree) becomes to all intents and purposes a *reality* to the person. That is, a false premise ('The room is getting colder,' etc.) is accepted uncritically (without conscious, analytical inductive reasoning) and then whatever would (deductively) follow from that premise indeed does follow (that is, the room would be perceived as getting colder, with certain physical changes occurring involuntarily in the subject). A hypnotized subject may respond in ways that are perceived by him to be perfectly logical, and yet which are obviously irrational to any observer who can perceive the falsity of the premise.

It thus follows that the subconscious mind acts on what it believes or perceives to be true, and this belief could be based on a declarative statement rather than on inductive or critical reasoning. This elementary fact, known and demonstrated by all experimental and clinical hypnotists, provides the basis for an easily understood concept of the origin of many mental aberrations and psychosomatic ills. When the mind is, for practical purposes, in a state of hypnosis (that is, a state of restricted awareness and receiving verbal stimuli uncritically) it perceives simple declarative statements as factual and these perceptions will profoundly affect all future thought and behaviour.

This state of mind which is characterized by uncritical hypersuggestibility often happens apart from the formal purposeful attempts known as hypnotism. Everyone has, in fact, been in a hypnotic state many times in his life. These states of mind are self-induced by intense concentration and mental absorption, or spontaneously induced by environmental circumstances which strongly affect the emotions,[8] such as bereavement, fright, confusion or mental trauma,[31] or under intimidation or drugs (such as in time of war with its prisoner-of-war camps, 'brainwashing', etc.)[20]

Psychiatrists have insisted that the first six years of life are crucial in forming the personality, and that by age six many psychological and personality factors are unalterably established.[13] It has been pointed out by modern hypnologists that the mental states of childhood and hypnosis have much in common.[1] The small child is imitative and hypersuggestible, able to identify mentally but not discriminate, and may be considered to be in a state of perpetual hypnotic trance.

The declarative statements that lodge themselves in the subconscious under any of the above circumstances will have all the effect of hypnotic and post-hypnotic suggestions, and are reinforced by habitual behaviour, repetition of the original statement stimulus, and self-verbalizations.[8,16] This hypnological interpretation of psychopathic etiology encompasses all that is known of the role of guilt, repressions and psychic traumas in neurotic and maladaptive behaviour, and confirms and completes rather than contradicts the traditional psychiatric concepts.

The origins of spontaneously induced states of hypersuggestibility are easily understood as an inevitable part of normal life and its often unusual stresses. Early childhood conceived as analogous to the trance state, and the involuntary trances momentarily brought about by traumatic experiences,[1,13] establish the fact that there are many times in life when the mind is capable of uncritically accepting what may actually be gross absurdities. What is the origin of these absurd declarative statements which unfortunately have the force of hypnotic suggestion? The answer to this traces irrational value systems and mistaken basic philosophies of life to their source so the maladjusted client can see that the assumptions from which his behaviour has 'logically' stemmed are themselves false.

Such origins are found in the minds that surround us as well as in our own. In childhood, we are stimulus receivers,[28] hypersuggestible, imitative, adaptable and continually moulded and fashioned by parents, relatives, siblings and peers.[2] By direct statements, authoritative commands, or by sarcasm and insinuation, the child's subconscious is ceaselessly being impressed for better or for worse.[24] Even after the critical faculties are developed and some intellectual discrimination becomes habitual, trauma,[29] confusion or other factors previously mentioned may temporarily suspend conscious thought long enough for statements by others to penetrate the subconscious. Another source of these statements is that of our own minds. We think in verbal symbols and, in effect, constantly 'talk to ourselves'. Far from being ridiculous, this sub-vocal self-verbalization is essential to clear thinking and lucid expression.[16] Self-verbalization, when related to emotional or personal aspects, can have the force of autosuggestions normally used in self-hypnosis.[8]

Studies in hypnotic suggestibility and assorted hypnotic phenomena indicate that the hypnological definition of 'suggestion' can encompass direct commands, authoritative statements, insinuations and even non-verbal cues.[32] Non-verbal communication is a seldom considered but vital factor in the study of communication theory. Thus a glance, a look of displeasure, or any gesture generally understood to express or repress an emotion may be perceived by an impressionable mind as intended to convey a value judgement. These perceptions, whether true or false, if self-verbalized, will be reinforced; if they unusually affect the imagination, they may have autohypnotic force.[3]

The following list contains examples of common expressions which can be heard daily in average homes, schools and businesses. Fortunately, they usually fall on deaf ears and are greeted by indifference, rebellion or amusement because they are critically evaluated on a conscious level and summarily rejected. If they should, under conditions favourable to hypersuggestibility, penetrate the deeper levels of awareness and be accepted as true statements by the subconscious, they would influence a person's behaviour and thought patterns on an unconscious level.

'Can't you ever do anything right?'
'You can't do anything right!'
'You're losing your grip!'
'What's the matter, can't you hear (or see)?'
'Clumsy! Butterfingers!'
'You're so awkward!'
'Stupid!'
'You're no damn good!'
'You're just like your father (or mother, etc.)!'

'You're useless!' ('Just like so-and-so.')
'You'll never amount to anything!'
'You're a dirty little liar!'
'That's a disgusting thing to do!'
'You couldn't do such-and-such if your life depended on it.'
'If you can't do better than that, don't even try!'
'You're just in the way around here!'
'Get lost!'
'Do you have to stand there like an idiot (blushing, trembling, stammering, stuttering, slouched over, staring, etc.)?'
'If I were you, I'd be scared to death (or mad, sad, etc.)'
'We could do without having you around!'
'Nobody asked for your advice! Keep it to yourself.'
'Shut up and mind your own business!'

There is no end to the uncomplimentary, demeaning and negative things we hear every day. Imagine the havoc if we took them literally and then consider the solemn truth that the subconscious mind takes everything quite literally. Imagine how you would habitually feel and act if you believed any of those statements to be absolutely true about you. Imagine what might conceivably happen to you if, under the influence of drugs, hypnosis or some emotionally sensitizing experience, any of those negative thoughts were implanted in your subconscious, *perhaps without your knowledge,* [20] and reinforced from time to time. Imagine how you'd think, feel and behave if you were absolutely convinced on an unconscious level of the truth of any one of those statements.

If you can conceive of these possibilities, you have a profound insight into the tragedy of the countless maladjusted, disappointed, unhappy people who feel strangely compelled to live out their lives on a basis that is as irrational as it is frustrating.

Hypnotherapy is merely the wise and ethical application of certain mental principles which daily affect every human being. It provides a rational way to eradicate the irrationalities of our lives. [3,8] It provides a way to control purposefully for our well-being the very force of suggestion which also can, and sometimes does, accidentally damage us. The harmful effects of suggestion on a mind made susceptible in any of the ways mentioned can be reversed through hypnosis. The power of suggestion is inadvertently and irrationally utilized by life in ways that often harm us; hypnosis is a scientific way to use the same powers of suggestion to help us. What improper suggestions have caused, proper suggestions can correct.[31] The facts and forces used in hypnosis are those which affect us also through tradition, ritual, society, advertising, education — and all of the words, gestures and actions that comprise and form our total life situation.

The mechanisms of the mind which are also used in hypnosis are those through which the good and the bad of experience have been internalized into the making of our characters and personalities. Like mass and energy, hypnosis *is* and will be as long as human minds exist. Humanitarian hypnosis should not be suppressed, eradicated or controlled by legislation because its processes and phenomena are a part of nature. The hypnotic receptivity of the mind is an integral part of *the way things are*, and when understood and employed by ethical people of good will, the principles and techniques of hypnotism can alleviate the sufferings of a great many people.

In addition to sympathetic counselling, hypnotherapy can be used to displace the erroneous life assumptions (Irrational idea 1, 2, 3, etc.) by employing the statements of the 'rational ideas' in the form of hypnotic suggestions. These have been stated in the first person so that they may also be employed as autosuggestions in a programme of self-improvement through self-hypnosis.

If the mental health of the world is to be improved, it must obviously be accomplished by some manner other than merely increasing the number of psychiatrists and professional psychological helpers. Simple statistics indicate the futility of that approach and, even so, the limitations imposed by time and money as well as by the necessity for establishing priorities mean that most people needing treatment will not receive it.[14,27] That is to say, the psychotics will take precedence over the neurotics, the hospitalized over the ambulatory, the greater disturbed over the lesser disturbed, the violent over the passive, etc., to say nothing of the limitations imposed by economics and geography.

Some self-help for personality maladjustments is a necessity. If self-treatment is impossible, then many people will never get any treatment at all. If self-improvement is impossible, then most people will never experience any real improvement. To assert that everyone who feels the need for help is 'too far gone' to be helped without expensive professional assistance is to assert that either: (1) they are too ignorant to understand how to re-establish a normal life, or (2) it is impossible to explain rationally the what and why of therapy in a manner intelligible to the person of average intelligence. It is my belief that neither assertion is valid for the vast majority of troubled people. If sufficient importance were attached to preventive mental health and the treatment needs of the masses, steps would be devised to inform and guide them in the techniques necessary for the achievement of healthy and well-balanced personalities for themselves and their children.

In an age when communication theory and techniques are developed to a higher degree than ever before in history, it should not be too difficult to conceive of this as an easily attainable goal. [14] Television, with its vast educational and constructive possibilities, will probably continue to be a 'cultural wasteland' dedicated principally to commercial aims. [21] Because hypnotic inductions have been done successfully even via closed-circuit television, radio, recordings and telephone [5,11] it is not unreasonable to assume that mass communication media could serve the public in terms of ordinary directive psychological counselling, marriage counselling, etc. Perhaps a form of pay TV could be used to provide psychoprophylactic help for subscribers on a mass basis at nominal cost.

There have been those who, while advocating hypnotherapy, have questioned the therapeutic practicality of self-hypnosis. [19] This scepticism seems to be based on a limited understanding of what constitutes self-hypnosis or due to a lack of imagination about the general applicability of hypnosis to common personality problems. Some perhaps have claimed too much for self-hypnosis, emphasizing the rare and dramatic phenomena of age-regression, automatic writing, etc., [6,17] which certainly are not routine procedures in general hypnotherapy and are undoubtedly beyond the capabilities of most people through self-hypnosis. It is the inclusion of self-hypnosis in the field of hypnotherapy that increases its probabilities of success and preserves its gains; hypnotists have discovered that they get better results when they teach clients self-hypnosis. Cures can be permanent because the practice of self-hypnosis reinforces the therapeutic suggestions and enables the client to repel the negative suggestions of his associates and surroundings. [34]

Although outstanding physical and psychosomatic cures have occurred through the sole agency of self-hypnosis or its equivalents (religious, spiritual or esoteric healings which are generally agreed upon to work by the same mechanism as hypnosis),[30] severe personality problems and neurotic syndromes seldom improve by self-hypnosis alone, although there have been exceptions. In addition to the use of self-hypnosis, the irrational philosophical assumptions and fallacious value systems which have provided reinforcement for the symptoms must be challenged, exposed and corrected.

The fallacious assumptions which aid and abet maladaptive life patterns could be most effectively attacked on two fronts: rational psychotherapy and hypnotherapy using self-hypnosis. Such a concerted attack would provide a reorientation of the mind on both conscious and subconscious levels, leading to a balanced, integrated and synchronized interaction of the intellectual and emotional aspects of the personality. Such designed interaction should serve not only to accelerate the treatment process, but to secure permanent change.[34] Inasmuch as the self-verbalizations necessary to perpetuate habit patterns have been recognized as having crucial importance, it follows that autosuggestion, applied consciously and self-hypnotically, would facilitate personality improvement immeasurably.[7,18,15]

The 'rational ideas' presented earlier were phrased in the first person and in positive terms in a manner consistent with reason, and therefore they form model autosuggestions which are in accord with established hypnological principles.[3] Therapists will find that a programme of prescribed autosuggestions for persons suitably trained in self-hypnosis will ensure quick, effective and lasting results even in cases where rational psychotherapy alone would most likely fail. The 'rational ideas' are given to provide a therapist or a person using self-hypnosis with the contents of such a prescribed programme.

(The study upon which this section is based was done years ago, as reflected in the bibliographical references on pages 121-123. Since that time, however, absolutely nothing has appeared in the literature which contradicts or even modifies the thesis presented here. The scientific knowledge supporting the recommendations in this book have been commonly known among serious students of behaviour for many decades!)

The Principles of Self-Hypnosis
For reasons which ought to be abundantly clear by now, self-

hypnosis offers the scientific way to engineer intelligently one's personality according to a design of one's own choosing.

Self-hypnosis is essentially the only kind of hypnosis there is! All hypnosis is basically self-hypnosis, for only that which is accepted by the mind of the subject ever becomes effective in hypnosis. The suggestions given by a hypnotist accomplish nothing unless they simultaneously become the autosuggestions of the subject! It is really what the subject tells himself which produces the effects of hypnosis.

All authorities agree that there is no danger whatever in hypnosis unless injudicious suggestions are made. Therefore, self-hypnosis should be the safest kind of hypnosis imaginable. However, there is one caution that should be made for the sake of some people who are highly suggestible: when you have achieved the state of self-hypnosis, *do not listen to your subconscious — tell it!*

This is because some people, perhaps 5 per cent of the population, are naturally deep-trance hypnotic subjects. A certain number of these people believe themselves to be 'psychic' and capable of experiencing all kinds of extrasensory phenomena. They easily induce a deep hypnotic trance and then, because of wishful thinking and hypersuggestibility, they may hallucinate through autosuggestion. In the trance state, these people find that these induced sensations are so vivid they easily become convinced of their literal reality. To people already predisposed to believe in their 'psychic powers', it is easy to see how they could be led to believe in ever-increasing delusions. Because there is no way to vouch for the soundness of the belief systems held by the entire readership of this book, it is necessary to emphasize this caution to everyone.

It is a rule of vital importance: *Don't listen to your subconscious mind under hypnosis — tell it!*

There is a sense in which you can get information from your subconscious through hypnosis, *but this requires special training* which is beyond the scope of this book.

Self-hypnosis is both a science and an art. As a science, it follows definite laws which can be learned; as an art, it must be practised.

If you do not practise self-hypnosis faithfully, you will never be proficient in the art of it.

This book will teach you both the science and the art of self-hypnosis, but if you do not practise you will derive no benefit from studying it.

It does not take long to learn all there is to know about self-hypnosis. Far from being a difficult subject, it is simplicity itself. One does not have to join a secret society to learn self-hypnosis. One does not have to travel around the world, climb mountains in Tibet and study at the feet of a Great Master in a legendary Shangri-La. Just follow the instructions given here and you will become an expert.

The art of self-hypnosis is not difficult to master, providing you understand it properly and then practise it faithfully. The basic idea to remember is that you are both the hypnotist and the subject; in other words, you have a dual role to fulfil.

In self-hypnosis, you talk to yourself mentally. That is to say, you think the words silently but you 'hear' yourself talking. You can mentally hear yourself talk — fast or slowly — clearly or slovenly — or in any dialect you choose — with complete ease. This is natural and easier to do than to describe.

A skilled hypnotist speaks rather slowly and with clear enunciation. As your own hypnotist, you must talk silently to yourself in the same way. Do not rush. There is a temptation to get in a hurry when you are hypnotizing yourself. It cannot be done that way. When you are hurried, you sometimes feel it is sufficient just to 'think the thoughts' without actually articulating them mentally. However, you are the hypnotist, so you must articulate clearly to yourself mentally and be completely unhurried.

A good hypnotist adapts the speed of his induction to the mood and personality of the subject. He waits until the subject responds to one level before he proceeds to the next step. You are your own hypnotist, so do not rush ahead of your own reactions as the subject.

Naturally, you are also the subject in self-hypnosis, so be a 'good' one. You do this by co-operating with the suggestions given. You concentrate on the words and you do not let your mind wander.

Remember that you are playing this dual role. As the subject, be sure you respond to your own suggestions before you, as hypnotist, go on to the next step in the induction. For example, if you (as hypnotist) tell yourself (as subject) that the nerves and muscles in your face are relaxing, etc., be sure that you (as subject) do eliminate all frowns and squints before you (as hypnotist) continue to the next step.

If you will go back and re-read the last few paragraphs you will know all you need to know about the basic premise underlying self-hypnosis.

The objective is to relax your body completely until you feel every nerve and muscle has relaxed as much as it is possible at that session. This is usually characterized by a feeling of numbness or detachment, sometimes perceived as a heaviness or even a lightness. In some cases there may even be a slight tingling sensation. When relaxation is complete, it sometimes feels as if you are 'a mind without a body'. This detached feeling, usually perceived as a numbness, detachment, heaviness or lightness, is the physical description of the 'trance' state.

This condition of 'trance is difficult to explain, but it will be easily recognized on the basis of the foregoing description. Every time you practise self-hypnosis, your goal is to achieve this 'trance' state, or the state of complete relaxation which is characterized by a slight sensation of numbness or detachment. It usually begins with your feet and legs, then reaches your arms and hands, and then spreads quickly throughout your entire body.

As soon as you have reached that degree of relaxation, *at that point* you may give yourself the suggestions for your well-being that you have decided upon. It is not necessary to continue with the induction. There is a temptation for some people always to doubt if they are 'deep enough' for the suggestions to work. They perpetually postpone giving the self-improvement suggestions in the mistaken belief that they must 'go deeper'. This is entirely false. Use the relaxed state you've achieved. As you continue to practise you will naturally achieve deeper relaxation.

The objective is to achieve the trance, give yourself the suggestions, and then terminate the trance. *The object is not to prolong the trance.*

The trance, in self-hypnosis, always tends to extinguish itself and is difficult to maintain for long periods. A hypnotic trance is actually a state of mind between being sound asleep and wide awake. It has been described as a 'hammock slung between wakefulness and sleep'. No one in the history of the world has ever failed to come out of a hypnotic state. It is an impossibility to 'get stuck' in a trance, as it constantly tends towards complete wakefulness on the one hand, and sound natural sleep on the other.

There are two positions recommended for self-hypnosis: lying down or sitting up. When you practise lying down, loosen tight clothing and lie with your arms at your side with your legs uncrossed. When you practise sitting, sit up straight with both feet flat on the floor, hands held loosely in your lap, and your head erect so that your back and neck are in a straight perpendicular line. At a certain point in your induction you may feel your head pulling backwards (or forwards or even sideways) as neck muscles relax. If this happens, just let your head sag for a moment until the tension is gone from your neck, and then slowly bring your head back to a perpendicular position and keep it there. You will find this position is the most comfortable.

After some practice with self-hypnosis lying down, you may find it is too easy to fall sound asleep and too difficult to maintain the trance long enough to get around to giving the self-improvement suggestions. When you find this happening, you should then practise self-hypnosis in the sitting position. The sitting position is very practical, for then you will be able to practise nearly everywhere.

The Progressive Relaxation Method

We will begin with the most popular and familiar induction method known as 'progressive relaxation'. Later you will learn an instantaneous method; however, following the sound learning principle of progressing from the more familiar to the less familiar, we begin with the progressive method.

Take your position (either lying down or sitting up, as described) and take three or four deep breaths. Breathe in slowly and deeply, then exhale quickly and go limp. Do this slow inhalation and quick exhalation three or four times, then close your eyes and keep them closed. Talk to yourself mentally, 'speaking' slowly and distinctly as follows:

My body is already beginning to relax. (Pause) As my muscles relax, a pleasant sensation of numbness will tend to come over me. (Pause) It usually begins with my feet and legs growing numb, just slightly. Next my hands and my arms will grow numb. And then a very pleasant sensation of numbness will spread over my entire body, and I will begin to enter a state of complete mental and physical relaxation. It is a wonderful feeling to relax, and I am going to relax from my head to my toes. I will begin with my mind.

I will not be distracted or disturbed by any outside noises. If I hear a noise, it will not disturb me at all. I will listen to every word I say mentally and think of nothing else, as I relax my mind and body completely.

My mind, in a few moments, will become lazy. It will become so lazy that I won't care to think of anything or do anything. I will think of nothing except utter darkness, a complete blank, but I will hear every word I say to myself, and not only 'hear' each word, but actually feel the meaning of each word, and live each word as I go along.

My mind is relaxing now. And as my mind relaxes, the relaxation has begun to spread to every part of my head and scalp. Every nerve and muscle in my head and scalp is relaxing. I can feel the tenseness leaving my head and scalp. Now the skin and flesh on my forehead is softening up, smoothing out, relaxing. Now there isn't a bit of tenseness left in the muscles of my face, and there isn't a trace of a frown or wrinkle in my forehead. And as I am breathing freely and easily, I am relaxing the muscles in my throat. (Swallow) And I am relaxing my jaws by separating them slightly. (Separate them) And my lips (separate them), just letting them hang loosely, comfortably. And even though my eyes are closed, I am relaxing my eyes even more. (Pause)

Now I am driving out all the tension from the muscles of my chest, and on up my neck to the back of my head, then to the top of my head. Then down, deep down between my shoulder blades, and right down my spine to its base. Every nerve and muscle in that region of my body is relaxing. And as those nerves and muscles relax, a very pleasant sensation of numbness and detachment is spreading over my entire body, and I am going deeper and deeper into complete relaxation of my mind and body.

Now I am driving out all the tension in both of my shoulders and arms, and the relaxation is travelling on down to my fingertips. I can feel the tenseness leaving my arms and my hands.

Now I am driving out all the tenseness from the nerves and muscles in my stomach and abdomen, and the relaxation is spreading around my waistline to the small of my back. (Pause) It feels so good as the nerves and muscles in the small of my back soften up and relax. It is so restful, so comfortable. And as I am breathing freely and easily now, just the way I do when I'm deep asleep, a very pleasant sensation of numbness and detachment is coming over me, and I am going deeper and deeper into complete relaxation of my mind and body.

Now I am driving out all the tenseness from the muscles in my hips and thighs. The relaxation is travelling down through my knees (pause) and down through the muscles of my calves, and down through my ankles and into all the small muscles of my feet, and right on down to the tips of my toes.

It feels so good as all the tenseness leaves my entire body from my head to my toes. Every nerve and every muscle is relaxing more and more with every breath I take. And with every moment that passes, I am going deeper and deeper into complete relaxation of my mind and body.

By this time, if you have played your dual role well, you will have begun to feel a rather interesting sensation of complete relaxation. It may or may not be especially pronounced but at this point you will probably be as relaxed as you are going to be at that session, short of falling asleep. You will also be experiencing a state of mental peace, serenity and tranquility. Now you may forget your body and further relax your mind by saying to yourself:

I am going to relax even more than I am at this moment. I am going to count from ten, backwards, all the way down to zero. With each lower count, I am mentally doubling my relaxation. Beginning with the count of 10 . . . (Pause about ten seconds between counts, mentally doubling the relaxation, just imagining the relaxation becoming twice as much with each lower count . . . 9 . . . 8 . . . 7 . . . 6 . . . 5 . . . 4 . . . 3 . . . 2 . . . 1. (Now double all your relaxation) . . . Zero. Now I am in a state of complete rest and relaxation. Now I am enjoying perfect peace of mind. Nothing can disturb me, nothing can distract me. I am in absolute control of my emotions, my desires, and my five senses.

At this point you will be in a hypnotic trance, varying from light to medium depth. *This is adequate for all self-improvement purposes.* Although you will feel surprisingly 'awake', as indeed you are, you will now influence your subconscious mind with every word you 'say' or think.

You may now give yourself the suggestions you have decided upon. *Never practise self-hypnosis without a definite purpose and plan in mind!* If you follow this rule, self-hypnosis cannot be overdone. Repeat the suggestion(s) as many times as you like, but do not elaborate on it.

If you are practising while you are in bed ready to retire for the night, there is nothing more to do except just let yourself drift off into a natural sleep. You may want to give yourself a suggestion to the effect that you will sleep deeply and soundly throughout the night and awaken in the morning completely refreshed and full of energy to go about all your daily duties and heartily enjoy every minute of it. With that thought in your mind, you can fall asleep for the night.

However, if you are practising your self-hypnosis sitting up or at some time during the day, you will have to terminate the trance. This 'awakening' process is quite simple and you should make it a pleasant finale to your session.

Before you terminate the trance, and regardless of the depth

require the amount of time they have become accustomed to. We are creatures of habit and it is difficult to imagine that anything will happen to us that hasn't happened before. It's hard to believe that self-hypnosis can be done in far less time than is usually advocated by those who teach or practise it.

To break this 'time barrier', it is necessary to have a scientific understanding of exactly when hypnosis occurs in any method, then isolate the factors which produce that moment and identify the shortest possible way to accomplish it.

In any method of hypnotic induction, there is a 'magic moment' when the hypnotist, at least, says to himself: 'Now the hypnosis itself has begun'. What is the nature of this magic moment and when does it actually occur? It is first necessary to distinguish between ordinary relaxation and 'hypnotic' relaxation. Ordinary relaxation is merely the conscious lack of noticeable tension. Many times we think we are relaxed, and indeed we are in this ordinary sense, but it is far different from hypnotic relaxation. 'Hypnotic relaxation' is more than the mere absence of tension; it is the awareness of the presence of a certain type of relaxation which feels like a positive force which might be overcome by making an effort, but the effort doesn't seem worth making. The hypnotic relaxation seems almost like a comfortable 'force-field' around oneself, forestalling any effort or desire to disturb it. ('My arm is so relaxed I can hardly move it. I think I could probably move it if I really wanted to, but I just don't want to try. It feels so comfortable.') It feels like not only has *tension left*, but a *positive relaxation has appeared* in its place. This is the meaning of 'hypnotic' relaxation. At what precise moment does this occur, and why?

The oldest form of hypnotic induction (in written history) was the practice of Mesmerism. In the late 1700s, Dr Franz Anton Mesmer discovered he could put people into a trance by making slow hand movements downward over their bodies. He believed these were 'magnetic passes' which conveyed 'animal magnetism' and eventually 'magnetized' a person. The method often took several hours to achieve its purpose. The downward passes over the face eventually caused a rather strange phenomenon to occur: the person's gaze became fixed, the eyelids fluttered, the eyes rolled upward, the eyes closed, and the entire musculature relaxed. The person was then said to be 'magnetized'.

After the theory of Mesmerism was largely discredited by men of science, a new method of putting people into a trance was discovered some seventy-five years later in England.

Dr James Braid of Manchester discovered that by having people gaze at a bright light or a shiny object held slightly above eye-level, sooner or later the same phenomenon would occur. The eyelids would flutter and close, *and at that moment* the entire musculature would relax. The result, although obtained differently than by Mesmer's method, was the same. It was obvious that no so-called 'magnetizer' was needed, and because Braid wanted to dissociate himself from the discredited Mesmerism, he coined a new term: 'neuro-hypnotism', which soon became known as 'hypnotism'. Unfortunately, the term was a misnomer based on the Greek word for 'sleep'. Braid soon recognized his error but the translation of his book in many languages resulted in 'hypnotism' soon becoming an international word. The subject of hypnotism was thus forever contaminated by the 'sleep' concept.

Braid's eye-fixation method often took an hour or more. Verbal suggestions were used to shorten the procedure, but it still took too much time. For many years hypnotists (and the public) erroneously believed that the super-relaxed hyper-suggestible state was produced only by either hand-passes or eye-fixation on shiny objects.

The recognized 'father of modern hypnotism' was a French physician, Dr Hippolyte Bernheim. Oddly enough, hypnotists continued to overlook something he clearly stated in his book: the purpose of eye-fixation was not, as commonly supposed, to tire the optic nerve but to *tire the muscles of the upper eyelid*! This oversight retarded the discovery of the instantaneous method of hypnotic induction for several more decades.

An American hypnotist named Dave Elman had read Bernheim's book more carefully. He observed thousands of hypnotic inductions by every conceivable method and concluded that the 'magic moment' of hypnosis never occurred until the eyelids fluttered and closed in a characteristic way. If this were true, he concluded, this particular kind of 'eye-closure' was the 'opening wedge to hypnosis'. He correctly reasoned that by teaching people to do with their eyelids what was required, all the lengthy preliminaries of hypnotism could be eliminated entirely!

This theory stood up under scrutiny. Mesmer's downward hand motions had been simply a non-verbal suggestion to relax the eyelids, because the eyes tended to follow the hand movements.

Each time the person again raised his eyelids, they didn't open quite as much as before. After repeated 'passes', the eyelids relaxed, fluttered and closed. At that moment, hypnotic relaxation occurred. The trance had begun! (Had Mesmer made upward motions, the eyes would have tended to open wider and wider, and hypnotism would never have been discovered through that method!)

Braid's eye-fixation method never would have hypnotized anyone either if the person's gaze had not been directed upward. Looking straight ahead or downwards does not tire the muscles of the upper eyelids, because we are so accustomed to those positions. (Eye-fixation in a sideways direction is too uncomfortable to be a practical method; it strains the muscles of the eyeballs rather than tiring those of the upper eyelids.) For over a century and a half, hypnotists managed to hypnotize with their cumbersome time-consuming methods without ever understanding why they produced hypnosis. It required a new understanding to abbreviate the induction technique.

The rationale for the amazing Elman eye-closure technique is quite simple: when the eyes are relaxed, they are closed. (We sleep with the eyes closed.) It takes effort to keep the eyes open; it takes no effort to close them or keep them closed. It is certainly possible to contract muscles to close the eyes (as people do when they tightly close the eyes) but no effort is really necessary. All that is needed to close the eyes is to relax the muscles of the upper eyelids which keep them open! Furthermore, when the eyelids close *in this fashion*, the entire body will relax. It is impossible for an untrained person to maintain tension in the body when the eyelids are completely relaxed! (You fall asleep when you 'can't keep your eyes open'.)

So much for the reasoning behind the eye-closure relaxation mechanism. Now for the demonstration.

Close your eyes and then open them. The effort you make to open them is perhaps the smallest effort you can imagine, but it logically takes effort to open the eyes. It is important to realize that when your eyes are relaxed and closed, it does take a tiny effort to open them — because your task in self-hypnosis is *to create a sense of relaxation so great that this tiny effort seems too much of an effort to make*! Notice that this is *your* task; no one can do it for you. It really is simpler to do than to explain; this explanation is just so you will know why you must do it.

To prove how easy it is, close your eyes and then see *how slowly* you can open them. Then close them and open them *twice as slowly* as before. Repeat this and open your eyes twice as slowly each time. (Imagine you are trying to set a world's record in slow-motion eye-opening. People all over the world are watching a close-up television picture of your closed eyes as you set the slow-motion eye-opening record of all times. Determine that it will take you hours to open your eyes.) What you will notice is this: your eyelids reach a 'sticking point' where they seem glued in place *by the relaxation*. (Not by effort!)

What you probably will not notice is something of supreme importance: *at that moment*, you have become instantly and completely relaxed!

Now you are ready to practise the instantaneous relaxation method of self-hypnosis by hypnotic eye-closure:

1. Close your eyes.
2. Relax your eyelids to the point where the muscles 'just won't work'.
3. Test them to make sure they 'just won't work'.
4. Let that relaxation sweep down your body all the way to your toes.

If you do these steps properly, you will be in the hypnotic state — the same state as all the people hypnotized by Mesmer, Braid, Bernheim and every other hypnotist who ever lived! However, it's possible you didn't get it the first time if you didn't follow instructions.

If your eyes popped open, it means one of two things: either you didn't relax them 'to the point where the muscles just won't work', or you tested them to make sure they *would* work instead of testing them to make sure they *wouldn't* work'. It's vital that you understand what is meant by testing them to make sure they *won't* work!

It isn't that you can't possibly open your eyes if you decide to do it and then try. However, you can't open them *without giving up the relaxation that keeps them closed*. The idea is to *hold on to that relaxation no matter what*. A simple illustration will clarify this important point.

Suppose I said, 'You know, it's very strange to realize that you cannot get out of the chair you're sitting in. For that matter, I can't get out of the chair I'm sitting in. As *a matter of fact*, neither of us can rise from these chairs — unless, of course, we *give up the relaxation that's keeping us in these chairs!'*

It's perfectly obvious that in order to get out of a chair you must first 'give up' the relaxation that's keeping you there. To rise, you must give up the relaxation, *then* make the effort before you can get up. Think of relaxation as a positive force which keeps you in the chair. If you chose to 'hold on to the relaxation', you would remain unable to get up *under that circumstance*.

How do you 'test' your relaxed eyelids to make sure they won't work? After you have closed your eyes and relaxed the eyelid muscles 'to the point where they just won't work', you can raise your eyebrows as high as you like, but those muscles won't open your eyes if the eyelids are relaxed. That is how you test your eyelid relaxation to make sure you've got it.

Do not confuse this procedure with the so-called 'challenges' of a hypnotist who tells a subject that he cannot open his eyes. The eye-closure relaxation phenomenon is not the same as eyelid catalepsy induced by suggestion. No one is testing you; you are testing your own eyelid relaxation to make certain you have really achieved it.

After you have 'tested' it in this fashion, you 'let that relaxation sweep down your body all the way to your toes'. By 'that relaxation', you understand it to be the same kind of relaxation as in your eyelids. In other words, the kind of relaxation 'where the muscles just won't work' — an instantaneous 'floppiness' of every muscle in your entire body. Now to recapitulate: close your eyes, relax the eyelids to the point where the muscles just won't work, test them to make sure they won't work, and let that relaxation sweep down your entire body.

At that point, you will experience that unique quality of relaxation known as 'hypnotic' relaxation. The hypnotic state has been achieved in about fifteen seconds. It is right now, *at this point*, that your autosuggestions become true hypnotic suggestions which programme your subconscious.

When you wish to 'come out of it', simply think: 'When I open my eyes, I will be fully alert and feeling wonderful.' Then simply give up the eyelid relaxation, open your eyes and notice how good you feel. You should hold on to the pleasant feeling of relaxation you've achieved; there is no need to 'snap' out of it. Enjoy the after-glow.

You should realize that the 'depth' of hypnosis has nothing at all to do with the duration of the induction. With a little practice, you'll find that you can go very 'deep' in seconds. ('Depth' is a matter of your mental involvement in what you're doing, nothing more.) Once you've achieved the state, it is of course possible to deepen your perception of the physical and mental relaxation. You can do this by the countdown method of the progressive relaxation, mentally doubling your relaxation with each lower count. Or you could think: 'With each breath I take, I'm doubling my relaxation.' Then simply breathe normally and mentally double your relaxation with each breath. You'll soon find you can quickly go as 'deep' as you want to.

There is a great deal more to the Elman technique which is beyond the scope of a book on self-improvement through self-hypnosis. You have read all you need to; from here on it is a simple matter of practice.

You should practise this instantaneous relaxation method as often as you think of it. Try it under all kinds of circumstances, even when you think it is too noisy or hectic to relax. Follow the method and you'll be pleasantly surprised to find you can relax completely under circumstances you would have thought impossible. Indeed, it would be impossible without this amazingly simple and infallibly effective method!

Another marvellous advantage to this instantaneous method is that you can do it surrounded by other people and they will never know you're doing it! Because it only takes a few seconds, you can easily do it numerous times a day with great benefit each time. Tension multiplies throughout the day so that at the end of a day we feel not only the tensions generated in the last hour, but the compounded and multiplied effect of accumulated tension. If you practise the instantaneous relaxation method of self-hypnosis every hour on the hour (which is simple to do because it only takes half a minute), at the end of a day you would have only one hour's worth of tension to get rid of! Make a habit of this and you'll have far more energy at the end of each day. Even without giving yourself specific self-improvement suggestions, these mini-sessions of total relaxation will benefit you greatly.

Safety Rules to Keep in Mind

All human activities in which we engage, whether at work or play, have certain safety factors which must be observed. Self-hypnosis, being a normal activity, also naturally has certain safety factors which ought to be observed if you are to proceed with sure success. There are absolutely no medical contraindications to self-hypnosis. It cannot be overdone, providing you follow these basic precepts:

1. Always have your suggestions planned in advance. Know exactly what you are going to say to your subconscious, and exactly how you are going to say it. *Make your practice a planned procedure.* Do not improvise.
2. Do not experiment with yourself. Do not leave things to chance, but practise according to plan. Do not give yourself suggestions which distort your perceptions of reality. Do not induce hallucinations, visual or auditory. Do not tell yourself that you cannot do something you normally can do. (For example, do not say: 'I cannot open my eyes, I cannot move,' etc.)
3. Do not use hypnosis to tax your normal strength. It should be used to increase strength, energy, etc., in emergencies only. Common sense tells you that self-hypnosis is no substitute for the observance of normal health rules.
4. Unless you are a physician, do not presume to know how to treat physical or mental illness with hypnosis. Self-hypnosis for *therapy* (without professional assistance) is in the same category as self-medication, and runs the same risks. Use your knowledge of self-hypnosis to improve yourself; that is, to enhance your natural and normal qualities and abilities.
5. Use your skill in self-hypnosis to benefit yourself in practical ways. Based on years of study and personal observation, the author believes that *the use of hypnosis* in studying parapsychology, psychic phenomena, ESP, etc., is a detour to genuine self-improvement and generally a waste of time.

If you keep these safeguards in mind, you can enjoy self-hypnosis to the full and you will be able to utilize the powers of your subconscious mind to help you in a multitude of positive ways to project yourself *into* reality, rather than as an escape *from* reality. More will be mentioned in this regard later.

Part Three

The Programme You Must Follow

Prerequisites to Progress

At the very beginning of this book, a definite emphasis was made on the importance of deciding the kind of person you are going to become. Part One presented you with information intended to give you greater insight and appreciation of yourself. By knowing how your unique personality has developed, and the various factors that influence your daily actions, you can better plan for the *future self* you choose to become.

After learning something of your *perceived self*, how it developed and how it influences your behaviour by causing you to do only those things which tend to protect, defend, maintain or enhance this 'phenomenological self,' you studied your *suggested self* which is the key to self-improvement.

Part Two not only explained the mechanisms by which this *suggested self* is formed and maintained, but also described in detail the method of self-hypnosis by which you can consciously influence your subconscious mind. To a large degree, your past and present self-concepts were formed by the influence of suggestion — from other people as well as from your own autosuggestion. Self-hypnosis is a way to begin taking control over the quality of suggestive influences on your subconscious which will form your future self-concept. Two effective methods of self-hypnosis have been explained: one the traditional progressive relaxation method, and the other a new instantaneous relaxation method.

This present section deals with the methodology by which you can put all this knowledge to use. Before you begin practising the practical remainder of this book, there are a few more theoretical considerations which will be of great help to you. They are prerequisites for your assured progress in self-improvement.

There are three steps you are now ready to take in the transition from theory to practice. They are:

1. formulation of a definite goal;
2. insulation of your mind from negative influences;
3. opening your mind to your experience in a new way.

The formulation of a definite goal will be considered shortly in more detail, but a few words here will clarify this essential prelude to all self-improvement. Your goal must be something you can imagine, describe and visualize. It is not enough to put it into words (although you must do this) because some people have a great gift of putting nice-sounding words together without saying much of anything definite. Your goal must be something you can *visualize*. You must be able to see it in your mind's eye. You must 'see' yourself as you wish to be. You must 'hear' yourself as you wish to sound. You must 'feel' yourself as you wish to feel. You should make this imagined fantasy more real to you than other people's reality is to them! You must enlist your imagination's powers to make your idea of what you want to become vivid in every way to the greatest degree possible. The subconscious mind is influenced primarily by emotions and mental pictures, and by words only to the extent that they convey these.

The insulation of your mind against negative influence is of paramount importance. Our minds are subtly influenced by the minds around us and negative associates can hinder the development and achievements of the most positive person. It is a handicap which must be eliminated from the life of one who is serious about attaining the highest success and satisfaction in life.

This mental insulation cannot be accomplished by isolation; you cannot avoid all of the negative people in the world, for you would soon become a hermit. However, you can take certain precautions which will minimize the negative influences which normally would be brought to bear upon you.

You can mentally build a wall around your mind. Dr Napoleon

Hill, author of many success books and articles, says he has built three walls around his mind. The outer wall is rather low, and has several doors in it. Anyone who has a reasonable demand upon his time can enter through these doors. A second wall, however, is much higher and there is but one door through which can pass only members of his family and a few intimate associates. Then there is an inner wall, very high, with no door at all. Inside this wall is the ego of Napoleon Hill, and no one is permitted to enter or extend his influence there. This is a picturesque way of describing a positive mental attitude that you would do well to imitate. Keep your mind open when appropriate, and keep it closed when appropriate.

There is another way to avoid negative influences which is as simple as it is powerful. All you have to do is *keep quiet about your goals*. You can safely share some of your smaller sub-goals with others, but maintain absolute secrecy about your major goals and never share them with anybody except your spouse (and sometimes you will have to be a little guarded even there). The reason for this secrecy is that the sidelines of life are crowded with negative people who like to stick their feet out and trip others, especially positive people. Negative people seem to take a perverse delight in discouraging the positive, constructive and hopeful plans of others. Some negative individuals are simply ignorant of the devastating effects of their negative thinking; others are malicious about discouraging every faint glimmer of optimism wherever they find it. If you have the slightest reason to doubt that another person is fully sympathetic to your major positive goal, then keep it a secret. In this way you do not open yourself to attacks by adversaries, gossips and assorted petty people who habitually wallow in their negativism and malignantly inflict their pessimistic outlooks on everyone they can influence to any degree at all.

A second reason you should keep quiet about your major goals is less understood by most people. When you talk about doing something, you are not doing it. Talking about your plans gives you the impression that you are making progress, when actually the opposite is true. You want to build up an inner pressure in your subconscious which will empower its exertions on your behalf, and you do this by following the plans in this book. When you constantly talk about your goals, you deplete this mental pressure as well as divert it from your purpose. The world is full of those who talk about what they intend to do 'someday'. They discuss their intentions in great detail with anyone who will listen. They become so stimulated by expressing themselves that they never buckle down to the hard work involved in doing the things they plan. A year later they will bring it all up again in conversation, muttering 'I still think it's a great idea, don't you?' Talking isn't doing. Just talking about self-improvement never improved anyone.

The old steam-driven locomotive is quickly becoming a thing of the past, but it serves as a good illustration for those who still can remember those antiquated trains. A small engine was pulling a long train up a hill. It was a very steep grade and the fireman frantically shovelled coal into the engine's furnace to build up enough steam to make it over the top. The strain was great, but the little engine slowly made progress to the top of the hill. When the crest of the hill was a few dozen yards away, the engineer was so excited he blew the whistle in celebration. The whistle tooted shrilly as the steam blasted through it. The train suddenly slowed and started moving backward! The fireman had to shovel coal furiously to build up steam again in the engine's boiler. Finally, the train chugged lamely over the hilltop and sped down the other side.

The point of the story is this: The steam that makes the whistle blow doesn't make the engine go!

When you talk about your plans, you're just 'letting off steam' — steam you should be using to realize your plans. In simple self-defence, positive people should take a vow of silence about their dreams and plans for meaningful self-improvement.

If you think about it, you will probably recall that you have been robbed of precious moments and memories over the years simply because you listened to negative people. Learn the lesson, and from now on keep your secrets and don't give others an opportunity to discourage you in the attainment of what can be yours. Prudent silence is your best protection and it will maintain the inner pressures you need to 'climb the hill' you have before you.

The picture you have in your mind of your *potential future self* and what it can accomplish is your most priceless possession. Guard it well!

The third transitional step is to *open your mind to your experience.* This is difficult to explain except by describing what is not meant by it.

There has been an unfortunate emphasis in our society on drugs which supposedly 'expand the mind'. These 'psychedelic' or 'mind-manifesting' drugs are no doubt a great breakthrough in modern psychiatry, and under proper scientific controls they offer great promise in the search for better understanding of our minds.

It seems that the desire to transcend experience by chemical means is deeply ingrained in human nature. In all countries and throughout all ages, people have been willing to smoke, drink or otherwise ingest anything that held a remote promise of 'expanding' their consciousness. The search for transcendental experience is a common denominator among all mankind. There is nothing wrong with that desire, but it is crystal clear that sustained creativity or tangible achievement does not come from drinking, smoking, sniffing or injecting anything!

The only benefit derived from psychedelic experiences, however arrived at, seems to be the sense of unity with all things and all people that is momentarily perceived by the person. All distinctions between objects and people seem to be artificial and the person deeply feels a oneness with the universe and its contents. Particularly, one perceives that the relationships between people are a form of role-playing and one feels a sense of liberation at having suddenly 'seen through the game'. This is a description of the positive psychedelic experience. The same can be gained by a philosophical commitment to the belief that this unity is a fact. Unfortunately, the vagaries of human nature and the unpredictability of drugs being what they are, there are occasionally negative and nightmarish reactions as well in store for those who seek mind-expansion through chemicals.

Self-hypnosis can be a natural psychedelic experience. It is a misconception to attribute stupefaction to hypnotic experience; on the contrary, it can be an adventure in true consciousness-expansion. Self-hypnosis is the most ancient method of obtaining a transcendental experience known to man. However, the mental discipline required disqualifies those types of people who have never learned, or have no desire to learn, to discipline their minds.

A true transcendental experience should be a flight *into* reality, not a flight *from* reality. Sensible goals and wholesome motivations are essential to a valid and positive psychedelic experience.

The position of the author regarding the use of psychedelic drugs is reflected in the observations of the famous semanticist, S. I. Hayakawa, who commented in the December 1963 issue of

E.T.C., the Review of General Semantics:

But perhaps my basic reason for distrusting the dependence on 'mind-expanding' drugs is that most people haven't learned to use the senses they possess. Speaking only for myself, I not only *hear* music; I *listen* to it when it is around, so that I find Muzak and other background music, intended to be heard but not listened to, utterly intolerable. When I am, in Carl Rogers' terms, open to my experience, I find the colors of the day, whether gray and foggy and muted or bright and sunlit, such vivid experiences that I sometimes pound my steering wheel with excitement. A neon-lit supermarket is often too much for me — so terribly rich in angles and colors and dizzying perspectives that I must deliberately narrow my perceptions to the things on my grocery list lest I take forever to do the shopping. Paintings and sculptures and ceramics get me so intensely excited that I often come out of a museum higher than a kite. In short, I *use* my senses — at least some of them, some of the time. And I say, why disorient your beautiful senses with drugs and poisons before you have half discovered what they can do for you?

Thus, the three steps you must take in transition from theory to practice in your self-improvement programme are the formulation of a definite goal, the insulation of your mind from all negative influences, and the daily habit of opening your mind to your experiences, as described above. Having begun this, we are now ready really to get down to business.

Self-Concept, Self-Control and Positive Thinking

We have considered that one's self-image, or concept and evaluation of oneself, is basic to one's mental health. The sense of value, importance or worth one attaches to the self, as perceived in relation to the body, social contacts, family and ethics, will have an obvious and incalculable effect on one's life. The self-concept, when understood by the individual, can pinpoint existing deficiencies which require constructive attention.

One's self-image is the result of combined life experiences as perceived by oneself. Because it is the result of one's own perception of reality (not reality itself), it may be distorted beyond reality. No two people perceive and evaluate their experiences identically, a fact which makes superfluous the arguments about hereditary or environmental determinism; due to their differing perceptions, no two people actually can have the same psychological environment.

All this is further complicated, usually to one's detriment, by the fact that our perceptions and evaluations are frequently influenced by other people's reactions. The imitativeness and intimidations of childhood tend to mould one's self-concept according to the distorted perceptions and values of those closest to the child during the formative years of infancy and childhood. The havoc and damage caused by neurotic parents and teachers upon impressionable children who are groping to formulate a self-image from life (as they are taught to see and understand it) is frightening to contemplate.

Although the self-concept may be thought of as either the cause or the effect of behaviour, it is indisputable that it is the determining factor in achievement and happiness. The inadequate and unhappy individual cannot succeed as long as he has a crippled self-image, for all resolutions and efforts will tend only to compound the fractures of an already shattered personality. The rehabilitation and reconstruction of one's self-image can be achieved only through significant, meaningful and positive life experiences *which are perceived of as such*. It is this essential and powerful perceiving which is so dramatically helped by hypnosis. Self-hypnosis is an indispensable ally in the creation of a positive, wholesome and integrated self-concept or self-image.

Self-control is an integral part of self-improvement; indeed, there would be no need of any improvement programmes if ego strength were sufficient to handle realistically and suitably all our anxieties and frustrations. Self-control, as understood by those who most need to improve themselves, is an onerous burden, a factor which increases rather than diminishes frustrations. The kind of self-control characterized by gritting the teeth, clenching the fists, and in general assuming the 'stiff upper lip' attitude is inherently self-defeating. True self-control comes from the subconscious. It is a *control of the self by the self*, not a tiresome subjection to more self-imposed restrictions. It is not a control by outer forces exerted on the inner being; on the contrary, it is the *inner self exercising control over the outer forces*. More than the concept of 'mind over matter', it is the control of the inner mind over the outer mind and thus over a wide range of experiences.

This inner mind, variously called the subjective mind, the preconscious, the unconscious, the 'it', the subconscious, etc., is evidently the controlling force behind not only most behaviour but most conscious thought as well. However defined or conceived, this subconscious seems to rule a surprisingly (we might be tempted to say a frighteningly) large part of one's life, and self-hypnosis provides a scientific way to deliberately and systematically influence in a purposeful way this ordinarily inaccessible part of the mind.

Positive thinking, that panacea of Pollyanna-ish self-help books and articles, is a concept difficult to grasp and even more difficult to practise for those whose personalities are already warped by years of negative thinking. As tiresome as the phrase 'positive thinking' has become, it is the key to wholesome personality growth and personal achievement.

Misunderstood as an unrealistic technique to avoid the harsh realities of life, it would be deserving of contemptuous scorn, but correctly conceived as an optimistic and constructive approach to life, it deserves serious attention and studious application. Perhaps no one appreciates the power of positive thinking upon health and happiness more than do hypnotherapists, who have the unique privilege of seeing its efficacy demonstrated in the cases with which they work. Those cynics who minimize the concept of positive thinking as inadequate in the achievement of any significant personality change are considering it only in relationship to the conscious mind; they are correct in the belief that positive thinking on a merely intellectual level has only a limited usefulness. However, through the procedure of self-hypnosis the implanting of positive thinking principles in the subconscious produces a continuing wholesome effect on the total personality.

You will learn the true meaning of 'positive thinking' later when you are taught how to make suggestions in self-hypnosis. It may be quite different from what you have been led to believe.

Many of the other precepts contained in self-improvement books can be useful, providing they are accepted at deeper levels of the mind. For example, bibliotherapy, a treatment method which utilizes a guided reading programme of select books which bear on a person's needs, is effective provided the person's intellect is adequate to comprehend the material, and providing the treatment sessions provide ample opportunity for discussion with a more knowledgeable person. This kind of intellectual approach can be immeasureably strengthened if its effects are internalized through simultaneous hypnotherapy. Post-hypnotic suggestions can motivate the person to read the material, enhance his appreciation for the subject matter, and predispose him to remember the contents. Discussions carried out on the trance level can enable the subject matter to be related to the deeper needs of the personality in an extremely vivid way. This integration of hypnosis and bibliotherapy opens up many challenging possibilities, for self-hypnosis can likewise be used to enhance and internalize the benefits of a guided reading programme.

Shaping Your Goal

Your *future self*, or *potential self*, will be the *suggested self* you formulate. It will be formed along the same lines as your presently perceived self was formed, a process which you understand by now.

Your 'self-in-relation-to-the-environment' is what you must re-form according to your desires and beliefs of what would be in your own best interest. We will now take each of the categories of the self-concept we have discussed earlier and, using them as a guide, use the following information in devising a personalized written plan.

The Physical Self

This means your view of your body, state of health, physical appearance, skills and sexuality (not what others might think of you in these ways, but how you think of yourself in these categories in terms of positiveness or negativeness).

For example, you might score yourself on a negative-to-positive scale of self-satisfaction at a point in the middle, or tending to one extreme or the other. There may be some things about your body, health, appearance, skills and sexuality that you like (feel positively about) and other things you may not like (feel negatively about). Again, your physical self-concept has nothing whatever to do with objective reality or other people's opinions, but how you feel about yourself in these categories.

Once you have defined for yourself your physical self-concept as you presently feel about it, then list the characteristics of your *potential physical self* as you wish it to be in the future. Be specific about the things you want to improve and feel better about a year from now.

Then list the steps that common sense tells you are under your conscious control which you must take in order for this *future physical self* to become a reality. For example, you may need to exercise more, eat less, develop some particular skills, take better care of your appearance, etc. These steps under your conscious control require only that you practise them until they become habitual.

Finally, list the steps which must be taken to achieve this *potential physical self*, which conceivably might be under the control of your subconscious mind. For example, you may need to exercise or diet, but for some reason this seems impossible for you to do consistently. These steps would normally be under conscious control, but you somehow feel the need to enlist the aid of your subconscious. Be specific in listing the things you need subconscious assistance to achieve.

The matters you list under this latter category must later be put into the form of suggestions you will give in the state of self-hypnosis!

After giving all this serious and thoughtful study, you are ready to organize your thoughts on the following worksheet.

Physical Self Worksheet

1. My present physical self as I perceive it:

    +3 Very satisfied
    +2 Fairly satisfied
    +1 Partly satisfied
    −1 Partly dissatisfied
    −2 Fairly dissatisfied
    −3 Very dissatisfied

2. My potential physical self as I visualize it:

    ....
    ....
    ....

3. Steps I must take to achieve this potential physical self *that are under my conscious control*:

    ....
    ....
    ....

4. Steps which must be taken to achieve this potential physical
    self *which conceivably might be under the control of my subconscious mind:*

    ....
    ....
    ....

The Moral-Ethical Self

This means how you perceive yourself from a moral-ethical frame
of reference. That is, what you feel is your moral worth, your
relationship to God, your feeling of being a 'good' or 'bad' person,
and your satisfaction with your religion (or for that matter, your
satisfaction with the lack of it). Rate these matters on a negative-
to-positive scale according to how you feel about them.

Note: It is possible for a very devout person to have a negative
moral-ethical self-concept and an atheist to have a positive moral-
ethical self-concept! Whether it is positive or negative depends
solely on the degree of your satisfaction or dissatisfaction with
how you see yourself in this regard. Do you feel positive or
negative about it? Why? Be as specific as you can.

Now follow the same procedure you did for the physical self-
concept on the next worksheet.

Moral-Ethical Self Worksheet

1. My present moral-ethical self as I perceive it:

    +3 Very satisfied
    +2 Fairly satisfied
    +1 Partly satisfied
    −1 Partly dissatisfied
    −2 Fairly dissatisfied
    −3 Very dissatisfied

2. My potential moral-ethical self as I visualize it:

    ....
    ....
    ....

3. Steps I must take to achieve this potential moral-ethical self
    that are under my conscious control:

    ....

4. Steps which must be taken to achieve this potential moral-ethical self *which conceivably might be under the control of my subconscious mind*:

The Family Self

This refers to your feelings of adequacy, worth and value as a family member: how positively or negatively you see yourself as a son or daughter, father or mother, brother or sister, etc. The family self-concept also includes the 'extended family' of intimate associates. (A person who has never been part of a natural family nonetheless has a family-type relationship with people who substitute for a family in the emotional sense.) Your family self-concept is your perception of yourself in reference to your natural family members *and* to your closest and most immediate circle of associates.

After careful consideration of these factors, fill out the following worksheet.

Family Self Worksheet

1. My present family self as I perceive it:

    +3 Very satisfied
    +2 Fairly satisfied
    +1 Partly satisfied
    −1 Partly dissatisfied
    −2 Fairly dissatisfied
    −3 Very dissatisfied

2. My potential family self as I visualize it:

3. Steps I must take to achieve this potential family self *that are*

under my conscious control:

....

....

....

4. Steps which must be taken to achieve this potential family
    self *which conceivably might be under the control of my subconscious mind*:

....

....

....

The Social Self

This means your perception of self in relationship to 'others' in
a more general way and your sense of adequacy and worth in
your social interaction with other people in general, your 'social
life'.

Rate yourself on a negative-to-positive scale in every aspect
you can think of which pertains to this category. Then fill in the
following worksheet.

Social Self Worksheet

1. My present social self as I perceive it:

                              +3 Very satisfied
                              +2 Fairly satisfied
                              +1 Partly satisfied
                              −1 Partly dissatisfied
                              −2 Fairly dissatisfied
                              −3 Very dissatisfied

2. My potential social self as I visualize it:

....

....

....

3. Steps I must take to achieve this potential social self *that are
    under my conscious control*:

....

....

....

4.   Steps which must be taken to achieve this potential social self *which conceivably might be under the control of my subconscious mind*:

....

....

....

The Personal Self

This means your sense of personal worth, your feelings of adequacy as a person and your evaluation of your personality *apart from your body or your relationships with others!* Many people have such an emotional investment in their bodies and appearance, or their family or social relationships, that if these were taken from them by some terrible misfortune then they would have nothing left. What is left after you have lost your health, your skills, your sexuality, your appearance, your family and friends, and your faith — this is what is meant by your 'personal self'. How would you rate your inner resources minus all these things? (Think of Job in the Bible. What would have happened if he had lost even his faith in God? Supposing he had, what would have been the qualities of his personal self-concept which might have enabled him to cope with his difficulties? Imagine yourself in such a dire situation, and consider what your personal self-concept is at this moment.)

Now go through the steps previously described and fill out the final worksheet.

Personal Self Worksheet

1.   My present personal self as I perceive it:

+3 Very satisfied
+2 Fairly satisfied
+1 Partly satisfied
−1 Partly dissatisfied
−2 Fairly dissatisfied
−3 Very dissatisfied

2.   My potential personal self as I visualize it:

....

....

....

3. Steps I must take to achieve this potential personal self *that are under my conscious control*:

   ....

   ....

   ....

4. Steps which must be taken to achieve this potential personal self *which conceivably might be under the control of my subconscious mind*:

   ....

   ....

   ....

When you have finished these worksheets you will have accomplished several important things. You will have honestly searched your soul and put down on paper exactly how positively or negatively you think of yourself in these categories which make up your phenomenological self. You will have clearly defined your physical, moral-ethical, family, social and personal self-concepts. You will have determined which areas you want to change and you will have decided exactly what you want the end result of your self-improvement plan to be — you will have visualized your future potential self-concept in those particular categories.

More importantly, you will have analysed the disparity between what you are and what you want to become, and formulated definite steps which must be taken to eliminate the disparity. Some of these steps will be made by simple decision-making and conscious habit-forming, while others will require help or reinforcement from your untapped inner resources. Many of these steps to change will overlap. All the steps you have listed under item 4 on your worksheets will indicate exactly what the content of your autosuggestions must be during self-hypnosis.

Actually filling out these worksheets and getting it all in written form should not be laborious if you think of it as a fascinating process of self-revelation and an exciting adventure in growth and self-improvement. You should give a great deal of thought to each worksheet as you decide the kind of person you really want to be. Many people are so limited in their self-improvement goals that the end result is hardly noticed as an improvement by the people who know them best. The discipline of actually filling out these worksheets eliminates the superficial thinking which results in such shallow attempts at self-improvement.

These worksheets provide you with a specific plan to attain specific goals in specific ways. No one would think of building or remodelling a house without having a detailed, well-thought-out, carefully planned set of blueprints. These worksheets are your blueprints for planned self-improvement. The wonderful thing is that you can review and revise your 'blueprints' from time to time during 'construction', as it were. We never finish building ourselves into what we could become and it is wise and helpful to review our progress periodically and revise our plans if necessary.

Having carefully and conscientiously worked out the various aspects of your *potential self* as indicated, you have enumerated the stepping-stones to its achievement.

You have listed the steps which you must *consciously* take in order to achieve the self-concept you desire. To accomplish this phase of your self-improvement programme you need only to remind yourself of these steps frequently enough to make them habitual. This demands character and effort, but it is well within your power. After you have followed faithfully those conscious steps for a few months or less, they will become so habitual that you will be astounded at the difference they make in your life.

You have also listed other steps which must be taken which seem beyond your conscious power. To achieve these goals you must influence your subconscious mind and it in turn will produce the desired results in your experience. To accomplish this phase in your self-improvement programme, you must utilize *self-hypnosis, which is the only known way you can deliberately influence your subconscious mind.*

These two approaches to self-improvement, the conscious and the subconscious, should be pursued simultaneously. Deliberately doing things until they become habitual, and faithfully using self-hypnosis to shape the subconscious mind according to your plan, are the twin approaches to the achievement of your *potential self* or *future self*. You can now see why it can be referred to as your *suggested self*. Your suggestions, reaching your subconscious mind via self-hypnosis, bring it into reality.

You and you alone can devise the blueprint by which you will re-construct your personality and shape your earthly destiny. No one else has that right, but no one else has that responsibility; no one else has the ability to do so. You now have the *plan* and the *method* by which you can attain your goal. Now you must practise the method sufficiently and apply it to your plan.

The principle ingredients of self-hypnosis are *relaxation, concentration* (*controlled attention*) *and visualization*. Some courses recommend elaborate mental and physical exercises which allegedly develop these abilities. I personally practised many of these as a boy and found them more entertaining than practical.

The best way to develop these qualities is to practise them daily in practical ways for a definite purpose. If you faithfully practise the programme suggested in this book, you will have no need of supplementary exercises of any kind.

When you actually practise self-hypnosis on a daily basis for self-improvement, you soon discover what visualizations work best for you. For example, an accountant who suffered from insomnia due to worries about piled up work at the office discovered the most helpful visualizations for him through a little practice. In self-hypnosis, he visualized a cloth sack which he imagined contained the work which remained for him to do the next day. He visualized tying this sack tightly, putting it inside a box which he tied securely, and then locking the box inside a large desk drawer. He visualized himself leaving the office, closing the door, locking it and walking out of the office building with a smile of relief. After practising this personalized visualization for one week, he was able to 'leave his work at the office' (in the emotional sense) and sleep like a baby every night thereafter.

The particular visualizations you devise for your own needs will serve you far better than any you could read in a book. Some people want a kind of 'recipe book' for self-improvement which contains the 'right kind of suggestions' to use in self-hypnosis. It simply isn't done that way. Self-improvement involves self-involvement and the visualizations and suggestions you make up will be the best ones for you!

As you practise self-hypnosis, you will discover a wonderful thing happens to you: *relaxation will become a way of life.* You will discover that you have a new sense of bodily awareness which will enable you to detect and diminish tension in your body the moment it appears. Many times during the day you will mentally check your body for unnecessary tension and you will soon develop the knack of relaxing those tense areas instantly. You will do this inconspicuously and undetected by others. Thus you will develop a healthful serenity at the same time that your associates may be developing destructive reactions to the same stresses.

Your daily and nightly practice of self-hypnosis will soon enable you to relax instantly. You will fall asleep quickly every night and you will sleep comfortably throughout the night, enjoying pleasant dreams. You will experience sleeplessness only as long as you choose to; you will be able to tranquillize your mind and body the moment you direct your mind to the task.

Your powers of concentration will increase simply because, by practising self-hypnosis, you will come to understand the real meaning of concentration. True concentration is effortless, and can only be achieved by a forgetfulness of one's own body as well as of the surroundings. A person with a scowling face, squinted eyes and furrowed brow may be *trying* to concentrate, but he certainly doesn't succeed until he becomes effortlessly absorbed in the object of his attention. Your practice of self-hypnosis will develop the corollary ability to relax completely, narrow your perceptions, and effortlessly focus your entire attention on any subject you wish, regardless of where you are or what others may be doing. You will find that this controlled attention is accomplished without strain and therefore you will be able to do 'mental work' for long periods of time without fatigue or distraction.

The practice of self-hypnosis will also develop your ability to visualize things relevant to your goals more clearly. The power of imagination (visualization) is the method by which the subconscious is impressed. 'Pictures' are the language of the subconscious; we speak to it in word-pictures and it speaks to us in its own unique symbolism. Words are effective in influencing the subconscious only to the extent they convey clear and vivid pictures to the imagination.

As you become expert, you will be able to practise wordless autosuggestion by continually flashing desirable mental images or pictures to your inner mind. This is 'positive thinking' in the truest sense — getting your mind away from what you don't want and on to what you want — a continual procession of optimistic images marching through the mind, profoundly influencing the subconscious and thereby intensely affecting your mind, body and circumstances.

In the preceding paragraphs I haven't said 'self-hypnosis' will do these things; it is the '*practice* of self-hypnosis' which does them!

Scheduling Your Practice

To develop skill rapidly in the method of self-hypnosis, the following practice schedule is recommended. Follow the instructions given previously on how to do the progressive relaxation method and the instantaneous relaxation method until you master both of them. Practise the progressive relaxation method lying down just before you fall asleep at night. Do not concern yourself with prolonging the trance or with giving yourself constructive suggestions at these times. Work rather at getting complete relaxation so you find yourself actually falling asleep for the night. Soon you will be able to relax so profoundly and quickly that by simply assuming a comfortable position, taking a few deep breaths and just thinking of relaxation, you will fall sound asleep in a matter of four or five minutes! Practise this procedure nightly for two full weeks. Never just 'go to sleep', but *put yourself to sleep* every night of your life!

Of course, hypnosis is not sleep and the real object of self-hypnosis is not to go to sleep, but you will be learning to relax by following a specific technique preparatory to sleep. This is a helpful conditioning period for people who are extremely tense and nervous. It isn't as important for those who are naturally more relaxed.

After a week or so of nightly practice, you will have developed the knack of relaxing your body to a point of pleasant numbness within a minute or two. When you have reached this degree of proficiency in the practice of self-hypnotic induction (remember that this 'numb' feeling is the most commonly experienced phenomenon of the trance state) you will learn to recognize the trance coming over you (or you going into it, whichever way you prefer to think of it) and you can begin *at that moment* to give yourself the positive suggestions you have decided upon.

By then you will find it extremely practical to practise self-hypnosis in a sitting position. If you use the progressive relaxation method, the change in position may require you to shorten the rather lengthy mental 'verbalizing'. If you practise the progressive relaxation method in a sitting position at least once daily for one week, by the end of that time you should be able to induce the state within two or three minutes.

Also practise the instantaneous relaxation method during this time. It is so brief it will not require additional time from your daily schedule; it can be done for one minute as many times a day as you desire. Many people find the instantaneous method easier from the beginning. If you do, by all means use it exclusively. Except for very tense individuals who find it difficult to let go of tension, the instantaneous relaxation method is the superior one from the start. Everyone should aim at mastering it as soon as possible. Once mastered, it can then be used exclusively.

You can increase your skill in self-hypnosis, both in terms of speed and depth, by a simple but powerful technique known as *fractionization*. Before you terminate each session, always tell yourself that the next time you practise you will immediately enter a deeper and sounder state of relaxation. Then upon 'awakening', you immediately begin another induction! Repeat the process several times in one practice period. In other words, you practise several successive inductions, each time giving yourself the suggestion that the next time it will be easier, quicker and deeper. For example, if you have a half-hour at your disposal and you can induce the trance within fifteen minutes, you do it twice within the half-hour. Likewise, after you can do it in five minutes, you will be doing three inductions within fifteen minutes. When you can do it in one minute, you can do it five times in five minutes. Soon you will find that ten seconds will be ample time to induce the hypnotic state!

To recapitulate: (1) practise self-hypnosis in bed every night for two weeks; (2) during the same time period, practise it in a sitting position for fifteen minutes a day for one week; (3) continue to practise it in bed nightly regardless of your other practice sessions.

Following these simple instructions, the 'worst' hypnotic subject will become an expert in self-hypnosis within twenty-one days! Since you go to bed every night anyway, the nightly sessions do not take time from your regular schedule and the short daily sessions are easy to work into the busiest life. At the end of three weeks, you will be able to use the instantaneous relaxation method numerous times daily. By then you will find it interesting, relaxing and rewarding to practise. It will not be something you 'practise', but something you just 'do' as often as you think of it.

You'll be able to sit up straight, close your eyes, take a few deep breaths, do the eye-closure, think of deep relaxation, and deepen the state by counting or simply breathing as you double the relaxation each time. Then you are ready to give suggestions to your subconscious mind. Your entire self-improvement session need not take more than three minutes!

No one can truthfully say there isn't enough time for self-hypnosis. It takes less time than drinking a cup of hot coffee or tea, and everyone seems to find time for that!

Within one month from the time you begin to practise, you will have acquired a life-long skill that you will be able to use to your advantage *any time, any place.*

Just as soon as you have mastered the method, you can apply it to your plan for self-improvement, shaping your subconscious towards whatever goals you choose.

Emile Coué's system required the repetition of the phrase 'Every day in every way I am getting better and better,' a formula which Coué asserted was sufficient for all purposes, for the subconscious could then interpret it according to whatever need existed. There is great truth to the Coué system, but now you are prepared to do even better.

How to Formulate Suggestions

The 'rational ideas' and the material from your worksheets provide you with the content for your suggestions. But you must know the science of *phrasing* the suggestions for maximum impact on your subconscious.

The first rule is to make your suggestions positive. This means they must be positive in *form* as well as in *content.* 'I will not be nervous and jittery' is positive in its intended content, but it is negative in its phrasing! *This is the wrong way to make a suggestion.* Because the subconscious mind is affected by pictures, a negatively phrased suggestion is likely to accomplish the opposite of what is intended! If a child is carrying a glass full of water and you shout 'Don't spill it!', the picture to the subconscious is 'Spill it!' The water will likely be spilled. 'Don't be nervous' is translated by the subconscious as 'Be nervous,' for the picture conveyed is that of 'nervousness'.

Remember that positive thinking is getting the mind off what you don't want, and getting it onto what you do want. What you should suggest is not the absence of nervousness, but the opposite of nervousness. The right way to make the suggestion in self-hypnosis is: 'I will be calm and confident.' The subconscious hears and pictures 'calm and confident', and brings that to pass.

'I will not eat fattening foods' is interpreted by the subconscious as 'Eat fattening foods' because it presents a picture of fattening foods. Likewise, 'I will not be angry' is interpreted as 'Be angry,' etc. Consider the contrast with the following: 'I desire only nutritious, natural food. I eat small, reasonable portions, which I enjoy thoroughly. I always feel full and satisfied. I enjoy more physical activity, and I feel rewarded when I exercise. I control my desires and habits, and do only those things which are good for me. I am confident in everything I say, think or do. I like people and they like me,' etc. These are examples of suggestions which are positive *both* in content and phrasing.

In hypnosis, negatively phrased suggestions are considered to be negative suggestions, regardless of their intent. It is simply the way the mind works. Negative words ('not', 'don't', 'won't' 'shouldn't', etc.) simply underscore the thing negated in the phrase. From a hypnological point of view, the reason the Ten Commandments have not found wider acceptance in actual practice is that eight or nine of the ten are phrased negatively. 'Thou shalt not do this-or-that' is heard by the subconscious as 'Thou shalt do this-or-that.' In refreshing contrast, Christ summarized the Commandments in two positive statements: 'Thou shalt love the Lord thy God,' and 'Love thy neighbour as thyself.'

Always make your self-hypnotic suggestions *completely* positive (in both content and phrasing), and also make it a practice in your conscious thinking. That's what it means to be a positive thinker and live a positive life!

The second rule is to make your suggestions something you can see yourself doing. See yourself feeling, thinking, acting the way you suggest. Effective suggestions can be wordless, but never blank to the imagination. When you 'flash' a positive picture to your subconscious, you are making a wordless hypnotic suggestion. People sometimes say, 'I could never see myself doing that!' If true, it means they will never do it. You must transform your self-improvement suggestions into that which can be desirably visualized or imagined as taking place.

The third and last rule is to make your suggestions brief. Write them out. Then condense them. A page may be shortened to a paragraph without losing its essential meaning. The paragraph can be condensed to a sentence. That sentence may be shortened to one word. This can result in an appropriate 'codeword' which (to your mind) encompasses the meaning of an entire page of accomplish 'miracles' with the self-concept.

Then, devote one week of daily self-hypnosis sessions to each of the other categories of the self (that is, Physical, Moral-Ethical, Family, Social and Personal) and notice the rapid improvement in your experience. Following this schedule, you will spend two full months on programming your subconscious to produce the *potential self* you have designed.

To summarize your *entire* practice schedule:

1. Practise the progressive relaxation method in bed every night for two weeks, and also practise the instantaneous relaxation method several times daily during the same period.
2. Practise self-hypnosis inductions in a sitting position with the instantaneous relaxation method for a total of a half an hour daily (using 'fractionization') for one week, continuing the practice in bed.
3. Then, under self-hypnosis, give yourself positive suggestions daily regarding the one category of your *potential self* you consider most important. Continue this for thirty days.
4. Do the same for one week with a second category.
5. Do the same for one week with a third category.
6. Do the same for one week with a fourth category.
7. Do the same for one week with a fifth category. (If you feel you need to.)

In just eleven weeks you will have begun to overhaul your personality to a remarkable degree. By the end of three months' practice, your *perceived self* will then coincide perfectly with your *suggested self*, for your *future* or *potential self* will have become a present reality to you. Naturally, this is not the end, but a new beginning. It provides the basis for bigger and better things to come.

By that time, your mental marksmanship will be so good you will be able to apply the method of self-hypnosis to whatever plan you choose to work on for the rest of your life.

Go back and re-read the destructive self-suggestions listed previously (the 'irrational ideas'). If you have been guilty of self-indoctrination with any of these negative and foolish suggestions, begin applying the correct suggestion (the 'rational idea') that corresponds to the wrong one. Use the positive suggestion in your self-hypnosis sessions every day for one week. Review this list from time to time to see if you have slipped into any of the errors mentioned. Systematic use of those correct suggestions in your daily sessions will improve your mental health considerably.

In general, it is best to work with one problem area exclusively until it is solved. When you try to bombard the subconscious with too many diverse suggestions, you are reverting to a 'shotgun approach' which, although better than nothing at all, is far inferior to a planned, methodical 'rifle approach'. Pick your target, make your plan, and then stick with it until you achieve that specific goal.

You will find that two weeks of daily self-hypnosis sessions should be ample to get results with most problems. If you seem to reach an impasse, examine the suggestions you have been giving to your subconscious mind and perhaps you can improve them. *Sometimes a minor change in phrasing can make a dramatic difference in results.* One man developed a strange hand tremor whenever anyone was watching him. His hand shook so violently if he thought someone might be observing him that he was unable to drink from a glass or cup in public. He tried self-hypnosis, giving himself the suggestion 'I am calm and confident,' but to no avail in correcting that specific problem. He re-evaluated the matter and devised the following modification: 'I am calm and confident *at all times, in all places, and in all company.*' Within a week, the hand tremor vanished and never returned!

Do not forget to take the conscious steps you know must be taken to achieve your goals. Make a habit of the right actions which reason would dictate to be proper in your self-improvement programme. When you have the right attitude through a strong motivation, you will be surprised how easy it is to form the right habits!

It isn't necessary to 'erase' negative thoughts and actions by attacking them directly. Just as it isn't necessary to erase a tape recording in order to record something on it (it is naturally erased as it is re-recorded), positive suggestions work the same way in your subconscious. Programming your mind with positive suggestions through self-hypnosis naturally 'erases' the thoughts, feelings and actions you want to get rid of.

Apply self-hypnosis to your problems and goals daily, not only at a set time, but at any time and place you can squeeze it in. Learn to have brief sessions in all kinds of locations so you will be prepared someday for an emergency or unexpected circumstance. Never omit the nightly session, and always fall asleep with some positive, desirable thought uppermost in your mind so the subconscious can work peacefully on it throughout the night.

Develop a positive mental attitude at all times. Keep your mind happy and optimistic. Insulate yourself from negativism wherever you find it.

Keep in practice with self-hypnosis daily throughout your life. If you are in-between specific goals, use the general suggestion recommended by Coué: 'Every day in every way I am getting better and better.' Incidentally, Coué taught children to use positive autosuggestion by reciting: 'I am growing every day, a better boy (or girl) in every way.' When you use this generalized suggestion, be sure to visualize what you mean by 'every way'.

The first dreamers of aviation found that the hardest thing was not to fly — it was to get off the ground. The greatest difficulty in self-improvement for most people is not in moving, but in getting started!

If you diligently follow this programme, it will get you off the ground so you can fly, so to speak. It will get you started so you can keep going. But as was mentioned in the beginning, it is *you* who must start; it is *you* who must keep moving! The physical Law of Inertia says that stationary objects stay stationary unless acted upon by a greater force, and that moving objects tend to continue moving until opposed by an equal or greater force (such as friction or some barrier). There is also a Law of Inertia in human behaviour: nothing moves unless you push it, and once it gets started it is easy to keep it moving! Life's improvements are like pushing a car. At first it seems to require great effort as you rock it back and forth. But once the wheels turn over, it is much easier pushing to keep it moving. You will discover a wonderful truth about this as you continue to follow this programme: once a problem situation begins to budge, it soon starts rolling; and once started, it tends to pick up momentum!

A once-popular song lyric said: 'When you're hot, you're hot; when you're not, you're not.' The common saying is: 'Nothing succeeds like success.' Once you are moving in the right direction, everything good seems to come your way. Things which once seemed impossible suddenly become easy to do. A very timid woman was astonished at her progress overcoming her shyness through self-hypnosis. What happened was that when she became the tiniest bit more self-confident, people reacted to her more positively and this in turn emboldened her to become even more confident. Soon her entire personality and all her relationships had improved dramatically. In like manner, once you begin making some progress in the direction of your goals, you will find the process accelerates beyond your expectations. The slightest progress in the beginning is cause for unbounded optimism, for it assures continued progress at a faster rate.

Life's inevitable setbacks are never real cause for discouragement. When the first ground-to-air missiles were invented, they were guided by the heat from the targeted aircraft's jet engines. These missiles did not go in a straight line, but followed a zig-zag path as their heat-sensors compensated their course by detecting when they were getting 'hotter' or 'cooler' in their pursuit. (This early zig-zagging missile was called the 'Sidewinder', after a snake that slithers sideways towards its destination.) In your self-improvement programme, you may experience some 'zigs' and 'zags' as you approach your goal. As long as you are moving towards your goal you will achieve it, for your subconscious will compensate to keep you on track!

(The Sidewinder Missile became obsolete when enemy fliers discovered they could throw it off track by dropping heat-flares. The heat-sensing missile would then follow the flare instead of the plane. This was countered by developing more sophisticated missile-guiding technology.) It's important to realize when you are simply zig-zagging towards your self-improvement goals due to minor setbacks, and when you are actually on a detour which leads you in a different direction. To eliminate this possibility, you should evaluate your progress periodically. Sometimes you will find that a sub-goal you have unwisely chosen is actually a detour which leads you away from your major goal. Simple awareness of this possibility should prevent it from happening.

Once you start moving towards success, it is important to keep moving and to conquer new horizons in self-improvement. Self-hypnosis can be used to enrich every activity of your life every day. Because it is so easy to become more than a little fanatical on the possibilities of expanded and self-directed mind-power, the author has refrained from giving a lot of self-hypnosis 'success stories'. Many of them would sound utterly fantastic and unbelievable to you at the beginning stage. But if you practise and get serious about your goals, *and apply this method*, you can be assured that you will soon be able to write *your own success story*! It will no doubt seem miraculous to others.

The world is full of people who 'know all about' hypnosis and self-hypnosis because they took a course or read a book or two. They may even have practised it for a time but soon gave it up. Their minds and lives are undistinguished in spite of their supposed knowledge. They have in their possession an Aladdin's Lamp but they seldom rub it. Determine to be one of the few who make this wonderful power a 'way of life', helping you to be and do whatever you want to be and do!

Your Success Mechanism

It is said that 'Knowledge is power,' but this is only partly true. Knowledge is power only when it is employed in the service of a burning desire to accomplish a specific goal.

It is also said that hypnosis is powerful, but this too is only partly true. Hypnosis is a state of mind, a tool, a technique, a method. Self-hypnosis is indeed a key to your subconscious mind, but *all the power is in your mind*. It has always been there, and is there now, waiting to be used.

Microcomputers captivated the public's imagination when they were first introduced; they are rapidly becoming so commonplace in our society that they are taken for granted. Suppose a friend were to show you a tiny black box which he kept carefully guarded. In answer to your question, he replies: 'This is a highly miniaturized portable computer of extreme accuracy and complexity, with an accuracy so fantastic it has near-infallibility. It helps me solve complex personal problems. It helps me to study, to concentrate and to remember. It gives me an advantage in all competition. *It is my personal success mechanism!* By using this 'success mechanism', I can have complete control over my mind, my emotions and many of my bodily functions. It is priceless, this 'success mechanism' of mine, for it is *the only one in existence!*'

You would probably give up everything you own to get one of those success mechanisms and it would be well worth whatever sacrifice it took. The message of this book is that *you already have a success mechanism* — it is *your subconscious mind!*

Your activated brain, your mind, is unique and priceless. Your very body and all its organs exist, in the most literal sense, solely to support your brain. Your brain will be the last organ in your body to die; every other organ will sacrifice itself, even to the last beating of your heart, to keep the brain alive a few moments longer. Your lungs may be kept breathing and your heart may be kept pumping blood by artificial life-support equipment, but medical and legal experts agree that when your brain dies (and only then) will you be literally dead. This brain, which is far more complex than any computer could ever be, has somewhere within it all the functions we call the subconscious mind. It can scan your past experiences, synthesize data in your memory bank, provide you with creative insights, and do a host of other incomprehensible things too wonderful and numerous to mention, even if we could. It is your success mechanism. Use it well!

WOOLWICH
CASHBASE
Terms and Conditions of Issue

1. The Cashbase Card must only be used in accordance with these Terms and Conditions of Issue.

2. The Cashbase Card is not transferable and must be used only by the person to whom it is issued ("the Cardholder"). Each Cardholder will receive, in addition to the Cashbase Card, a secret Personal Number. In the case of a Cashbase account in joint names, a maximum of two Cardholders will be permitted and withdrawals will be allowed on the authority of either Cardholder.

3. On opening the Cashbase account, the Society is irrevocably authorised to debit withdrawals effected by means of the Cashbase Card to the Cardholder's account.

4. The Cashbase Card must be signed by the Cardholder immediately on receipt.

5. The Cashbase Card remains the property of the Society and must be destroyed or returned to the Society on closure of the Cashbase account. The Society may suspend or withdraw the right to use the Cashbase Card and may refuse to issue, renew or replace any card.

6. The Cardholder must keep his Personal Number secret and must not disclose it to any other person whether an employee of the Society or not. The Cardholder must not keep a record of the number in any way which might enable it to be identified with the Cashbase Card or account. The Personal Number must never be written on the Cashbase Card, or kept with the Cashbase Card.

7. The Cardholder shall take all possible steps to ensure that the Cashbase Card is kept safely and that it is not passed to any other person. The Cardholder must not allow the Cashbase Card to be used by any other person.

8. The Cardholder may not use the Cashbase Card before or after the period for which it is stated to be valid, or after any notification is given by the Society of its cancellation or withdrawal.

9. If the Cashbase Card is lost, stolen or mislaid or the Personal Number is disclosed to any unauthorised person, the Cardholder must immediately notify the Society's Cashbase Control, (telephone 01-301-4949) at any time day or night, and confirm the same within 48 hours in writing to Dept. C.C., PO Box 124, Bexleyheath DA7 6BL. Lost cards subsequently found after notification must be destroyed by the Cardholder.

10. The Cardholder is responsible for any use of the Cashbase Card whether or not he or she has authorised it and the Society may debit the account holder's account in respect of any payment made to any person using the card unless the account holder can show
(a) that he or she had notified the Society that the Cashbase Card had been lost, stolen or mislaid more than 24 hours before the payment; or
(b) the Society has not exercised reasonable care in making the payment.

11. The Cardholder may not withdraw more than a total of £250 in cash from any Cashbase machine in any one day.

12. The Cardholder may make withdrawals at any Woolwich branch in cash or by cheque on production of the Cashbase Card, subject to the Society's Rules and the normal branch limit.

13. Cash or cheque deposits may be made at the Cashbase machine or at any Woolwich branch or agency. Deposits made at a Cashbase machine shall be subject to subsequent confirmation by appointed Woolwich branch staff. No withdrawals will be allowed against unconfirmed or uncleared deposits.

14. The Society may withdraw or terminate the Cashbase machine facilities without notice. The Society shall not be liable for any contingent loss or damage alleged to have resulted from the failure or malfunctioning of the Cashbase system or in respect of the inaccuracy of any data furnished by the Cashbase system.

15. The Terms and Conditions of Issue may be altered by the Society at any time, without notice, in accordance with the Society's Rules.

16. Investments in a Cashbase account represent shares in the Society. Cardholders are members of the Society, bound by its Rules and the current Terms and Conditions of Issue. Current copies of the Society's Rules may be obtained from any Woolwich branch.

17. No transfer of a Cashbase account shall be effective unless made in a form approved by the Board and registered in the books of the Society.

18. The minimum holding in a Cashbase account is £1.00.

19. The rate of interest on a Cashbase account may vary from time to time. Any variation will be publicised in the Society's branch offices and by advertisement in selected national newspapers in accordance with the Society's Rules. Interest shall be calculated on a daily basis, from the day following receipt of the investment, up to and including the day of withdrawal. The amount of interest payable on the account will be automatically added to the account annually on the 30th September.

WOOLWICH
CASHBASE

Notes on the Terms & Conditions of Issue

Introduction
Every Cashbase Account holder is subject to the Terms & Conditions of Issue of the Account. It is important for you to understand these Terms & Conditions and to know what they mean to you. We have done our best to ensure that they are as jargon-free as possible and presented in a way which is simple to follow. The following notes highlight some of the main features.

Security
Many of the account conditions are concerned with security. Each account holder should take all reasonable steps to ensure the safety of their card and Personal Number. In particular, you should always sign your card as soon as you receive it and never allow another person to use it. You should also always keep your Personal Number secret and never keep a record of it with the card. If, for example, you keep the number with the card, and lose them, someone else could gain access to the money in your account.

Lost/Stolen Cards
If you lose or mislay your Cashbase Card, or are unfortunate enough to have it stolen, you must notify us immediately. Cashbase Control can take your telephone call at any time, day or night, so you should never delay telling us. This is most important. A delay in telling us of a lost, stolen or mislaid card could leave you open to financial loss.

Deposits/Withdrawals
You can deposit money in cash or by cheque into your Cashbase account in a number of ways; through a Cashbase machine, at a Woolwich branch, or at any Woolwich agency.

Cash withdrawals may be made at a Cashbase machine and at any Woolwich branch. Cheque withdrawals can be made at a branch only. Cardholders may withdraw up to £250 each day at a Cashbase machine, as long as there is sufficient money in the account. You must keep at least £1 in a Cashbase Account.

Interest
Interest is calculated on a daily basis and is added to the Cashbase Account on 30th September each year. The rate of interest may change, but the current interest rate will always be on display in any Woolwich branch.

WOOLWICH
EQUITABLE BUILDING SOCIETY

Chief Office: Equitable House, London SE18 6AB
Investment Department: 30 Erith Road, Bexleyheath, Kent DA7 6BP
Branches and agencies throughout the country
Member of The Building Societies Association

Appendix:
Spiritual Improvement

This is for those who are spiritually oriented and who think of self-improvement as a process of becoming more ethical, more religious or more God-like.

Rather than inject a metaphysical interpretation into the previous discussions of personality, self-improvement and self-hypnosis, it has been scrupulously avoided for a reason. This has not been in any compromise with truth, but simply as a concession to those readers whose past experiences might have regrettably prejudiced them against religious or spiritual interpretations. There is no reason they should be denied the instruction whereby they can shape their subconscious minds for constructive ends. The teachings of this book effectively apply to all human beings, irrespective of their personal spiritual philosophy or religious beliefs. The Bible teaches that the sun shines and the rain falls on the godly and ungodly alike. Like other blessings, surely hypnosis exists for everyone.

Hypnosis can be explained adequately in purely materialistic terms; its mechanisms are neurological and its phenomena are perfectly natural. There is really nothing the least bit supernatural about hypnosis. However, to explain anything adequately in material terms is not necessarily to say all that can be said on the subject. Certainly man is not less than his body, but he may be considerably more. Biology is the study of 'life', and when we speak of life we necessarily refer to biology. However, when we speak of life, we usually mean a great deal more than mere biology.

Spiritual values are part of human life and no serious student of human nature can ignore the implications of the combined wisdom of the ages which always has recognized a transcendent idea or principle called 'God', and a human's relationship to God.

Normal Guilt

In clinical practice, the author sometimes has felt in the midst of an ethical dilemma when dealing with patients who suffered from the oppressive burden of guilt. Guilt feelings are psychologically destructive, but not all guilt is pathological. Guilt feelings are neurotic only when undeserved or out of proportion to their cause. Guilt complexes are not experienced by most guilty people; on the contrary, one can scarcely find a truly morally guilty person who has any 'complex' about it at all! You could interview all the criminals in all the world's prisons and not discover a single person with a guilt complex. Only 'good people' — the sincere and scrupulous — ever suffer from 'guilt'. It is considered neurotic only when there is no real cause for it or if it is felt to a disproportionate degree in relation to what caused it.

For example, a person who suffers increasing guilt feelings because ten years earlier he stole a postage stamp is obviously feeling inappropriately guilty. Worse yet are those who feel constantly guilty without knowing why; they can't imagine what terrible thing they must have done to feel so miserable. Such 'guilt' is a legitimate concern for psychotherapists and hypnotherapy has been very helpful in such cases.

However, many people who suffer mental anguish from guilt feelings are suffering the logical consequence of their wilful and continued violations of common moral and ethical standards. They have cheated and violated the integrity of others and deliberately trespassed against their own religious or moral convictions until the burden of guilt (via the subconscious mind) produces emotional or psychosomatic problems which require treatment. Unless such persons are willing to straighten out their lives, they must either keep their symptoms or lose their ethics altogether.

It is the author's conviction (considered an eccentricity by many, no doubt) that therapy skills are a gift from God and should not be used simply to make people more comfortable in the pursuit of unethical exploitations of their fellow men. Any 'adjustment' to life that requires the abandonment of personal principles is, in itself, unethical and immoral.

It will be the assumption of this section that you are a person who places value on religious and spiritual values and that therefore you are willing to conduct yourself according to principles which are consistent with universally accepted standards of right and wrong.

Spiritual values, ethical values and religious values may not be synonymous terms, but we are concerned here with spiritual self-improvement apart from religious dogma, and with the personal growth of the individual's 'soul' rather than with church affiliations.

Although it may be superfluous, it should be asserted that there is no conflict between hypnosis and religion. The Roman Catholic Church has officially approved hypnotherapy for its members, and if other church groups have mental reservations about hypnosis it is due to their ignorance of the truth. Hypnosis and self-hypnosis have an essential relationship with all activities in which the mind is engaged and therefore it is inextricably tied to people's religious lives as well.

Religious Practices and Hypnosis

To some extent, the object of all religions is to alter consciousness (creating a sense of the supernatural and transcendent feeling of worship), promote inwardness and subjectivity (self-examination, other-worldliness), re-structure value systems (instruction, indoctrination, 'growing in grace'), remove or alleviate guilt and fear through what psychotherapists call ventilation, abreaction, catharsis or symbolic expiation (confession, penance, supplication, exorcism), strengthen inner controls (sanctification, consecration, 'separated life'), possession by divinity (being Spirit-filled, 'on-fire-for-God'), harmonize interpersonal relationships ('love thy neighbour'), and redemptive service to the world (testimony, witnessing, evangelism, altruism, philanthropy).

The means towards these ends have taken various forms well-known to hypnotists as consciousness-altering techniques: rhythmic movements, chanting, repetitious singing, monotonous movements, postural change, immobility, use of symbols, imagery, group identification, solitude and isolation, unquestioning belief in authority, etc.

There have been famous personages in the history of hypnotism who were also clergymen, notably Father Gasner, Father Maximillian Hell, and the Portuguese monk, Abbé Faria. During the early days of hypnotism (Mesmerism), these men played important roles in the theory and practice of hypnotism for healing purposes.

Other famous hypnotists ran afoul of the Church due to misunderstandings. James Braid of Manchester was called a 'child of the devil' by a prominent English clergyman of his day. Jean Martin Charcot, foremost neurologist of his time and director of the famous Salpêtrière hospital in Paris, was the first man of international repute in medicine to popularize the use of hypnosis, yet he often found himself caught between the Church and his fellow physicians. When he replaced nuns with secular nurses, the Church denounced him as an atheist, and when he declared it might be worthwhile to study the miracles at Lourdes in order to gain knowledge which might be helpful in treating mental illness, he was ridiculed as too religious by his medical colleagues!

The importance of 'eye-closure as the opening wedge to hypnosis' has been explained earlier in this book. It is interesting to note that Protestant Christians are the only religious group that habitually close the eyes in worship and prayer. Buddhists do not; Muslims make obeisance to the ground but do not close the eyes. Jews stand in prayer and move back and forth or from side to side, but usually with open eyes. Roman Catholics, with numerous eye-fixation points in front of them, seldom close the eyes in prayer. One might assume that bowed head and closed eyes is the way one is 'supposed to pray'. The Bible recommends no particular posture for prayer, and simply depicts people at prayer, usually standing, eyes raised to heaven, or occasionally prostrated or kneeling — but nowhere is it mentioned that the eyes were closed! It is fascinating to consider when and how Protestants learned the secret of eye-closure. Far from being frivolous, it is a serious question which penetrates a mystery worth studying.

The use of eye-closure in religion probably originated in the revivals of John Wesley, the founder of Methodism. Forced out of the pulpits of the establishment churches and obliged to preach out-of-doors where listeners were deprived not only of the usual eye-fixation points provided by the religious symbols, candles, etc., at the altar, but were also subject to the discomforts and distractions characteristic of open-air gatherings, the preacher had to rely on volume, enthusiasm and theatricality to hold an audience's attention, even more so to convert them. At the conclusion of the sermon when it was time to urge the listeners to repent and publicly confess their conversion (which was, of course, the object of preaching to the masses out-of-doors in the first place), it was imperative that each person be undistracted. What could have been more natural than to say 'Bow your head and close your eyes' under the pretence of prayer, and then to continue urging for repentance? This provided a few moments as a postscript to the sermon, to recapitulate and individualize the salient points (like the 'close' of a 'sales pitch') given under optimum conditions for a favourable response.

The practice was tremendously successful. Thousands upon thousands were converted, new denominations were started, and churches, schools, orphanages and hospitals were built after the Wesleyan revivals began. It was soon discovered by imitation and trial-and-error that although not every preacher was as eloquent and charismatic as certain outstanding leaders, yet if the 'bow your head and close your eyes' routine followed the sermon, the number of converts increased. The practice soon became a standardized, routine technique indispensable to mass evangelism. When it was used, people were converted; when it was not used, lives remained unchanged. With time, variations and elaborations were made on the basic theme: that is, heads bowed, eyes closed, the hand raised, stand up, come forward, etc., and the 'altar call' became the indispensable Protestant ritual for numerical growth.

Not only is the eye-closure the 'opening wedge to hypnosis', one could also say it is the opening wedge to life-changing decisions made in religious groups!

Far from recommending that clergymen stop using this hypnotic technique, I recommend they should be urged to its more widespread use! It would be constructive if a skilful use of the scientific principles of suggestion were employed at the moment of eye-closure in religious services. Certainly much fear and guilt have been implanted unnecessarily. Fears and guilts repressed in the subconscious are the source of numerous neurotic and psychosomatic illnesses and the most credible person to deal with these emotions might well be a respected clergyman rather than a remote secular therapist.

After she learned the instantaneous relaxation method of self-hypnosis, a religious woman remarked that she almost felt guilty because what the saints of history achieved only after years of arduous struggle — that is, a mystical sense of the ineffable — she was able to achieve in less than half a minute! Modern hypnosis is an effective, scientific means to affect human behaviour, and since both science and religion presumably seek the truth, there can be no essential contradiction between them. The author believes that worthy ends deserve effective means. It is up to you to take it from there.

Meditation

All mystics of history who claimed intimate knowledge and experience of God had one method in common: meditation. Stripped of philosophical pretence, meditation is a mental activity characterized by physical relaxation, narrowed perceptions and visualization of lofty themes. Meditation is controlled attention or effortless concentration. This attentive mental absorption should easily be recognized not merely as similar to self-hypnosis, but identical to it!

People in ancient times could spend hours in the quiet outdoors and contemplate the starry heavens in relative solitude. Without the noises and distractions of mechanized civilization, relaxed mental absorption was easier. The life of shepherds and nomads lent itself to a certain amount of philosophizing and people who chose to think of God and His works could do so to their heart's content.

Such meditation (or hypnoidal contemplation) was made easier by circumstances and, more importantly, by the attitude of others. Meditation was a type of thinking that people did best. *Meditation was respectable*.

When societies were predominantly rural, people had time to meditate on spiritual things. Before civilization became so advanced that people had devised ways to keep themselves awake all night, sundown and eventide were times of quiet meditation. Meditation was the kind of thinking everyone could do and it was valued.

Modern urban life in the Western world has been described as a complicated system of keeping ourselves both busy and nervous. 'Keeping busy' is considered to be a modern virtue and meditation is the opposite of keeping busy. Meditative thinking looks like a waste of time to most people, and therefore not quite respectable.

By contrast, the countries of the East have practised meditation as a valued part of the shared culture for centuries. No matter how crowded the household, each member was expected to spend some time in private 'spiritual' meditation. Certain techniques to assist this type of mental activity developed over the ages and in those cultures where it was valued the most, every person received some instruction in the art of meditation.

Because so little value is placed on meditation in modern Western civilization, there is no technique widely taught for its attainment. Meditation is one kind of thinking that is not highly valued; it is, in fact, discouraged.

The decline of meditation and the decrease in 'spirituality' in the world are mutually the cause and mutually the effect, the one of the other.

If you wish to be more 'spiritual' — that is, to experience subjectively the ideals you believe in, you must cultivate the art of meditation, for it is this kind of thinking which results in spiritual growth and improvement.

The art of meditation and the art of self-hypnosis are one and the same! To be sure, monks, mystics and yogis have developed elaborate methods of meditation, but the various elaborations and embellishments which have accumulated by accretion over centuries are not at all necessary. Stripped of all the irrelevant hocus-pocus, the irreducible residue of practical technique boils down to nothing more nor less than self-hypnosis. You have been taught the most practical methods of self-hypnosis in this book. You have already mastered *the* technique of using your mind by which spiritual improvement is also accomplished. By learning to apply the method of self-hypnosis to your religious values, you can experience spiritual reality and growth!

To the spiritually minded person, self-improvement is a religious duty as well as a privilege. You become a *co-creator with God* when you 'make something of yourself', which is a uniquely human prerogative.

Metaphysics Simplified
The subject of metaphysics, on which innumerable volumes have

been written, is quite understandable to the student of self-hypnosis. Metaphysical principles are really very simple and will become crystal clear after a brief review of what you have already learned about your mind.

The subconscious mind acts upon the rest of the mind and the body. It is the non-self-conscious source of life. The subconscious does not reason inductively because it has no interest in knowing 'why'. It just knows how to do what it does — namely, to maintain the basic life processes and act upon suggestions. The suggestions are accepted as commands because the subconscious cannot say 'No'; it just does what it is told to do. It works automatically, one might say almost mechanically. It does not know or care *why* it does what it does; it only knows *how* to do it. It can be told *what* to do.

The basic assumption of metaphysical teaching is that the subconscious mind is universal; that is, there is no such thing as 'my' subconscious mind and 'your' subconscious mind — there is only one subconscious mind, and we are merely partakers of it. Each person is an individualized centre in this universal subconscious mind, just as a wave is an individualized manifestation of the ocean. It is distinctive but of the same essence. This subconscious mind, being universal and independent of any individual, is considered as infinite 'Mind'.

Because it works mechanically according to the suggestions or commands (or thoughts and images) given to it, it is not capricious, but renders to each person exactly as he or she thinks. It works in an inexorable and inflexible way and for this reason it is called 'Law'. Thus we read in metaphysical books of Infinite Intelligence, Universal Mind, Spiritual Law, etc., which are basically synonymous with the term 'God'. However, because the term 'God' has certain historical and theological connotations which are unacceptable to many metaphysically oriented people, they choose to refer to God in terms of an impersonal Force.

Metaphysically speaking, God is more than 'subconscious' because this Mind also thinks Its own thoughts. That is, It is creative. Creating is achieved by imagining or 'image-ing' in Mind, which is brought into manifestation through the Law of Mind. God is Mind — not a mind, but all the mind there really is. Mind is forever thinking and thus creating. This Infinite Mind does not reason inductively, for It has no need to search for truth, for It is Truth and Mind and Law all in one.

It logically follows that things are caused by ideas. That is, things are ideas brought into manifestation through Universal Law. Thus, when we think, we are thinking *into* this Universal Mind which, acting as Law, will bring forth the equivalent of our thoughts. We bring forth our own good or evil by the habitual quality of our thoughts.

Because this subjective Universal Mind is in all people, each one can influence others, not intentionally, but causally. There is apparent evil in the world only because of the combined negative and false thinking of the human race. Universal Mind is Law; it doesn't care or know what It is making but just keeps on creating according to the thought-patterns It receives; It is totally impersonal. However, it logically follows that through positive enlightened thinking we can have a healing influence on the race.

Evil, sin, sickness, poverty, unhappiness and all negative circumstances exist as experiences but not as realities! They are neither person, place nor thing. They are really the objectifications of thoughts and they can therefore be corrected by correct thinking.

By knowing the Truth and using the Law, you can alter the circumstances of your life. It works by Law anyway, so you might as well go about your life intelligently co-creating with Infinite Mind.

Certain corollaries of metaphysical teaching are that we have access to thoughts far beyond our own past experiences via the subconscious, for it is really a universal and infinite intelligence in which all people share. That being so (it is assumed), we can sometimes communicate by telepathy through that medium.

This is the subject of metaphysics simplified. Whether you choose to believe it or not is a matter for your personal discretion. Certainly just spelling words with capital letters doesn't make the concepts true. Like everything else, if you try it and find it practical (that is, if you can demonstrate the Truth, as they say) then you will naturally continue to use it. It really doesn't make a great deal of difference (if any) what you actually believe about it, for *if you practise self-hypnosis you get results* whether it is your personal subconscious mind or a Universal Mind that does the work!

Metaphysical teaching is more philosophical than religious. It's a way of thinking about thinking. You do not have to change creeds or churches, but just add its concepts (the method of self-hypnosis, practically speaking) to your present way of religious thinking.

(I myself am a churchman in a large orthodox denomination and recite a historical church creed every week with sincerity and conviction; any metaphysical insights I may have are easily fitted into my overall philosophy of life.)

If mankind was created in the 'image and likeness of God' (whatever that means), then a study of the human mind may teach us some limited truths about the mind of the Creator. The hypnological interpretations of psychology and the metaphysical interpretations of life are compatible and have much in common. Whether they are identical is a moot question and of little practical importance — if you practise self-hypnosis!

Experiencing God

If you wish to experience more of God, as you presently conceive of God, then a starting point is to recognize that it can be done, for others have done it. Although such people are unique as individuals, just as you are, they are not unique in this ability. They simply have certain assumptions and follow certain techniques — all of which are the assumptions and techniques of self-hypnosis.

If you wish to experience God, the following questions must be asked and their answers considered:

1. *What* God? Obviously, because of the way the mind works, you will only experience the God you believe in.
2. *Where* will you experience God? You can only know and experience God through your mind, for that is the only way you know anything at all. Faith and feeling are two different functions of the mind and you will know God through your mind only by the thoughts of God you have in your mind.
3. *When* will you experience God? The only answer to that is: whenever you choose to begin.
4. *How* will you experience God? Throughout history people have known God in certain ways which are common to all religions, namely through:
    (a) worship — private and group;
    (b) study — reading of sacred Scriptures;
    (c) meditation — inward contemplation of teachings;
    (d) service — sharing spiritual and temporal blessings with others.

Basically, spiritual experiences are *from the inside out*. This is simply to say that it must work via your subconscious mind, and you work on your subconscious mind through self-hypnosis.

You can ensure that your subconscious mind is filled and fortified with spiritual truths which then will be translated into your total lifestyle. What are these spiritual truths with which you can fill your mind? They can be 'meditations' or 'affirmations' found in devotional books of your religion or you can devise your own which are consistent with your beliefs, and use these as suggestions in your self-hypnosis sessions.

Personally I recommend the use of appropriate Scriptural verses, for these have stood the test of time. Whether you believe them to be the literal 'Word of God' or only the distillation of the great spiritual insights of wise and good men throughout the ages, in any case they come highly recommended and you can use them with confidence.

Many years ago the author was asked by some Christian ministers to make a set of programming suggestions which could be used by all Christian groups for spiritual growth. To minimize resistance to the suggestions, it was decided to use Scriptural verses after the usual hypnotic induction. The result was rather novel, so it is included here:

I want you to know that God wills for you to *enjoy health, happiness and prosperity*. As you are breathing freely and easily now, I am going to put certain suggestions into your subconscious mind and these come from God through His word, the Bible.

It is God's will that *fear* in every form *be removed from your life*. Fear not, only believe . . . Fear not, it is your Father's good pleasure to give you the mastery. . . . Perfect love casteth out fear. . . . I will fear no evil, for thou art with me . . .

God wishes you to *have confidence*, and He says to you: in quietness and confidence shall be my strength. . . . the Lord of hosts is with me, the God of Jacob is my refuge. . . . Be still, and know that I am God. . . . Be strong, and of a good courage. . . . the Lord thy God, He it is that goeth with thee, He will not fail thee nor forsake thee. . . . I know whom I have believed, and I am persuaded that He is able to keep that which I have committed unto Him against that day . . .

It is the will of God that your *faith be increased*. Have faith in God. . . All things are possible to him that believeth. . . . Great is thy faith, be it unto thee even as thou wilt. . . . Thy faith hath made thee whole . . .

As you are breathing freely and easily now, with a wonderful sense of peace pervading your entire body, God speaks to you out of His word to assure you of His *grace*: By grace are ye saved through faith. . . . Let us come boldly to the throne of grace that we may obtain mercy and find help. . . . The God of all grace settle, stablish, strengthen and perfect you. . . . The grace of our Lord Jesus Christ be with you . . .

God wills for you to have *healing*: The leaves of the tree are for the healing of the nations. . . . The Sun of Righteousness is risen with healing in His wings. . . . The prayer of faith shall heal the sick. . . . He forgiveth all my iniquities, He healeth all my diseases . . .

It is God's will that you *have peace* at all times, and God through His word speaks to your subconscious mind, instructing you: Great peace have they who love the law, and nothing shall cause them to stumble. . . . Thou wilt keep him in perfect peace, whose mind is stayed on Thee. . . . Peace I leave with you, my peace I give unto you. Let not your heart be troubled, neither let it be afraid. The peace of God which passeth all understanding shall keep your heart and mind through Jesus Christ . . .

God wills for you to *develop strength*: They that wait upon the Lord shall renew their strength. . . . The Lord shall give strength to his people. . . . They shall go from strength to strength. . . . The Lord is the strength of my life, of whom shall I be afraid? . . . I can do all things through Christ who strengtheneth me . . .

As you are breathing freely and easily now, completely relaxed, the Spirit of God which wishes to *deepen your love* speaks to you in the depths of your heart, saying: This is the first and great command, thou shalt love. . . . By this shall all men know that ye are my disciples, if ye love one another. . . . We know that we have passed from death unto life, because we love. . . . He that dwelleth in love, dwelleth in God, and God in him . . .

It is the will of God that you *obtain happiness*: A merry heart doeth good like a medicine. . . . If ye know these things, happy are ye if ye do them. . . . Happy is he that hath the God of Jacob for his help. . . . These things have I spoken unto you that my joy might remain in you, and that your joy might be full . . .

It is the will of God that you be able to *rest and to sleep* well and perfectly. He says: Come unto me all ye that labour and are heavy laden, and I will give you rest. . . . There remaineth therefore a rest for the people of God. . . . I will lay me down in peace and sleep, for Thou maketh me to dwell in safety. . . . He giveth his loved ones sleep . . .

The hypnotic session is then brought to a close in the usual manner with the customary health suggestions. You can record these suggestions on a tape recorder and use it in your daily or nightly sessions, if you wish.

To the spiritually minded person there is nothing that is not God-related, and therefore all self-improvement is spiritual improvement. You cannot grow as a person without growing spiritually for the object of religion is wholeness as well as holiness. By becoming a better person you are growing spiritually and by improving your relationships with people you are no doubt improving your relationship with your God.

Prayer is the spiritualizing of your thoughts, and the controlled attention which you have developed through self-hypnosis will help you to pray more effectively.

Self-hypnosis cannot provide you with a creed or a religion; it will enhance the creed and religion you already have. Your subconscious mind may not literally be God, but it certainly is the part of your mind through which God can become more real in your experience.

'Thou shalt love the Lord thy God with *all* thy mind.'

References

1. Ambrose, G., Van Pelt, S., and Newbold, G. *Medical Hypnosis Handbook*, Hollywood, California: Wilshire Book Co., 1960.
2. Aveling, F., and Hargreaves, H. 'Suggestibility With and Without Prestige in Children'. *British Journal of Psychology*, 1921-2, 12, 53-75.
3. Baudouin, C. *Suggestion and Autosuggestion*. Translated by E. and C. Paul. New York: Dodd, Mead & Co., 1922.
4. Bernays, E. *The Engineering of Consent*. University of Oklahoma Press, 1955.
5. Bryan, W. 'The Use and Abuse of Hypno-Aids'. *The Journal of the American Institute of Hypnosis*, Vol. 6, No. 4.
6. Caprio, F., and Berger, J. *Helping Yourself With Self-Hypnosis*. Englewood Cliffs, NJ: Prentice-Hall, 1963.
7. Coué, E. *Self Mastery Through Conscious Autosuggestion*. New York: American Library Service, 1922.
8. Coué, E. *How To Practice Suggestion and Autosuggestion*. New York: American Library Service, 1923.
9. Dunlap, K. *Habits, Their Making and Unmaking*. New York, Liveright, 1949.
10. Ellis, A. 'Rational psychotherapy; the treatment of a homosexual with rational psychotherapy; the treatment of a psychopath with rational psychotherapy, etc.'. reprinted in Eysenck, H. *Experiments in Behavior Therapy*. New York: Macmillan. A Pergamon Press Book, 1964.
11. Estabrook, G. 'A standardized hypnotic technique dictated

to a Victrola record'. *American Journal of Psychology*, 1930, 42, 115-16.

12. Freud, S. *The Ego and the Mechanisms of Defence*. London: Hogarth Press, 1937.

13. Freud, S. *An Outline of Psychoanalysis*. New York: Norton, 1949.

14. Freud, S. *The Question of Lay Analysis*. New York: Norton, 1950.

15. Hakebush, Blinkowsi and Foundillere. 'An attempt at a study of development of personality with the aid of hypnosis'. Trud. Inst. Psikhonevr. Kiev: 1930, 2, 236-72.

16. Johnson, W. *Verbal Man: The Enchantment of Words*. New York: Collier Books, 1965.

17. LeCron, L. *Self Hypnotism: The Technique and its Use in Daily Living*. Englewood Cliffs, NJ: Prentice-Hall, 1964.

18. Livingood, F. 'Hypnosis as an Aid to Adjustment'. *Journal of Psychology*. 12: 203-7, 1941.

19. Marcuse, F. *Hypnosis: Fact or Fiction*. Baltimore: Penguin Books, 1959.

20. Merloo, J. 'Television Addiction and Reactive Apathy'. *Journal of Nervous and Mental Diseases*. Vol. 120, 1954.

21. Merloo, J. *The Rape of the Mind*. New York: The University Library, Grosset & Dunlap, 1956.

22. Miller, J. 'Unconscious Processes and Perception'. Chapter 9 in Blake and Ramsey, *Perception: An Approach to Personality*. New York: Ronald Press, 1951.

23. Nirenberg, J. *Getting Through To People*. Englewood Cliffs, NJ: Prentice-Hall, 1963.

24. Papov, E. 'Suggestibility and Automaticism in School Children'. *Propilaktecheskaya Medetsina*. 1926, 5, 68. Reported by Coffin, T. 'Some conditions of suggestion and suggestibility: a study of certain attitudinal and situational factors influencing the process of suggestion'. *Psychological Monographs*. No. 4, 53, 1941.

25. Rhodes, R. *Hypnosis: Theory, Practice, and Application*. New York: Citadel Press, 1950.

26. Rowland, L. 'Will Hypnotized Persons Try to Harm Themselves or Others?' *Journal of Abnormal Social Psychology*. 1939, 34, 114-15.

27. Salter, A. *Conditioned Reflex Therapy*. New York: Farrar, Straus, 1949; Capricorn Books, Putnam, 1961.

28. Salter, A. *The Case Against Psychoanalysis*. New York, Holt, Rinehart & Winston, 1952.

29. Sperling, G. E. 'The Interpretation of Trauma as Command'.

Psychoanalytic Quarterly. Vol. 19, 1950.

30. Thigpen, C., and Cledkley, H. 'Some Reflections on Psychoanalysis, Hypnosis, and Faith Healing'. Chapter 7 in Wolpe, J., Salter, A., and Reyna, L. *The Conditioning Therapies: The Challenge in Psychotherapy.* New York, Holt, Rinehart & Winston, 1964.

31. Van Pelt, S. *Hypnotism and the Power Within.* New York: Wehman Brothers, 1954.

32. Weitzenhoffer, A. 'The Production of Antisocial Acts Under Hypnosis'. *Journal of Abnormal Social Psychology.* 1949, 44, 420-42.

33. Weitzenhoffer, A. *Hypnotism: An Objective Study in Suggestibility.* New York: Science Editors, John Wiley, 1963.

34. Wolberg, L. *Medical Hypnosis.* New York: Grune & Stratton, 1948.

Index

HOW TO MANAGE YOUR GLOBAL REPUTATION

A Guide to the Dynamics of International Public Relations

Revised and Updated Paperback Edition

Michael Morley

NEW YORK UNIVERSITY PRESS
Washington Square, New York

First published in the U.S.A in 2002, by
NEW YORK UNIVERSITY PRESS,
Washington Square
New York, NY 10003

This book is printed on paper suitable for recycling and
made from fully managed and sustained forest sources.

Library of Congress Cataloging-in-Publication Data
Morley, Michael.
How to manage your global reputation : a guide to the dynamics of
international public relations / Michael Morley.
p. cm.
Includes index.
ISBN 0–8147–5679–4 (pbk.: alk. paper)
1. Public relations—Corporations.   I. Title.
HD59.M64   1998
659.2'89—dc21
                    98–13360
                       CIP

10   9   8   7   6   5   4   3   2   1

Printed and bound in Great Britain by
J.W. Arrowsmith Ltd, Bristol

How to Manage Your Global Reputation

Contents

Preface

There is no better time to make a career in international public relations. The planning and implementation of concerted multinational public relations programs are still in their infancy. Global programs are, in truth, still a dream.

Similar conditions prevailed in 1967 when I met Dan Edelman and we agreed to establish a joint venture in the UK. London became the first city outside the USA with an Edelman office.

Friends pursed their lips. Won't this be a bit risky? What about the competition?

I had the arrogance of youth. I also had a mission to improve what I felt was a generally low standard of practice in British PR at that time. My reply, which I am still convinced was true, was: "Look, I only have to be mediocre by my own standards for our company to be an outstanding success." So it turned out, although I like to think we were better than mediocre.

And so it can be for those who really make an effort to succeed on the worldwide stage.

I hope this book helps.

You will quickly ascertain that this is not an academic work. It is in small part a memoir, a measure of historical color to help understand how we arrived at today's situation, some anecdotes and mostly, I hope, helpful information and tips. It is less a work of scholarship than lessons from first-hand experience.

This revised edition has had to take into account huge changes that have reshaped the world in which we live and the techniques we use to communicate: the Internet, religious fundamentalism, global terrorism, increasingly strident NGOs seeking to de-rail globalization, the concentration of power into a few communications conglomerates, the boom and bust of the "new economy" along with the rapid deployment of the Internet in a 24/7 mobile and continuously connected society. Each of these demands a volume or more of its own, but it is my hope that the basic concepts outlined here will provide a useful foundation for all engaged in, or aspiring to, a career in international communications.

I had to make some decisions which may be offensive to certain groups. In the interest of attaining some flow of prose, I use the male gender to cover the entire spectrum. Thus he means she as well.

In the matter of monetary units, I have decided to work in US dollars to achieve some standard. And in spelling conventions, I have chosen American English rather than British, based on the toss of a coin and the fact that an American spell check function is built into the hard drive of my laptop computer.

Acknowledgements

There are many to thank for their vital contributions to this book.

First, my wife Ingrid, who had the patience of a saint when, at distant intervals, I sequestered myself to do the writing. But, more important, she was at my side during all the ups and downs over these past 44 years when I was gaining the experience that is, I hope, distilled in the following pages.

Thanks to Dan and Richard Edelman for providing the environment for me to practice my craft and from whom I have learned so much, not just about public relations but about hard work and the business aspects of PR. And to my many colleagues and friends with whom I have worked over the years.

Special thanks go to the clients who have taken that huge step and entrusted their reputations and budgets to me and my firm. There have been moments (quickly suppressed) when I felt I should rebate some part of their fees because I learned so much from them.

What I have learned about international public relations I owe to having worked closely with a galaxy of outstanding practitioners, among them Jacques Coup de Frejac (France), Ramon Alvarez (Spain), Peter Czerwonka (Germany), Patrizia Antonicelli and Tony Muzi Falconi (Italy), Kaarina Alanko (Finland), Val McKenzie and Robyn Sefiani (Australia), Austen Zecha and Jeanette Robertson-Lomax (now Shahabuddin and living in Malaysia), Barbara Frischknecht (Switzerland, who died a few years ago), T.H. Lee (Korea) and Serge Dumont (China). David Davis, Rosemary Brook, Andy Knott and Susi Luss deserve special mention for many years of campaigning together. In recent years my professional horizons have been expanded by working closely with Pam Talbot, president of Edelman USA and Leslie Dach, a vice chairman of our company, Nancy Turett, president of Edelman Health Worldwide and John Weckenmann, a general manager at Edelman New York.

I have been encouraged in the venture by my daughter, Ann Wool, who assisted me for a few years before spreading her wings on international PR projects of her own. Although she is the only one of my three children to follow me into a career in PR, my son Andrew and elder daughter Helen have been an inspiration to me in this work.

Without the help of three people, you would not be holding this book in your hand. Cathy Johnson played an important role in helping me get started.

Paulette Barrett stepped in and not only acted as a sounding board and tough copy editor but condensed many of the case studies and pushed me to meet deadlines. Eneida Lamberty has organized the text, typed large sections which were initially produced handwritten and brought order to the text and the charts.

For this revised edition I acknowledge the valuable guidance and access provided by Jack Bergen, former president of the Council of PR Firms. I have drawn heavily on material generated in connection with the ICCO Conference, 2001, in San Francisco for which I thank John Pearce of MediaMap, Stephen Farrish of PR Week, Sandra McLeod of Echo Research, Mark White of Mainsail and Kay Branksome of Vocus. I am in debt to Jonathan Wootliff, a source of great wisdom on non-governmental organizations, Tom Steindler of McDermott Will and Emery for his guidance on the rules of lobbying in Washington, D.C. and Eric Vaes for his insight into the labyrinth of the European Union and the circumstances surrounding the rejection of GE's bid to acquire Honeywell by the EU's competition directorate. Maureen Taylor's paper on the Coca Cola crisis in Belgium was an invaluable source as was Jonathan Chandler's presentation to the International Public Relations Association Conference in Berlin (October 2001) on Coke's reputation recovery program. Nancy Ruscheinski and David Dunne were immensely helpful in the new chapter on the Internet. There are others, unnamed, who in one way or another have contributed directly or indirectly to this volume and I thank them, too.

Foreword

Never has public relations been so important to as many organizations as it is today. At the corporate level, we see public relations in action communicating corporate messages to the worldwide financial markets, shaping corporate images, telling "our side of the story" in times of crisis, and playing a key role in developing new identities and positioning for companies formed in the wake of mergers, acquisitions, and takeovers. At the brand level, public relations provides marketing support in the form of ideas for international, national, and local sponsorships, for cause-related marketing, and for brand-building via both consumer-directed and trade-directed communications.

It is not only for corporations that public relations has become more salient. A panoply of non-profit organizations, tourist development agencies, military services, and labor unions are among those who have harnessed public relations in their behalf.

Yesterday's public relations focused extensively on press releases; today's also involves video news releases and establishing and maintaining websites. Yesterday's focused on brand promotions; today's also emphasizes development and defense of corporate reputation. At its best, public relations is a component of corporate strategy.

This volume offers a comprehensive treatment of the field by Michael Morley, a highly experienced senior executive who has been engaged in public relations worldwide on behalf of companies and organizations for four decades. Morley's extensive collection of case histories is drawn from a wide range of industries and applications. They encompass programs in print and broadcast – and even the Internet. His frames of reference include both brand and corporate, and extend from individual firms to economic development agencies, trade associations, agricultural commodities, and causes.

Morley emphasizes the global character of business – and the public relations that support it – as well as the need to translate "big picture" programs into local initiatives. From a process perspective, he takes readers from strategy reviews through audits and issue identification/tracking to program development all the way to evaluation. He describes internal public relations organization and structure as well as the roles of the public relations agency.

From strategy to implementation, from the boardroom to the firing line, Morley provides insights for both the experienced and the aspiring in public relations.

Stephen A. Greyser
Richard P. Chapman Professor
Marketing/Communications
Harvard Business School

CHAPTER I

The Global Village — It's Here

The global village predicted 35 years ago by communications scholar and philosopher Marshall McLuhan[*] is here. The primeval forces that drive entrepreneurs to establish global empires have combined with those that enable them to achieve their ambitions.

The driving forces are the quest for survival, power, peace, pride and profit.

Survival

Company leaders know they must grow in size if they are not to be swallowed up by a bigger corporation. Even huge corporations that operate nationally or regionally are prey for the larger global corporate predators. The only solution for survival is to become global themselves, as fast as they can, through acquisitions, mergers or other forms of strategic alliances.

Power

Leaders of industry are just as hungry for power as presidents, prime ministers, generals and bishops. In today's business world, only the global corporation delivers the ultimate in industrial and commercial power.

Peace

Peace is a real motivation for those who believe that it may be easier to achieve or maintain when twinned with power. Many business leaders also believe that an economy in which nations are interdependent is a significant

[*] *The Global Village*, by Marshall McLuhan and Bruce R. Powers, published by Oxford University Press

force for peace and that global corporations have a pivotal role to play in bringing that about.

Pride

Pride is often an overlooked motivation for globalization. For some individuals, the status conferred by being leader of a global corporation is sometimes more important than the power or profit that position brings. National rather than personal pride is a clear driving force for many of the huge corporations that emerged in post-war Japan and more recently in Korea and other countries which needed to reach parity with – and then overtake – companies in the USA and Europe.

Profit

Profit needs little elaboration. It is the primary reason for the existence of business enterprises. To achieve maximum profits, the corporation must operate on a global scale.

Technology, privatization, the dismantling of protectionism, swifter, cheaper travel, less restricted movement of capital and labor, standardization and education have been important factors in helping business leaders achieve their global ambitions.

Technology

Technology has had a dominant impact on globalization. Its manifestations are the subject of many books on mass production, mass customization, production processes, supply chain management, training and so on. For public relations purposes, we need to recognize how technology has revolutionized communications, not just within business organizations but, most dramatically, in the media.

Privatization

With the retreat from Marxist socialism, many nations in the 1990s engaged in a wave of privatization of state-run and state-owned industries, opening the way to global alliances for institutions that had previously been strictly local.

Dismantling protectionism

Protectionist barriers have been taken down at a fast and relentless pace, notwithstanding media reports about counter efforts to prevent this trend in many countries. Free trade and groupings such as the GATT and its successor WTO, the European Union, Mercosul, Association of South East Asian Nations and North American Free Trade Agreement have enabled many companies to expand their international operations and stimulated mergers of nascent global corporations.

Travel

Travel is now faster, cheaper and accessible to more people than ever, facilitating the all-important, face-to-face meetings that remain a cornerstone of business, even in the global village. And that transport does not only carry people, it carries documents, packages and goods as well.

Standardization

Standardization has smoothed the way for products made in one market to meet the safety, size and ingredient requirements in a large number of other markets. With minor modifications, many products can be sold worldwide.

Education

Education has improved business leaders' knowledge of the history, traditions and languages of markets well beyond their home bases.

Capital

The free movement of capital has created a single market for investors who will move their funds from country to country and company to company to achieve the best rate of return.

Media impact

With the premise that the global village has arrived, the PR practitioner should examine closely how this will impact his work. The Internet, television, telephone and radio have converged to take us into the age of instant communications, worldwide.

In the length of time it took news to circulate within a village of 200 people 200 years ago, it is now possible for five billion people to become aware of an environmental disaster, war or the outcome of a major sporting event. The Internet alone can disseminate news of a faulty or dangerous product to a worldwide audience in minutes.

The existence and speed of the new media should not be the only subject of concern for the PR practitioner. Its ownership is of equal importance.

The past decade has seen the emergence of powerful international media holding companies – Rupert Murdoch's News Corp, AOL Time Warner, Disney, GE through NBC, Kirch and Bertelsmann in Germany, and Berlusconi in Italy. They all wield immense power nationally, regionally and, increasingly, internationally.

Companies that own media outlets are seeking to go global and to exercise greater control over content – news and programming sources. Those with their roots in print media have branched out into satellite and cable television, and vice versa. And all of them are making sure that they play a key role in use of the Internet as the newest medium of all.

The trend toward consolidation alarms many who fear a world in which the concentration of media places commercial and political power in the hands of too few people. Yet a counter trend can be observed. Small groups gain unprecedented power with the advent of 500-channel television, and the capacity to produce professional-looking newsletters, magazines and even books that can be printed in small quantities. There are now newsletters, books and television programs that can serve very small communities, whether they be regions, villages, dialect groups or people with a shared interest in a sport, hobby, religion, political movement or cause.

Here, too, the Internet is a new medium with little editorial control, that returns immense power to the individual who, for one reason or another, does not communicate through the traditional major media groups.

PR practitioners for a new age

In the face of such a panoply of communications tools and opportunities, what sort of PR practitioner will we be seeing? What are the characteristics of the highest-ranking public relations professionals in the coming millennium? How might you plan to develop your talents to take a leadership position in communications, and perhaps beyond?

As you will read elsewhere in this book, public relations began by drawing its talents from other crafts and professions, mainly journalism but also from advertising, law, sales and politics. To be sure, it attracted its fair share of buccaneers and charlatans, who gave PR a flair and glamour that attracted many more professionals. Now, there are legions of practitioners who studied PR in college and have followed a career in the business ever since. Many of them have spent and will continue to spend their working lives in one of the PR specialties described in chapter 7.

In the future, I believe that the PR profession will continue to attract recruits from other fields — and will be the richer for it. They will come from all the same walks of life as before but there will also be more entrants from a variety of scientific backgrounds who have discovered in themselves a skill in communicating about their specialist fields.

It really does not matter what you study at college. It is no disadvantage to take a public relations course or program, usually run by the schools of journalism at various universities. This provides practitioners with a fast start in being familiar with the techniques of communication and the needs and structure of the media. But you could as well major in computer science, law, English or another language (or languages), political science or international affairs, and start work immediately in a communications capacity or transfer after some period of practice in another field.

It will be easier for you to learn how to become a fine PR practitioner having studied, for example, medicine, than it will be for you to become a doctor after majoring in public relations at college. If you decide to study for a bachelor's degree in public relations, or a closely related field such as journalism or communications, your second degree or course of study should be in an alternative field that will enhance your career potential — for example, international affairs, business administration, political science or languages of the countries in which you are interested. Such study will give you an edge in your career.

In contrast, if your first degree is in a field unrelated to communications, you should consider a master's degree program in public relations. Yes, such courses do exist, e.g. at Stirling University in the UK, in Barcelona and at various colleges in the USA. Your career prospects will not be damaged in any way — indeed they may be enhanced — if you choose to combine two complementary courses for both a bachelor's and master's degree and neither has public relations, journalism, or communications as a major.

There are many excellent short courses in communications technique and theory which, along with workplace learning, will build on your studies to equip you to be an excellent practitioner.

How you plan your career development once you have entered the world of business or government will be as important to your achievement of the profession's glittering prizes as your basic education. The person who aspires to reach the pinnacle in international public relations will need to be multi-talented, with wide experience: Educationally qualified, a skilled communicator, a thoughtful and calculating strategist, technologically proficient, multilingual, avidly interested in current affairs, knowledgeable about political affairs in many countries, respectful of a variety of customs and etiquette, and experienced in working in a number of countries, with a spell in general management.

Technological proficiency

The successful PR practitioner will be technologically proficient in three ways.

First, he himself will be sufficiently computer literate and competent in keyboard skills so as to be in regular communication within his own organization as well as with key audiences. In the extreme example, he should be self-reliant enough to be able to undertake practical communications initiatives from his own desktop, laptop or hand-held personal computer without the help of an assistant. This will mean a lifetime of learning new tricks.

Second, in order to make choices, he must have sufficient command of technological developments, and the advantages, disadvantages and prices of competing equipment and enhancements available to organizations as the infrastructure of their communications departments.

Third, this knowledge must extend to the way in which technological advances are constantly reshaping the media, shifting importance from one technique to another, so as to develop strategies and tactics that respond to these changes in good time.

Technophobes will go the way of the dinosaur.

Languages

Proficiency in more than your native language is a major advantage. It signals both your respect for and interest in people of other nations, in addition to allowing you to work more easily in a variety of environments. And this says nothing of the joy, stimulation and fun you will get from the access you will have to other literature and conversations. You will save time and cost in obtaining translations, and you will put interactions with your colleagues and audiences in other nations on a different and stronger footing.

However, a warning: Do not imagine that a mere facility to speak foreign languages is sufficient to establish a worthwhile career in international public relations. I have known people with a knack for learning several languages who, sadly, had little of consequence to say in any of them, or were incapable of real communication. Better to learn the secrets of effective communications and practice them in one or two languages. And, in important business meetings – negotiating a contract, interviews with the media – always have a professional interpreter present. Executives who are highly competent but less than totally fluent in a foreign language can make embarrassing mistakes when they misinterpret the nuance of a word. The additional time taken for translation also helps you formulate a better answer.

Current affairs

As you will read elsewhere in this book, it is essential that you keep up with current affairs through regular reading and viewing of a selection of media. Only in this way will you be able to keep pace with the events that affect the lives of people in all the markets of importance to you and your organization. This reading program must involve publications from foreign countries.

I define current affairs as all important aspects of the life of any nation – politics, economics and business, arts, entertainment and sports.

Political affairs

Along with keeping abreast of current affairs, it is important that you familiarize yourself with the political structures in all key regions. Although ruling parties and their leaders may come and go (as your current affairs reading will show), the constitutions and political characteristics of many countries do not change. Even when seismic change has taken place, as has been the case in many of the countries of Eastern Europe, you should make it your business to know where power resides and where decisions of importance to your concern are made.

Customs and etiquette

Respect for the customs and etiquette of each distinct society, country, nation or religion is essential. Not only should these customs be learned, they should be practiced.

In the learning, you will often find the keys that open the door to improved communication, and that is your business. Without this knowledge, there can be no success, even for someone well qualified in all other respects.

International work experience

At a seminar of the Arthur W. Page Society entitled "Public Relations Leadership in 2001: Greater Importance, Greater Competition," Frank Vogl pointed out that "Globalization will impact every aspect of the PR Chief's work." Stressing that the communications function must reflect the new international approach apparent in so many major corporations, Vogl referred to an article in the *Wall Street Journal* on January 29, 1996, which said that "... the executive suite is going global. With nearly every industry targeting fast-growing foreign markets, more companies are requiring foreign experience for top management positions."

To illustrate its argument, the *Wall Street Journal* noted that, for example, Samir Gibara, president and CEO of Goodyear Tire & Rubber, had worked abroad for 27 of his 30 years with the company; Raymond Vialut, vice chairman of General Mills, was previously president and CEO of Kraft Jacobs Suchard in Switzerland; Michael Hawley, the president and CEO of Gillette, spent 20 of his 35 years with the corporation outside of the US; Harry Bowman reached the top at Outboard Marine after heading the European business of Whirlpool; and Lucio Noto, chairman and CEO of Mobil Oil, worked abroad for 17 of his 34 years with the corporation.

What's good for the CEO is equally essential for the global public relations practitioner. The top jobs of the future will surely be reserved for those who have worked in more than one market. This is confirmed by Peter Gummer (now Lord Chadlington), founder of Shandwick, one of the world's largest international PR networks: "I am confident that the future of this company will be based on working in a global relationship with 20 or more major clients paying fees in the millions of dollars annually. The only people who will be able to offer counsel and service at the level required by such clients will be those who have multi market and multi disciplinary experience. Right now few of these exist. There are great opportunities for all who groom themselves by working in three or four different markets."

Switch places

Even if you plan to make your career in an agency or consultancy, a spell of two or three years working in-house at a corporation, government department or other institution will be valuable experience. It will give you special insight into the minds of your clients and the pressures they face within their own organizations. Some in-house PR executives are skeptical of the advice given by their external counselors because they suspect it is given without accountability for the outcome. Your advice will be more respected if your client knows that you have at one time stood in his shoes.

For the practitioner who will spend his working life within an organization, a period of agency experience can be valuable. But a period working in line management is even more useful and pays dividends later in policy and positioning debates; peers will recognize that the views being expressed are not purely based on theory. On-the-job experience was a key requirement for the most senior PR position in United Parcel Service. So in 1988, when Ken Sternad was selected based on his performance in the PR department ever since he had transferred from journalism in 1977, he was sent into general management as a district manager in Baltimore for two years. In this position, he had to deal with sales, vehicle maintenance, labor issues and union negotiations, pick-up and delivery scheduling – all the nuts and bolts of the business of UPS.

Now, he is head of PR in a company with annual sales of $30 billion, over 300,000 employees and serving 200 countries around the world; his views are respected as coming from someone with a first-hand knowledge of the business and valued because he is a skilled communications expert.

It is increasingly unusual for PR practitioners to spend an entire career, or even a large proportion of their working lives, in a single organization. UPS is a singular corporation in many respects. But direct line management experience is immensely valuable in enlarging your professional capability.

CHAPTER 2

Corporate Reputation

A strong and positive corporate reputation is the holy grail of every public relations professional.

The management of corporate reputation can be defined as: the orchestration of discrete public relations initiatives designed to promote or protect the most important brand you own – your corporate reputation.

This reputation will be good or bad, strong or weak depending on the quality of strategic thinking, the management's commitment to achieving its stated goals, and the skill and energy with which all component programs are implemented and communicated.

Corporate reputation – or image, as advertising professionals prefer to term it – is based on how the company conducts or is perceived as conducting its business. A constellation of elements contributes to this reputation, as shown in the following diagram. Each element is discussed in other chapters of this book.

Chart 2.1   Corporate Reputation

When corporate reputation is secure, a flow of positive and tangible benefits accrues to the organization. And, it is an important shield in times of crisis.

Because businesses today operate in an environment of stress that often seems close to bursting into crisis, a carefully nurtured corporate reputation is all the more important.

Consider the market forces at play. Stock price performance has never been under such close and regular scrutiny, especially in the USA, where there is a quarterly disclosure of financial results by public companies. Chief executives are under extreme pressure to produce quarter after quarter of increasing profits and this militates against any venture and investment with a long-range pay-out. Corporate reputation is one such long-term investment.

Mergers and acquisitions across borders, often under hostile circumstances, are taking place at an accelerating pace, leaving many managements uneasy about an independent future and employees unsure that their jobs will be safe under different ownership.

Even though many candidates for political office seek election on a platform of "less government" (with the promise that there will be less interference in industry and business), in reality the tide of legislation and regulation is on the increase – even if that paradoxically means de-regulation.

As corporations contend with globalization of their markets, their organizations and their competitors, there are enormous strains and changes with which to deal. Externally, the simultaneous fractionalization and concentration of traditional media and the growth of new media are new complexities facing public relations professionals.

In such a turbulent climate, a positive corporate reputation can play a vital role in ensuring that an organization is on a solid footing. It will prove a powerful tool in what we might call "business climate stress management."

Following are some important examples of the benefits of a good corporate reputation.

Stock value

Shareholder value can be measurably improved. Corporate reputation and the confidence it inspires in investors will lead to a higher stock price for one company than for others that appear to be equal in all other respects but neglect the care of reputation.

Warren Buffet, chairman of Berkshire Hathaway, who has won legendary renown as a consistently successful investor, alluded to this phenomenon in a 1996 prospectus. With a touch of humor rare in such usually fact-filled and dry documents, he said he thought the stock in his investment company was really overvalued and he would not be a new buyer at that price. But he went on to say: "Berkshire believes that its reputation has added significantly to its value over the years. Berkshire further believes that its reputation, if it remains unimpaired, will produce substantial gains in the future as well."

Supporting that view is research data from Opinion Research Corporation (ORC), which conducts "Corperceptions," a periodic caravan survey of more than 4,000 business executives in several of the world's major markets. At the conclusion of its survey and analysis, "Corperceptions" gives each company a "Corporate Equity Rating," a score based on a number of criteria.

ORC CORPerceptions Criteria

1. Customer Focus
- Quality of products and service
- Value for $
- Responsiveness

2. Competitive Effectiveness
- Quality of Management
- Investment strategy/financial soundness
- Research and development focus

3. Market Leadership
- Vision
- Differentiation

4. Corporate Culture
- Social responsibility
- Ability to attract and retain employees
- Employee development

5. Communications
- Communicates effectively with all publics

Chart 2.2

ORC concludes that the better the corporate reputation, the higher the stock price. "There is a strong correlation between higher corporate equity ratings and higher price: earnings (P/E) ratios," says Dr. James Fink of ORC, illustrating the point with chart 2.3.

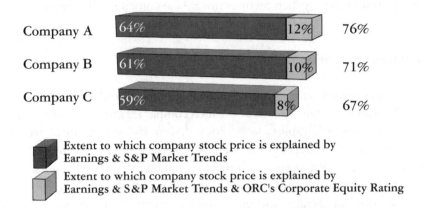

Company A	64% 12%	76%
Company B	61% 10%	71%
Company C	59% 8%	67%

Extent to which company stock price is explained by
Earnings & S&P Market Trends

Extent to which company stock price is explained by
Earnings & S&P Market Trends & ORC's Corporate Equity Rating

Chart 2.3 Corporate Reputation and the Stock Price

There is a large school of CEOs for whom the enhancement of shareholder value is the one and only goal. All other stakeholders are considered subsidiary. For these executives, the ORC Corperception data will be a convincing argument in favor of achieving a positive corporate reputation.

But a good stock price is just one of several important benefits. Moreover, present-day realities unequivocally underline the need to satisfy the needs of certain key stakeholders if the investor is ever to see a good return.

Customers

Customers are more loyal to the products of companies with a good reputation. This is especially true when marketing communications make a strong connection between the company and its branded products or services. When corporate and product names are identical, as with Microsoft, Coca Cola, Visa and IBM, corporate and brand images are synonymous, making management of the reputation doubly important.

"If the perception of a company is negative, consumers will downgrade the quality of goods and services the company offers. If you have a positive reputation, it is easier to introduce new products because the customers get a guarantee of a certain quality of service with the name," says Lawrence Wortzel, professor of marketing at Boston University's School of Management.

Faith Popcorn, futurist and founder of the research organization Brain Reserve, predicts that consumers will increasingly be influenced in the products they buy by their feelings toward the companies that produce them.

Partners and allies

Corporate reputation is exceptionally influential when it comes to the partnerships and strategic alliances on which companies must rely for success in the increasingly complex, technology-driven and international world of business. The best suppliers, consultants, advertising agencies, potential joint-venturists, even PR agencies, prefer to establish partnerships and strategic alliances with companies of good reputation. The chances of a successful relationship are greater and the partner company helps improve its own reputation by association.

Employee morale and recruitment

Employee morale and commitment are generally much better at companies with a good corporate reputation, and this, in turn, usually leads to high productivity and good customer relations. Beyond existing employees, the reputation of an organization is a powerful factor in recruitment at all levels. Companies in industries that rely on technology, for example, must attract student stars to ensure that they maintain an innovative edge. A good reputation can win the honors graduates; a tarnished image will drive the best talent to the competition.

Government relations

A company with a solid reputation is much more likely than one held in low esteem to be able to influence the legislative or regulatory government decision-making process. This could affect millions in profits and create or eliminate jobs.

Consider one of the most competitive industries that exist today – economic development. In no area of business life is competition fiercer than in the attraction of investment, factories, infrastructure, all with the goal of creating jobs and wealth.

Governments of countries, states, counties, cities and towns vie with each other to entice companies to establish operations in their jurisdictions, offering a variety of blandishments that include free or cheap land, tax abatements, the establishment of schools, technical colleges and universities to educate the workforce, and the building of homes and other infrastructures for the company's employees.

South Carolina is said to have spent over $50,000 for each job created, when it won an intense competition to entice BMW to establish its first US automobile production plant in that state.

BMW's stellar reputation had helped it secure a superb deal. It could have chosen from many suitors. It had great bargaining power within the framework of electoral politics – the creation of jobs in a fine company is a guaranteed vote catcher.

Crisis shield

The value of a good corporate reputation and the penalties of a poor one are never more evident than in times of crisis. In fact, it is sad to say that it often takes a serious crisis to awaken certain agnostic corporate leaderships to the need for actions and communications geared to improving corporate reputation; it becomes apparent in time of crisis that a good reputation can be a shield.

John Garnett, prolific lecturer and pioneering leader of the Industrial Society, described a good reputation or image as providing a company "with a reservoir of goodwill," a concept he learned during his period as a manager in Imperial Chemical Industries (ICI). This reservoir of goodwill should be deep enough to draw on in times of drought or crisis, allowing the company to continue operating without undue harm until the crisis is resolved.

When a company with a good corporate reputation is confronted by a crisis or serious problem, it gets the benefit of the doubt from its important audiences who may well say, "This is a fine, well-managed company, with a solid record. There is probably no truth in the rumors/allegations. Even if there is, they will put things right and get back on track without undue damage."

In the same situation, a poorly regarded company will be assumed to be guilty from the outset. It will have to struggle to communicate its point of view, and its explanations will lack credibility. It will likely have to pay a higher cost for the experience.

The value of a reservoir of goodwill in time of crisis is pointedly described by Rebecca Madeira, vice president of public affairs of Pepsi Cola Company, following an incident in which a hoax was played on the company. News reports said someone had tampered with cans of Diet Pepsi and there were products on sale containing hypodermic syringes. Pepsi quickly defused public alarm with massive, forthright communications about the integrity of its manufacturing, underpinned by its corporate credibility. Ms. Madeira said, "Your reputation is your trade mark; it can be your biggest asset or your biggest liability. It is an asset because you can show the consumers how you've been able to make billions of cans safely, with quality and a taste you can trust, for the past 95 years."

The Strathclyde statement

Whether called corporate reputation, image or identity, this is the subject of lively study and debate in business and academic circles. Descriptions abound. The following summary, known as the "Strathclyde Statement," is the result of a collaborative effort on the parts of John Barlow, professor of marketing at Strathclyde University, Glasgow, Scotland, and Stephen Greyser, professor of marketing at the Harvard Business School.

"Corporate identity management is concerned with the conception, development and communication of an organization's mission, philosophy and ethos. Its orientation is strategic and is based on a company's values, cultures and behaviors.

"The management of corporate identity draws on many disciplines including strategic management, marketing, corporate communications, organizational behavior, public relations and design. It is different from traditional brand marketing directed towards household or business to business product purchases since it is concerned with all of an organization's stakeholders and the multi-faceted way in which an organization communicates. It is dynamic, not static, and is greatly affected by changes in the external environment.

"When well managed, an organization's identity results in loyalty from its diverse stakeholders. As such it can positively affect organizational performance, e.g. its ability to attract and retain customers, achieve strategic alliances, recruit executives and employees, be well positioned in financial markets, and strengthen internal staff identification with the firm."

CHAPTER 3

Corporate Reputation Management

With the value of a good corporate reputation clearly established, your task turns to the process of managing this key asset, on a global basis.

The management of the corporate reputation of a major organization is the challenge that most practitioners of PR aspire to as they reach the zenith of their careers. The task carries with it great responsibilities. It also draws on a wide range of skills and experience in the different public relations specialties.

Reality and corporate reputation are inextricably linked. Not even the most skilled and seasoned PR professional can create and sustain a good reputation for a bad company. But at one time or another, most PR counselors are indeed asked to work this magic and some foolish practitioners believe they can do it.

In such cases, the role of the PR counselor or executive (a difficult one, admittedly) is to persuade management to change the reality by revising

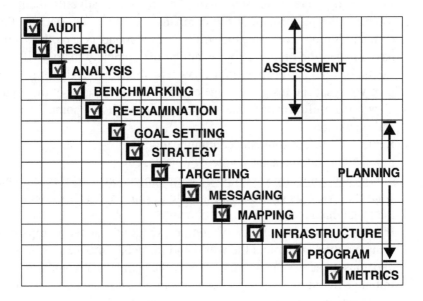

Chart 3.1   The Process

offensive policies and practices, and then to communicate these efforts so as
to improve the reputation.

The previous chapter should be a useful tool in persuading management
of the real benefits that will follow the establishment of a good reputation,
turning it into a corporate "must" rather than a "nice to have."

Your superiors and peers in management will be further encouraged if you
adopt a methodical approach to the process of corporate reputation
management. The process recommended has 13 steps, stretching from initial
audit to measurement of achievement, as shown in chart 3.1.

The first five stages or steps in the corporate reputation management
process are concerned with an assessment of the current situation in which the
company finds itself.

1. Audit

Start the process with an audit that should be largely internal.

- Collect and review as much existing data as you can about the
  company's ethos and way of doing business. It is possible, but unlikely
  in the case of most companies, that there are written statements on
  values, vision and mission. If they exist, get them into your data bank.
  Include corporate advertisements and even product advertisements to
  establish the promises that the company has made. Go back to the
  company's roots – examine the writings of the founders and others who
  have shaped the organization; examine the company history (if one
  exists) or what has been written elsewhere about them. All of this will
  give you a special insight into the evolution and character of the organization, a useful fundamental in the creation of its corporate identity
  and reputation.
- Review all current company communications tools – the annual report,
  newsletters and magazines, videos, website, etc.
- Survey the company's worldwide communications executives about
  what they view as critical issues. Include some non-PR personnel in
  the panel that receives your questionnaire.
- Interview a select number of senior executives in the company's
  principal markets around the world and in each of the main operating
  divisions, to assess the internal view of the company's reputation.
- Initiate a literature search (Lexis-Nexis or an equivalent database that
  is relevant to your company's field of activity) to establish how the firm
  has been portrayed recently in the media.

2. Research

■ Gather and consolidate all market and consumer research done by the various departments and operating divisions in your company. You will probably be surprised at the wealth of information that exists in various nooks and crannies, which can be useful in building up a composite picture of your organization's reputation. You may find market research that has been commissioned by the brand's marketing people and investor attitude data that has been supplied to the investor relations director by the advertising departments of business magazines and by brokerage houses. You will probably also find research commissioned on behalf of trade associations in which your company has membership. You might be the first person who gathers all this data in one place, and, by comparing components and cross referencing, you will be able to draw useful conclusions about the corporate reputation.

CORPORATE REPUTATION CRITERIA

Fortune Magazine	**Far East Economic Review**
Quality of Management	Management has long term vision
Quality of products and services	High quality of services or products
Innovativeness	Innovative in responding to customer needs
Long term investment value	Financial soundness
Wise use of corporate assets	Companies that others try to emulate
Ability to attract, develop and keep talented people	
Responsibility to the community and environment	

Chart 3.2

■ Review the free research that is available to you. Analyst reports (financial and industry) should be obtained and studied. Look especially carefully at the annual "report card" issues of the principal newspapers and magazines. For purposes of monitoring corporate reputation, the edition of *Fortune* on "Most Admired Companies in the USA" is required reading, as is the equivalent issue of the *Far East Economic Review*. The attributes considered in each survey are quite similar and as useful a checklist as any that exists for corporate reputation managers.
■ Check the availability of ready-made historical research, which might be relatively inexpensive to access. If your company is a leader in its

field, research material on it was quite likely included in cooperative or caravan studies conducted by organizations such as Opinion Research Corporation (ORC), Yankelovich, Market Opinion Research International (MORI), or Penn, Schoen and Berland, seeking to provide their clients with comparative data. A call to these companies and others in your area could yield a pleasant surprise – the existence of data at a substantial saving of time and money.

■ If there is no existing research, consider commissioning custom-made research or subscribing to the regular co-op or caravan studies conducted by reputable organizations. Give special consideration to MORI in the UK and Yankelovich or StrategyOne, Wirthlin Worldwide and Penn, Schoen and Berland in the USA, because they have demonstrated an ability to get responses from usually impenetrable groups of law makers, government officials, academics and the media. Similar organizations exist in many other countries, allowing you to build up a picture of your company in all your key regions. You are likely to find a widely differing reputation from market to market.

3. Analysis

■ Distill the findings of the mass of data that you have collected into a coherent report.
■ Check the regional and national variations in your corporate reputation. This will give you pointers as to where you must focus your efforts.
■ Write a short description of the company as it is perceived, based on what you have found out. Later, you will write a similar description of the company as you would like people to see it. Your challenge will be to develop strategies and programs that will progressively move perceptions from the present reality to the goal you set.

4. Benchmarking

Yours is not the first organization to have set off down this path. Others have done so and have achieved complete or partial success. You can learn by their experience. The process is known as benchmarking.

■ Make a list of up to 20 companies you most admire and wish to emulate. A majority should be operating in the same business sector as your own company. The others should have some relevance, and all should be operating on an international basis. Not all the companies you approach to participate in the benchmarking will agree to do it, which is why an initial list of 20 was suggested. Ten participants will be sufficient to provide you with information that will be invaluable in guiding you in the planning and executional stages that are to follow. Develop carefully thought-out questions that are specific enough to elicit concrete answers about how other companies enhanced or protected their reputations. These questions will initially be in the form of a written questionnaire. Personal interviews will follow to drill deeper; these may be done on a visit or by phone.

■ From the benchmarking, you will be able to determine which are best practices for the achievement of the corporate reputation you are seeking for your organization.

■ The rule of benchmarking is that participants get a "return on investment" by receiving a copy of your executive summary of the exercise. Without divulging the names of participating companies, provide a short description of each one.

5. Re-examination

You are now at the end of the assessment stage. It's time to re-examine and summarize the data that has been collected so far.

You may also decide to give an update to your management and colleagues in the corporate communications function. You will need their input and ideas in the planning and executional stages to come. In this re-examination, there are two important tasks.

■ Summarize your findings so far.
■ Undertake an analysis of your company's principal strengths, weaknesses, opportunities and threats, popularly known as a SWOT Analysis. Involve colleagues drawn from the communications function in your principal geographies and divisions. The analysis will provide you with a useful reputation balance sheet. Your charter, of course, will be to build on and communicate the strengths, eliminate the weaknesses, seize the opportunities and inoculate against the threats.

6. Goal setting

■ If your assessment phase indicates that your company is heavily handicapped in terms of its reputation, you will need to consider phasing your goals to make their attainment a realistic possibility. This can be done by grouping your goals under two or three headings: short, medium and long term.

■ Although goals should be broad and aspirational, at the same time they must be subject to measurement. So it is important to be specific as well. Eventually, when you come to the evaluation stage in the process, you must be able to measure whether you have achieved your goals or not. So rather than writing a woolly statement such as, "To improve our company's corporate reputation dramatically," write, "To ensure that our company becomes the most admired in its industry sector in the *Fortune*/*Far East Economic Review* annual survey." If you subscribe to Opinion Research Corporation's corporate reputation caravan study, your goal could be, "To increase our company's corporate equity rating by one full percentage point in the next two years and by two points in the next four years."

■ It is quite acceptable to state a single, overriding objective, as just illustrated, with subsidiary goals set against each important audience or stakeholder group – investors, employees, customers, government, and so on.

7. Strategy

■ Outline your strategies in the same way that you have structured your goals. Make sure not to confuse strategies with tactics – a common mistake. Here is an easy way to distinguish: Goal/Objective = Where I want to get to. Strategy = Overall, how I get there. Tactics = Specifically what I have to do to get there.

■ You must create different strategies for different markets around the world. Your research and analysis will have shown you widely differing perceptions of your company in the principal countries in which you do business. When United Parcel Service decided to embark on building a global infrastructure in 1988, it was already the world's largest package delivery company, based on its size in the three markets it served through its own resources: the USA, Canada and Germany. In the USA, the company was, literally, part of the landscape with its 120,000 delivery vehicles and 300,000 employees in their brown uniforms. Research surveys in America gave UPS a 100 percent awareness rating. Still, the company knew that it had to make structural changes internally and alter perceptions among its customers and other stakeholders to keep its leadership position in that market. In the "new" markets of

Europe and Asia, UPS was completely unknown. The challenge was to introduce the company there as a strong alternative to entrenched competitors. In Canada and Germany, there was a dual task of gaining wider recognition of the name UPS and reshaping some perceptions that had formed in these markets. Different strategies were devised for each region, but all were geared to meet the overarching goal.

8. Targeting

The fact that this is one of the final steps in the process does not diminish its importance. Effective targeting will ensure economy of effort and budget. More important, it will ensure that you succeed in improving your reputation among those audiences that matter most to your organization's success.

- Start by listing all your stakeholders and audiences. Then list all those who exert a major influence on the attitudes of those in the first part of the list.
- You may list media as an audience. While media is an audience in its own right, it is even more important as an interlocutor with key influencers and decision makers, and as a multiplier with broader consumer audiences.
- Prioritize your targets by general category, so that if budgets and resources are limited, you concentrate on those audiences that are most important.
- Prioritize within each general category. For example, not all customers are equal; not all influencers of governmental law-making are equal. Classify your targets into three levels of importance: A, B and C. Most attention and budget should be focused on the A list.
- Target by region and country of importance to your organization.
- Use the public databases that are available to you to build your target lists. You should also maintain your own regularly updated master database. Note on it each contact made by letter, mailing, e-mail, phone call or meeting.

9. Messaging

- Go back to Step 3, Analysis, and review the short statement you wrote to describe the reputation of your company as you feel it stands now. Prepare a new statement that reflects the company as you would like it to be seen at the culmination of this process. In addition to its role in message development, the new statement is necessary in the next step, Mapping.

■ Synthesize the key messages that will become the mantra of all those empowered to act as spokesmen for the company. The messages will be the building blocks for creating a new perception of the company. Divide the messages into those that are global and overarching and those that have special importance in specific countries. Repetition of the messages by spokespersons will allow them to penetrate the consciousness of stakeholders and other audiences you seek to influence, and you should not let up.

10. Mapping

■ Translate your descriptions of your company's reputation now and as you would like it to be into a road map, with a starting point and a destination. This will help you track progress.

■ Make individual maps for each area of reputation which you believe needs to be changed. For example, research may have shown that your company has especially weak scores for its attitude toward the environment and pollution, and trails its competitors in this regard. Plot the environmental issues map with as much specific detail as you can, including your competitors, as illustrated in chart 3.3.

■ Data you receive from ORC will be mappable, as will the information you glean from generally available studies such as the "most admired" lists that appear in various publications. If you subscribe to MORI, you will receive this data already mapped in convenient form.

■ In the map covering a company's "overall reputation" (chart 3.4), I have shown the curve rising first on the awareness axis on the basis that it is sometimes easier to gain awareness and a correct perception of a company at the same time than it is to change entrenched impressions. There is an opposing view which holds that you must change perceptions with those who claim to know you before starting on the missionary work of increasing awareness.

■ The worst starting position on reputation maps is at the top left of the upper quadrant. This is the place for a company that everybody knows ... and hates, with the awesome challenge of having to change everybody's current perception.

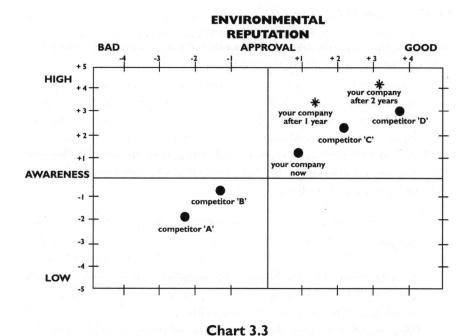

Chart 3.3

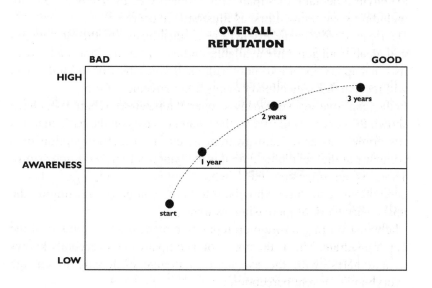

Chart 3.4

11. Infrastructure

Make sure you create the right departmental infrastructure to meet your goals. Alternatives are more fully described in chapter 12.

12. Program

With your research and planning completed, you must now develop and implement the program that will move your company along the road toward its goal.

■ Develop a memorable and inspiring creative concept, which symbolizes and encapsulates the reputation you seek for your company – a flag around which all your allies can rally. This concept or theme should be of a kind that can infuse all the action programs you undertake, binding them together.

■ Develop your action plan – or plans. Do not start with a piece of white paper or a blank computer screen. Use checklists of all the possible tactics available to you and pick those that are useful, while rejecting those that are not relevant. Only when you have screened all known techniques, should you start thinking about completely original techniques that might be developed to meet your particular set of circumstances. Here is a fairly comprehensive public relations toolbox which can be built into core programs for implementation by units of your organization around the world:

> Press conferences, editorial briefings
> Press kits, fact sheets, photographs, backgrounders, news releases
> Website
> CDrom
> Face-to-face meetings, presentation decks
> Position papers, white papers
> Op-eds
> By-lined articles
> Charts, graphs
> VNRs, b-roll
> Annual reports
> Spokespersons, speakers platforms, publicity tours
> Familiarization tours
> Seminars, workshops

Surveys and polls
Event sponsorships
Charity tie-ins

■ Develop country-specific and regional programs with your national PR directors.

13. Measurement

Your work will have been wasted – and your own job will be in jeopardy – if you cannot demonstrate that you have achieved success in meeting your goals. At the outset of the process, establish with your superiors how the work will be judged. If you have businesslike yardsticks for measurement, your proposals will most likely be accepted. If not, you will almost certainly have arbitrary criteria established to judge your performance, by people who do not have a close understanding of what is and is not possible in the world of communications.

■ You started with research. Continue, by monitoring your progress periodically to see if you are on track.
■ Check if you have met your goals in the "most admired" company ratings produced by the leading business magazines.
■ Re-audit your internal audiences to check how your colleagues feel the company is doing.
■ Conduct an annual Critical Issues Analysis to see which issues you have managed to defuse and control, and which are growing in importance. (See chapter 8, Issues Identification and Management.)
■ Conduct face-to-face interviews with key influencer groups.
■ Read your road map. Based on composite research findings, check how far you have traveled toward your destination of the reputation you desire.
■ Check that your stock price is at the desired P/E ratio.

CHAPTER 4

The Global Voice

Becoming a global corporation requires speaking with a global voice. This is not so easy as it sounds, and most companies find it difficult to establish the right messages and the right tone in which to express them. At this writing, there are no more than a handful of corporations with a commitment to becoming global in the fullest sense – Ford Motor, GE, IBM, Coca Cola and VISA are a few examples on this very short list. Nor are there many organizations that are truly multinational – the stage of development that immediately precedes the state of being global. Many corporations that believe they are multinational are really regional or super-regional, in the sense that they are well established in more than one region but fall short of being worldwide, or global, in their activities. Moreover, many are really national corporations that have expanded and added appendages in other countries, whose needs and views are not of any significance in the decision-making process.

Survival of concept

It will be interesting to see if the concept of the global corporation survives. To do so, it will have to overcome some powerful forces of economic nationalism and protectionism, as well as the internal pressure in many corporations, which together work to break up globalism into smaller pieces – either by geography or by the various lines of business in which they are engaged.

It will not be easy for most corporations, however big they are, to become truly global. This would mean a revolution in thinking which some will argue is against human nature. It means abandoning the enterprise's national identity, origins, center of gravity and community commitment, at least to a certain extent.

When hard decisions have to be made, say on the matter of selective plant closures in an economic downturn, the global corporation should, in theory, make its choices based on economic imperatives, even to the extent of closing facilities at the heart of its original home office. Sentiment, lobbying, industrial and political unrest can often be powerful factors in changing the best plan on paper into one that stands the best chance of being implemented.

An increasingly important movement dedicated to reversing the tide of globalization and its institutions – the IMF, WTO and the World Bank – first came to general notice at the G7 meeting in Seattle in 1999. This uneasy alliance of anarchists, political activists and established NGOs is becoming a formidable opponent that reflects and focuses widespread public fear about some of the consequences of globalization led by international corporations.

Balance

One of the most challenging problems facing today's business leaders is finding the right balance between the devolution of power to so-called autonomous units within a corporation and the exercise of power and decision making at the world headquarters, wherever that might be.

Today's fashion leans heavily toward a highly decentralized approach, with a large part of decision making placed in the hands of managers of national subsidiary companies so as to encourage a high degree of nimbleness and relevance, market by market.

Empowerment is a very fashionable word. By applying it to individuals at every level in the company, top management hopes to achieve the best possible performance from each person, unit, country and region. The aggregate will automatically ensure success for the corporate entity as a whole.

The decentralized model also makes it easy for corporations to establish uncomplicated and clear-cut criteria for success and, in turn, compensation and incentive packages for key managers. The best get promoted and the weak get weeded out.

Among the positive advantages of this system, there is another, less often mentioned defensive benefit. When things go wrong, central managements believe they might be able first to contain the problem at the local level without any bad effect on the main body of the enterprise; and if containment is not possible, the offending unit can be blamed for not adhering to corporate policy and its management can be changed before too much harm is done.

This is sometimes referred to as the "submarine principle." The naval submarine is built with up to eight water-tight compartments so that it can survive a hit on any one or two of them by enemy torpedoes.

Purpose

With global corporations still in the embryonic stage and the majority of multinationals operating in a highly decentralized manner, what is the purpose and role of a "global voice"?

A "global voice" is the subject of considerable study and attention by many of the world's finest corporations, even though the subject might be disguised under a host of other names, depending on the alma mater of the CEO or the dialectic jargon of the company. "One voice," "single voice," "key messages" and "must airs" are examples.

These corporations have recognized that a global voice is not optional nowadays; it is a corporate necessity.

Nor is it something that is only of concern for the global corporation; it is a vital necessity for every company that is engaged in international business, even if it operates in a highly decentralized way in other respects.

There are several reasons why this should be.

Media technology

The first and most compelling reason is the impact of technology on globalization of the media. The CNN coverage of Desert Storm was seen live by nearly every country in the world, as was the war in Afghanistan. This dramatically brought home what had been reality for some time since the advent of satellite TV: It is no longer possible to have substantially different messages for different markets or audiences. (I say substantially because the same technology also allows the opportunity to develop micromessaging to very small specialist audiences.)

Now, when referring to the media, it is necessary to include the Internet and all its various services, which are accessible by anyone, anywhere, at any time. Although, as the use of this medium grows and new service providers enter the market, it will be possible for corporations to depict themselves on home pages in a variety of forms and languages for different audiences, it will still be possible for the Internet surfer to access the basic portrait of the corporation from his PC in France, the UK, Ukraine, China or the Philippines.

As I write, certain governments are seeking to restrict access to the Internet for their subjects and it remains to be seen whether this is possible. I am certain that although a large section of any country's population will not seek to connect to "forbidden" sites, there will be plenty of enthusiasts who will be sufficiently motivated and skilled enough to find a way around any barriers.

The potency of the Internet as a global voice in its own right was amply demonstrated in the celebrated 1995 case of the faulty Pentium chip. A single complaint about the chip was aired on the Internet and built a crescendo of customer comments that the manufacturer, Intel Corporation, initially dismissed in quite a cavalier fashion. It ended with Intel offering to replace the Pentium chip for any PC owner who applied, a gesture with a possible price tag in the region of $450 million.

The impact of the Internet on the field of public relations is dealt with more fully in chapter 12.

Scrutiny

Increased scrutiny of the words and actions of corporations is another reason for a global voice. Governments, consumer protection organizations, non-governmental organizations (NGOs) and pressure groups of all kinds are making it their business to discover inconsistencies in multinational concerns. It is now far too dangerous to allow the corporate position to be articulated by local company officials without adequate guidance – or even direction, in some cases – from company headquarters. There are many examples of sister companies in different countries, subsidiaries of the same parent corporation, that have been found to subscribe to apparently contradictory philosophies and procedures. There are plenty of official and unofficial watchdogs ready to point out such anomalies to the public and hold the corporation up to ridicule with subsequent damage to its image and its credibility.

Among the predators who are happy to discover different standards (and explanations) within a single corporation are "venture lawyers" and, of course, the company's competitors in the marketplace.

For the lawyers, any hint of dissembling can open up financially rewarding opportunities for litigation in certain societies, such as America. Nor are these litigious activities any longer contained within national borders. One of the least instructive and most unpleasant sights in the immediate aftermath of the Bhopal disaster in India and after the downing of Pan Am 103 at Lockerbie in Scotland was the large number of American trial lawyers trawling among the victims for clients to represent in the US as well as the local courts.

For the competitors, such misadventures can be used as weapons with which to damage the rival company's reputation and sales for their own advantage. Few corporations in today's fiercely combative marketplace could resist the opportunity to take advantage of any misstep on the part of a competitor.

Benefits

If the threats were not enough to make the case for a "global voice," then the benefits that flow from a well-articulated and disseminated "global voice" should tip the balance.

It can be argued that it is the more decentralized multinational corporations that stand to benefit most. It is here, rather than in the old-fashioned, highly centralized or newer global corporations, that there is found a degree of local anarchy that can result in differing corporate cultures, policies and, therefore, messages being communicated. For such decentralized corporations, a single voice is of great importance in today's global village. But more often than not, they sound more like the Tower of Babel.

In an ideal world, the corporate or global voice should be descriptive of the reality. "The truth, well told" is an old advertising adage that might be appropriately applied to a well-executed global-voice concept for a company that strives for and achieves uniform excellence worldwide in every aspect of its business – in product quality, customer service, research and development, human relations, community relations.

The achievement of excellence, however, is not easy and takes steely resolve and time. For many companies, taking the first steps in this quest to establish a global voice can serve a different and valuable purpose – as a catalyst in the process of defining "the reality."

Mission statement

The precursor of any effective global-voice policy is the creation and adoption of a mission or vision statement that simply articulates the purpose and business of the enterprise: The corporate credo should be the guidelight for every executive and member of the company in whichever division or part of the world they may be.

Many sizable corporations still operate without the corporate mission being defined in this way. In a survey of 100 international companies conducted jointly by Edelman Public Relations Worldwide, Northwestern University and Opinion Research Corporation, 42 percent had no corporate values system, 75 percent of companies said they had no formalized mission/vision statement and 42 percent even worked without a written public relations plan. So it is not surprising that the subsequent development in more detail of such a corporation's viewpoint on various components of its mission should be inconsistent and inadequate. If the foundation is faulty, the building will crumble.

Assuming that the first step – the writing and adoption of a mission statement – has taken place, here are the further steps that should be taken in the development of a Corporate Global Voice.

Key messages

The next step should be to develop more fully into key phrases or messages the main elements of the company's policy on important topics. These are most likely to include comments about production processes, enhancements of shareholder values, policies toward employee development, commitment to product quality and excellence in many facets of day-to-day operations – in fact, all the things the company would like to say about itself to a benign reporter or government official making inquiries.

But an effective global voice must go much further and be able to articulate the company viewpoint on a range of external issues that might be raised regarding how the company's actions affect society in various ways.

Issues analysis

The identification of these issues is best undertaken by a systematic process of analysis, which is described in more detail in chapter 8. In essence, it involves surveying members of the communications and other staff in each of the company's various geographic locations and lines of business, and cross-referencing the data received with that easily obtainable from various opinion research organizations that regularly track public opinion. Even careful reading of the media and use of data-retrieval systems can freely elicit public-attitude data of a general kind that is helpful in this process.

From this process will emerge a list (upward of 50 topics is not unusual) of issues on which the company will need to formulate a brief position. A few, between six and ten, are likely to emerge as issues in most major markets and will require significant effort in preparing a global voice.

For chemical companies, these are likely to touch on pollution, use of non-replaceable fossil fuels, harmful effects when ingested, use of animals in testing of products, the disposal of waste and the possibility of explosions or environmental disasters.

For credit card companies, the issues of fraud, privacy, interest rates on outstanding balances and encouragement of use of credit by young people who have little chance to make payments are just a few of the universal problems that require uniform explanations and positions.

For tobacco, liquor and confectionery companies, all under varying degrees of control of distribution or advertising in many countries, there are a host of issues requiring global answers to obvious health-related questions.

The same is true of every company engaging in an international way of business, whatever its field (or fields) of endeavor may be.

Updating

Once the global voice policy has been started, it must be continued and constantly updated and refreshed. A periodic survey should be conducted to reprioritize the issues. It is almost certain that many will have receded in importance and others will have become more critical than ever. New concerns may be identified that have to be addressed for the first time, and old concerns may re-emerge in new ways.

CHAPTER 5

Think Global, Act Local

There is not likely to be a phrase you will hear in your career in public relations as often as "think global, act local." It is used to encourage international marketers and communicators to adapt their products or messages to be accepted in a variety of local communities around a region or around the world. The idea is that a good product, service or communications strategy can achieve global success as long as it is customized to meet local tastes.

A culinary equivalent might be a steak. An excellent piece of beef is described as tender, succulent and full of flavor. But, depending on where you are, some might prefer it rare or well done; grilled, fried or baked; plain or with bordelaise sauce, pepper sauce or forestiere. Without suitable adaptation, success will be elusive. When prepared for the regional palate, however, a fine piece of beef is likely to please.

But what about the fact that huge numbers of the world's people honor the cow and are offended by the notion that beef cattle are raised to end up on the dining table? Millions more are vegetarians. So mere customization, after all, is insufficient.

Post World War II

The internationalization of business in the post-World War II period and the parallel development of public relations have operated on this principle, which is generally seen as a refinement of the initial attempts by major corporations – mostly based in America in the early years – to export products or manufacture them locally, without any deviation from the products sold in the home country. This was: "Think global, act global."

It took a series of failures to achieve market penetration before businesses that were thinking global started acting local. Textbooks are full of examples of adaptations that had to be made to recover from these early reverses.

Manufacturers of home appliances had to learn that houses in Britain and many other countries in Europe were much smaller than in America, and the tiny kitchens could not accommodate the American standard size of refrigerator. Nor were houses built with basements in which the typical, large American washing machines could be installed. They, too, had to fit into the small kitchen alongside the refrigerator. This led quickly to miniaturization and local manufacture. The sizes and features of automobiles, which differ widely from continent to continent and country to country, are other well-known examples.

Hand in hand with the early attempts to think global, act global in product marketing went the efforts of corporate advertising and public relations departments. In the first wave, highly centralized communications were the order of the day. The advertisement that was created for placement in the *Cincinnati Enquirer* would have to suffice for the *Northampton Evening Telegraph* or the *South China Morning Post*, without alteration of a word or change of spelling.

The news releases written for and sent to city newspapers, whether the *New York Times* or the *San Francisco Examiner*, were also sent to the *Brighton Argus*, the *Sydney Morning Herald* and the *Daily Record* in Glasgow, sometimes without a local contact name and address. Even more remarkably, the same English-language communications were sent to media in France, Germany and elsewhere, in the naive hope that they would be welcomed, understood and published.

Ultimately, ads were adapted for individual markets and in some cases were even recreated to combat local competitors or to deal with specific local conditions, on the basis of accumulated experience and market research. Public relations was swift to adjust and start "acting local." Editors, journalists, opinion leaders, politicians, academics, pressure groups and civil servants are quick to voice opinions and they are the audiences or interlocutors for most public relations professionals. They have little time for catch-all communications that were obviously prepared for another audience in another country. At best, such efforts were disregarded and had no effect. At worst, they caused offense, creating a negative impression of the sender.

Early internationalists

The early internationalists were quick to learn. They employed public relations professionals, mostly recruited from the ranks of journalism, onto their staffs or into the emerging roster of consultancies and agencies that began to sprout up in London. Britain was well ahead of the other countries of Europe in this development, in large part because it was the primary location of the European headquarters of the major American companies.

This cadre of communicators had the dual function of educating their foreign "parents" in the customs, culture, sociology, politics and media of the local market, and reworking communications strategies and messages for local consumption. In the 1950s and 1960s, the development of public relations in Britain, at least, was as an adjunct to advertising although there were some very successful and prominent independent firms and individuals who specialized in public affairs. The largest consultancies were initially departments and, later, autonomous divisions of advertising agencies. It was late in the 1960s when the independent public relations consultancies began to rise to preeminence – until many of them were themselves acquired by ad agencies. One rationale for such acquisitions was that the major multinational clients of these agencies could be offered "the whole egg" (as Young & Rubicam described it). This meant one-stop shopping for clients, with integrated, or at least "bundled," services offered by advertising, research, sales promotion and public relations functions. Each agency had its own description of such combined marketing and communications support services. At Ogilvy & Mather, the concept was described as "orchestration": The client acted as the maestro, or conductor, of several instruments of marketing, bringing them all together in perfect timing, pitch and harmony.

The "think global" concept did not receive a warm welcome in every new market. The relentless rise of the multinational corporation posed a series of threats or, at least, perceived threats, to local communities in Europe and elsewhere. People and politicians became alarmed at what they felt was a creeping commercial colonization. From 1950 until 1985, the tension felt in Europe about the success of American corporations in foreign markets was matched by the alarm of Americans over Japanese inroads into the US automobile market, and in electronics, real estate and the entertainment industries in the 1980s and 1990s. To a lesser extent, America reacted with concern over foreign investment in US business and the consequences for the US economy. European companies, predominantly from Britain and Switzerland, were buying their way into ownership of US companies, many of them symbolic of the "American Dream."

The publication in France of Jean-Jacques Servan Schreiber's book, *Le Defi Americain*, signaled the peak of European reaction to the seeming takeover of the European industrial infrastructure by US-based multinationals, and the consequential impact on social, educational and family structures. Schreiber, a prominent French journalist, described the damaging effect he felt that American capitalist colonization had had in France and painted a scary picture of the future. He urged that the phenomenon be resisted at all costs. Among the effects was renewed emphasis on building the European Economic Community, now the EU, as a counterbalance.

On the other side, the less farsighted and thoughtful of the multinational companies reviewed their policies and joined the well-managed companies that had already adopted "act local" policies.

"Act local" benefits

Not only were these policies proven to be a useful defense against criticism of commercial imperialism, but they also turned out to have a variety of significant positive benefits. Some of the best new inventions and marketing concepts came from foreign employees in overseas units. Some overseas units outperformed the domestic operations when measured by growth and return on investment. And excellent young managers were being developed, many of whom ended up in key positions at the head office or went on to establish new subsidiaries in new markets.

And what did acting local involve? In essence, it meant that foreign-owned companies started acting as if they were members of the local communities in which they developed, made and sold their products, rather than as foreign invaders.

In actions, they sought to invest in production facilities and, in certain cases, even in research and development laboratories. They participated in local activities and increasingly became involved in education, and even the church.

PR actions

From a public relations or communications standpoint, these companies sought to make sure that the world was aware of their local involvement. They were at pains to be seen and accepted as local citizens rather than transient marauders who come, take what they want and then abandon the locality, rather like the Vikings.

The companies primarily publicized their actions to support the local community and host country. News releases and press conferences would put the spotlight on local acts: investment in new production facilities that would increase job opportunities, announcements of promotions and transfers of local executives, production records, funding of local charities, participation in local festivals, donations to schools and colleges, foreign earnings generated by exports from the unit, inventions or advances inspired by the local work force.

Some of the most serious examples of this full-blooded attempt to "act local" and to be recognized for doing so can be seen in the advertisements of many companies, notably IBM, which depicted individual nationals from several countries in each ad. The effect of the whole was to suggest that this huge multinational was, in fact, the federal headquarters of a number of independent and autonomous national entities run by locals. PR activities echoed this theme.

It certainly had its effect.

While foreign computer and technology corporations are forbidden by law from bidding for many US defense and other government contracts, IBM's lobbyists managed to get IBM/Europe classified as a European company, by virtue of its thousands of European employees, exports and importance to the European economies, so that it could bid for official contracts of the European Economic Community.

Think local

Yet the question remains: Does not the phrase "think global, act local" reflect an imperialistic economic attitude? At worst, it conjures up a colonial ambition in which the locals are satisfied with the offer of various beads and baubles, becoming pawns in a grand plan. Mostly, of course, it is common sense for executives cutting their teeth in the international business world and is sound as far as it goes.

But it may be much more effective – certainly for PR people and other communicators – to reverse the advice and "Think local, act global." This may seem just tinkering with words ("you end doing the same things, anyway"), but I beg to differ.

Tip O'Neill, the longtime Speaker of the US House of Representatives, is credited with saying, "All politics is local." He was right. In a democracy, ultimate power rests with the voter who might be moved by leadership and a dramatically articulated vision but most often has to make judgments based on local input and a "what's in it for me" attitude.

By "thinking local," you can reach a level of understanding of the mind-set of each group of people with whom you must communicate that will make your dialogue much more successful.

If you are able to "think local," or at least listen to and understand the advice of those who can, you will stand a much better chance of being able to put your case in terms that are comprehensible by and convincing to your local audience. Thinking local means much, much more than translating, customizing and even localizing news releases and other communications.

"Think local, act local" is the new credo of the world's most famous brand, Coca-Cola, adopted in the wake of crises which occurred in 2000 (see page 104).

It means understanding local history, customs, rituals, taboos and prejudices. It means knowing what does and does not make news. It means respecting that a local community's perception, motivation or priority represents a different outlook. It means patience.

Success in thinking local brings its own problems, however, the greatest of which is retaining loyalty to the global vision and mission of the organization. It can be a challenge to step from thinking local to acting global, when so often the two seem to be at odds with each other. This is where corporate resolve and commitment, tempered by compromise, are of the greatest importance.

Backlash

Japanese business leaders had to learn to think local before they could even act local.

As they achieved increasing success in penetrating the US market with sales of automobiles and electronics – as well as a host of other items – they felt the backlash of public opinion from Americans, who believed their jobs and way of life were under threat by a country that had been their recent enemy. In the next phase of Japanese globalization, the new-found wealth of the Japanese came back to be reinvested in America, in local manufacture or assembly of products, as well as in the purchase of prime real estate.

At the outset, the Japanese appeared not to be good corporate citizens in their many locations, something that caused concern back at headquarters. Efforts were made to find the reasons and put matters right. The firms recognized that they had to *learn* how to think local before they could act local.

Corporate philanthropy

Among the many differences between American and Japanese commercial practices, human relations, manufacturing procedures and cultures, one phenomenon became apparent: The Japanese were completely ignorant of the concept of volunteerism, community service and charitable giving that is such an integral part of American business life. Social responsibility in Japan manifests itself in other ways, such as provision of lifetime employment. Japanese corporations did not routinely make charitable donations or support community initiatives, seeing them as the responsibility of national or local government. What's more, the Japanese also are not accustomed to the private raising of large sums of money following natural disasters. Foreigners did this after the 1994 Kyoto earthquake, to help with the costs of medical care and repair to the infrastructure. The Japanese have no system for accepting and using such contributions, which, in turn, makes them appear insensitive and arrogant. Nevertheless, the Japanese were determined to understand what it takes to be a good citizen in their adopted country, and at the top of the list was the topic of corporate philanthropy, not to be confused with cause-related marketing.

This led to the creation of a specialized branch of consulting in which individuals and firms would advise Asian companies eager to understand this concept as applied in the United States. Some of these consultants could even act as the selectors of the beneficiaries of this corporate philanthropy on a local basis, which might be anything from the construction of a community swimming pool to the addition of a new wing to the library or uniforms for the marching band.

Understanding other cultures

If it has been hard for Asian managers and communicators to comprehend the European and American way, it was equally so for the Western executive to understand – and respect – the ways and customs of the Asian markets he sought to conquer.

Newcomers to the area of greater China, for example, are amused by and often deride the vital importance of *feng shui*. And the *feng shui* man is likely to be one of their first encounters, for he is the person who dictates – yes, dictates – the angle and placement of the reception desk, as well as the layout of the office or factory that is being rented or built. This skill is based on a combination of magical arts, including astrology, rather than his Western cousins' degrees in environmental engineering, ergonomics and industrial psychology.

Many Western companies have paid a heavy price with their local staff, suppliers and customers for ignoring the *feng shui* man, or for treating him as a figure of fun. It is a rare Chinese business leader – including any one of the scores of Hong Kong billionaires – who would inaugurate new premises without having taken the advice of the *feng shui* expert. Even such a wealthy person will meekly agree to the office allocated to him and will place his desk at the angle recommended.

McDonald's – a model of globalization – has had its own encounters with local custom. Its international expansion during a quarter of a century has evolved into a system that allows for a great deal of local modification of menu items, to appeal to local tastes, and even terminology. In Australia, signs at roadside read "MACCA's – 5KM ON RIGHT."

Such liberties were unthinkable in the 1980s. When the first McDonald's restaurant was opened in Kuala Lumpur, Malaysia, in 1983, questions were raised in the company's Chicago headquarters, and then incredulity at the answers, regarding an item that appeared on the invoice for the inaugural press and opinion-leader event: "Bomo Man M$500."

Who was this Bomo Man?

The Bomo Man, came the answer, is a key figure at every important, outdoor public event in Malaysia. He is a "rain man," but, unlike the better known rainmakers in the West, he performs a dance and casts spells to ensure that rain stays away during celebrations. McDonald's grand opening had taken place in perfect weather, thanks to the Bomo Man, the accounting people were told. The Malaysian partners of McDonald's had a hard time understanding what kind of ignorance could prompt the questions from Chicago. It was just as hard for the Midwest executives to believe they were looking at a valid expense.

Nonetheless, they paid the M$500.

McDonald's now faces a special challenge as the symbol of the USA and all things American. Its properties are the first to be targeted and damaged or destroyed at times when anti-American sentiment reaches fever pitch.

CHAPTER 6

The Barriers

It is a characteristic of many public relations people to be paranoid, intro-spective, and doubting. A few even add a measure of self pity.

Far too many people in public relations are convinced that they practice a profession that is in low esteem and that its growth is impeded. They feel relegated to a lower caste of management in their companies.

The facts prove differently. Public relations is fast growing as can be seen from the statistics given in chapter 14.

The numbers reflect the performance of an industry growing at well above the average rate. By another measure, college courses in public relations available in the USA number 150. This surely can only be reflective of a profession that is attractive from several points of view to aspiring youth.

There are some grounds, however, for public relations practitioners of a certain age and from certain countries to have feelings of lack of fulfillment. In spite of the fast growth of public relations worldwide, it is true that many barriers do exist to its growth. This is especially true in countries outside the USA and UK, where public relations is more deeply entrenched and practiced than in many other countries. There are a number of hurdles to be overcome in those nations where the concept of public relations is relatively new, and therefore suspect.

Special problems exist in totalitarian states and linger even when the total-itarian regime is overthrown or abandoned in favor of democracy.

Propaganda

One of the insults most abhorred by people in my profession is the use of the term propaganda, suggesting that it is synonymous with public relations. The word is invariably used in discussions when it clearly has a pejorative meaning.

The interchangeability of the terms propaganda and public relations was, in fact, a serious barrier to the development of public relations as practiced today.

After World War II, many people in Germany would have nothing to do with public relations. It is one reason why many of the major German concerns were so late to establish professional public relations departments and use consultancies and agencies. They equated public relations-style communications with propaganda; and they had seen or heard what that master of propaganda, Goebbels, had done to twist the truth and bring their country to war. They never wanted that to happen again. Ergo, "we will not engage in public relations activities for our company, it has an evil smell" was a common attitude in German commerce and industry for about three decades after the war had ended. Decision makers had failed to make the distinction between bona fide public relations and propaganda. Discussions and debates on this topic can engage PR people and journalists in arguments that go deep into the night. It is certainly not possible to resolve the question over a single bottle of wine.

Webster's Dictionary defines propaganda as: 1. a congregation of the Roman curia having jurisdiction over missionary territories and related institutions 2. the spreading of ideas, information, or rumor for the purpose of helping or injuring an institution, a cause, or a person 3. ideas, facts, or allegations spread deliberately to further one's cause or to damage an opposing cause; also: a public action having such an effect.

The Concise Oxford Dictionary's definition is: 1. association or organized scheme for propagation of a doctrine or practice; doctrines, information, etc., thus propagated 2. committee of cardinals in charge of foreign missions.

However, to me the distinction lies less in the meaning of the word propaganda than in the context in which it is practiced. I would like to propose this definition: "Propaganda is a form of persuasive communication that succeeds in states where there are totalitarian governments and cannot exist in a true democracy."

In other words, Goebbels was able to succeed when his voice or messages were the only ones permitted in Germany. No opposing view was allowed. No debate existed. It was perilous to voice any opinion contrary to the approved government view.

A similar situation existed in China under Mao Ze Dong, and in spite of gigantic steps undertaken in economic liberalization, the silencing of dissenting voices in Tiananmen Square showed that there had not been a full embracing of democracy. Public relations can be practiced in only a limited way in China and a number of other countries today.

The same can be said about the Soviet Union in the time of Stalin, the Iraq of Saddam Hussein and some of the Islamic states ruled by clerics, such as Iran under the ayatollahs and Afghanistan under the Taliban.

Censorship

The partner of propaganda is censorship. There are today some places which are "semi-propaganda" states. They are superficially democratic but the media is censored or restricted. Singapore is such an example. Censorship ensures that propaganda is the only form of communication and the distribution of several publications such as the *Wall Street Journal* and the *Far Eastern Economic Review* is strictly controlled.

In the USA there is concern at the concentration of media ownership into just a few hands, along with a similar trend in advertising agencies which hold great commercial power. Some fear for the objectivity of news and current affairs programming.

In many countries, the most dangerous form of media control exists – self-censorship. Although it is most prevalent in "semi-propaganda" states as mentioned earlier, it is also found in places thought to be the freest democracies.

In these cases, editors, broadcast producers and publishers consciously or unconsciously print or broadcast material that is benign to the state or, sometimes, commercial interests. In unwritten agreements, the media refrains from publishing material critical of the political or commercial establishment, its people and policies, in return for the right to publish at all. Even in strongly democratic nations there is a rush to self-censorship, with propaganda flourishing when a major crisis such as total war occurs. An example was Britain in World War II, when an unashamedly-called "government propaganda film industry" was established. Some of its products are still to be seen as re-runs on television. In the climate of those wartime years, any dissenting or opposing views were silenced.

Much more recently, since the war on terrorism was declared following the destruction of the World Trade Center in New York and part of the Pentagon in Washington on September 11, 2001, there has been much controversy in the USA over the willingness of some media to bow to pressure from the White House and Pentagon urging restraint on coverage that might allow opposing views to be aired.

For the international public relations executive, this means the need to be especially sensitive as to what can be achieved through the media and what messages must be conveyed to influencers by other means.

The galvanizing effect on the media when democracy replaces a totalitarian regime is amazing to witness.

An early European example was seen in Spain, where there was the restoration of a constitutional monarchy following the death of the dictator General Franco, in 1969. Even under Franco, Spain had a small cadre of public relations professionals who operated successfully but within the constraints of that strict regime. One of these practitioners, with whom I have had the privilege of working over many years, is Ramon Alvarez. He describes the change of government thus: "Overnight, newsstands appeared on the streets, each full of newspapers and magazines. Some of these had been published underground in previous years but others were completely new. The media in Spain took on a completely new lease on life and topics that had been taboo were now openly discussed in print. TV and radio, which continued to be government controlled, opened up more gradually in the years that followed."

The importance of the flourishing media in Spain was soon to be seen, as reactionaries in Spain who could not get used to the new ways of democracy sought to bring back the fascist regime via a coup which had its climax in the House of Parliament. The coup failed and many believe that it was because Spaniards had had a taste of the new media – and because they were informed of events hour by hour.

The experience of Spain was repeated in Germany, when the Berlin Wall came down, and there was a domino effect throughout Eastern Europe, culminating in the overthrow of communism in Russia itself. In the case of Eastern Europe, the media was an important cause for the rejection of communism, as well as the beneficiary when democracy arrived. In the Americas, recent political developments have led to the creation of a media that is much less pliable in the hands of the ruling party. Mexico is a good example.

The ability of people at all levels in society to receive TV signals and radio programs from neighboring – and far-off – democracies diminished the power of propaganda's single message.

In this age of channel surfing, how could pontificating party officials compete with quiz shows and soap operas newly available via satellite?

Overconfident self-reliance

Ralph Waldo Emerson said: "If a man can write a better book, preach a better sermon, or make a better mousetrap than his neighbor, though he build his house in the woods the world will make a beaten path to his door." It is perhaps the biggest lie in the annals of marketing. Similarly, "If you employ a public relations professional, everyone will think you are in trouble or have something to hide" is a most common myth in public relations and one that has actually deterred executives from gaining valuable advice and assistance that might have helped them avoid trouble.

In many countries, it is seen as sufficient to manage business in an efficient way and for the corporation to behave decently. Everything will then take care of itself and the company's reputation will stand high. In fact, some executives and journalists believe this so strongly that they accuse companies that do employ aggressive communications policies of being unduly self-promotional.

This barrier is very easy to understand, especially if you come from a culture that is reserved and repelled by people who are driven by a need for personal recognition and publicity.

Moreover, there is a technical reason which the media finds disturbing. If from time immemorial, senior journalists have dealt directly with the chief executive of the company, they do not usually take kindly to the insertion of an intermediary – a public relations professional – in the relationship, even though it might be to the advantage of both sides.

The media invariably views such an appointment as the erection of a wall between themselves and the company. It is regrettable that too few PR executives who take company positions have the personality and seniority to convince the media that they should be seen as a bridge, not a hurdle, in the relationship.

This is why such appointments should be made during a period of calm in a company's history and not at a time of crisis, lest the myth mentioned earlier come to be reality.

Measurability

The difficulties of measuring the effectiveness of public relations have been a serious barrier to its growth over the years. The many-sided nature of public relations and its special branches prevent measuring in a uniform manner. Different methods to evaluate whether the PR efforts have succeeded or failed are needed for marketing support, public affairs, corporate reputation, employee communications, and philanthropy. Even when the right method of evaluation is known, it is often not used for reasons of cost. Far too often, the cost of research studies to establish the success or failure of a program is greater than the cost of the program itself, and is therefore not undertaken.

In direct response advertising, success and failure are clear to see in the sales that are generated. In public relations, cause-related programs offer the potential of measurement through the speed with which funds are collected and the amount that is eventually amassed for the nominated cause. Similarly, in the arena of public affairs, success or failure is often recorded for all to know at the ballot box.

People in advertising have, over the years, done a much better job of convincing their employers or clients that the effect of advertising can be measured, and indeed, in some cases, just as with PR, there is a clearly measurable result.

In order to justify their huge budgets, advertising agents have developed sophisticated testing and measurement procedures and usually appear in joint meetings with public relations colleagues to have a greater mastery over the techniques of measurement. In truth, they are no more advanced than people in public relations.

The International Committee of Public Relations Consultancies Associations (ICO) has published a pamphlet on goal setting and measurement. Peter Hehir, then chairman of Porter Novelli International, whose brainchild it is, says: "I hope this provides clients and their agencies with a useful guide that will help them to establish realistic objectives."

In the US, the Institute for Public Relations and the Council of Public Relations Firms are collaborating to develop the first comprehensive model to measure the effectiveness of public relations programs. Research firm Wirthlin Worldwide is developing and testing several PR Outcome Models. The models would support the planning, execution and measurement of public relations by providing a means to forecast and evaluate the outcomes of PR programs and activities.

"Soft" image

Public relations' image as a "soft" discipline, lacking in intellectual under-pinning and research-based evaluation systems, is probably the most persistent barrier to its development. It is in this area that practitioners of the future should be devoting their greatest attention. The profession might then grow at an even more accelerated pace than in the recent past when, in spite of this and other barriers, the growth of the leading public relations agencies/con-sultancies has been much greater than that of the top advertising agencies.

Low esteem

A longtime hurdle for public relations was the relatively low esteem in which PR practitioners were held, but that is changing for the better, surely one reason the growth of PR has been so strong in recent years.

The profession is clearly very attractive to young people. Fast-increasing public relations undergraduate and master's courses around the world are oversubscribed. Yet, parents would probably have preferred their children to have chosen one of the established older professions such as the law, medicine or architecture. Nevertheless, the difference in the perceived status of public relations and more traditional careers is diminishing. The shift is not, unhappily, just because of the increased standing of public relations as a serious discipline, but because the "god-like" status and respect once accorded to doctors and lawyers has been fast dropping in recent years, as those professions slide from being vocational to commercial.

Strength in variety

The variety of public relations specialties and the ability of people from other professions to transfer to this field have given it great strength in today's society. I have known lawyers who have felt imprisoned in law firms, doing routine tasks, envious of us in public relations. While they have been trapped undertaking lengthy and boring interpretations of existing law or drawing up the papers for various transactions, they have observed that public relations people are often involved in the challenging and exciting business of helping to *change* existing law. There are now a number of lawyers practicing public relations and finding that their legal training is of great value.

The same is true of medicine. There are a number of doctors who feel they can achieve more for the health of a wider group of sick people by practicing their profession in the context of mass communications and have switched career to public relations counseling.

The troubling transfer

The notion that "anyone can do PR, because it is so easy" has caused many organizations to make a false start in public relations. This has slowed the acceptance of public relations as an important business discipline within countless companies and in the business community at large.

A typical story of a company recognizing that PR can be a useful business tool – and the all-too-common outcome – goes like this.

The CEO arrives one day and informs his management committee that, as part of improving management and market competitiveness, "we are going to go in for this PR thing I read about in *Fortune*/heard about from Joe at the golf club/that is being used by our main rival and is forcing down our market share/heard about at a conference I've just attended."

You can be sure the CEO did not learn about PR from an MBA course he took at one of the elite colleges.

Although PR now attracts many students to its specialist programs, it barely features in the curricula of the majority of MBA courses, according to "The Importance of Public Relations in Graduate Business Programs," a study I conducted for my company* in 1993. The initial finding of the study was depressing. Public relations came last in the rating of the most important elements for the career education of marketing professionals. Professor Miland M. Lele of the University of Chicago could not have made things clearer, saying: "I'll be frank, public relations isn't included in our curriculum."

However, there is also a promising situation: Half of those who teach marketing say that coverage of public relations now is too light in their curricula; at the same time, more than one-quarter believed it would increase in importance in the next five years. This might well have happened but, according to my conversations with leading post-graduate educators, the advances made have been slight.

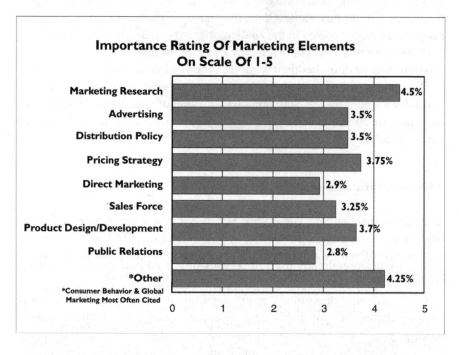

Chart 6.1

---

* The importance of Public Relations in Graduate Business Programs, a survey conducted by Edelman Public Relations Worldwide in 1993.

Methods of improving public relations study

Responding professors offer a wide variety of ways they think understanding of public relations can be improved. Case studies are by far the most frequently mentioned (38.4 percent) followed by textbooks (16.4 percent). Guest speakers, computer simulations and outside reading are also mentioned (see chart 6.2).

**Ways to Improve
Understanding of Public Relations**

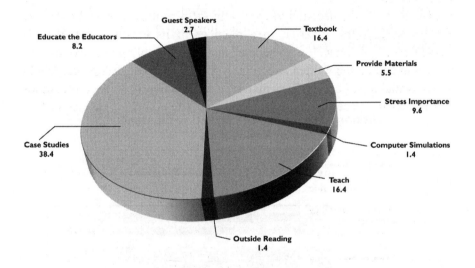

Chart 6.2

Case studies are already used in courses in almost half the schools (46.3 percent).

"I think the only opportunity in my department (marketing) is to develop teaching materials – probably case histories – that raise public relations management issues. I think faculty members would react very appreciatively to new, exciting, dramatic cases," said Peter L. Wright of Stanford University.

"To improve the understanding of public relations among MBA students, state-of-the-art case histories should be developed and used," Paul W. Farris, University of Virginia, agreed.

Important aspects of public relations

Within public relations, educators ranked crisis and issues management as the most important aspect of public relations for their students to understand and apply. Media relations ranked second, followed by corporate image and employee communications. Marketing was ranked fifth, followed by government relations and investor relations.

Eight in ten survey participants said that fewer than 20 percent of the required courses in their MBA programs are devoted to marketing. About the same number (81.3 percent) said it would be difficult to add a new required course to their curriculum, although most said it would be relatively easy to add an elective course.

Having made the decision to engage in PR activities, a typical company usually assigns the function to a member of its existing staff who is personable, "gets on well with people" and is reasonably persuasive in conversation and on the written page. Sadly, his likely most striking credential is his availability, because he is no longer as effective as he once was in his current position (perhaps a sales manager). The company has no wish to

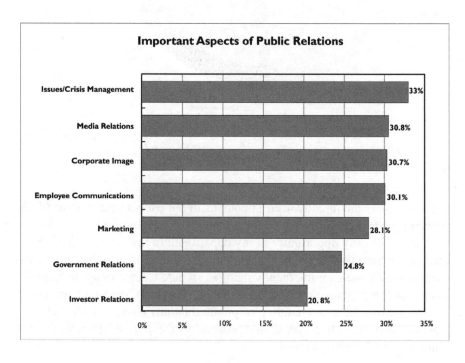

Chart 6.3

dismiss him but is watching out for opportunities to transfer him to other duties. The PR position sounds perfect!

Such transferees sometimes make a decent go of the job and prepare the way for the appointment of professional, trained staff, in due course. Others, I fear, put back the cause by several years, through no fault of their own.

The problem, which would be immensely helped by the introduction of some PR modules in the MBA courses, arises because there is little under-standing of the art and science of persuasive communication, its strategic purpose or the technology of message delivery, all of which are essential to the effective use of PR.

It is no longer true that "anybody can do it," if ever it was.

The hidden persuaders

Vance Packard's book, *The Hidden Persuaders*, published in 1957, had an important impact on the development of the entire field of persuasive com-munication, including public relations. The book turned out to be both a barrier and a force for growth of the field.

On the one hand, many people (well beyond the number of those who had actually read the book) were repelled by the sinister suggestion that people could easily be manipulated by various communications techniques, including subliminal messages. They wanted to have nothing to do with it.

Others recognized that understanding and using these techniques was the path to power and success in business or politics.

Before Packard's thesis, there had always been public concern about the potential for sinister manipulation of people – individuals and groups. The concern will continue as long as the earth turns. The public has a huge appetite for stories of possibly evil manipulators, such as the *eminence grise*, Cardinal Richelieu, and the boy king, Rasputin and the Tsar and Tsarina, and Svengali and Trilby.

More recently there has been much public debate in the USA, UK and elsewhere about the power of unelected political strategists and communica-tors who are no longer the hidden persuaders made famous by Vance Packard. Now they are themselves celebrities, whose views are discussed in the political columns and whose private lives feed the gossip columns of the media.

Their importance has increased, as have the complexity and balance of modern politics, along with the need to understand the way in which the media must be used for electoral success. Political leadership relies as much on expediency – polling to chart a course most acceptable to public opinion

– as it does on deeply held convictions. There is great concern that unelected advisers exercise too great an influence on policy decisions.

The whole topic was summed up in a remark made by Larry Speakes, White House spokesman in the Reagan Administration, who claimed that "When the President opens his mouth, it is my words that come out."

An American art

The American-developed art of electoral campaign strategy, surely a subset of the broad field of public relations, has been exported to politicians in many countries by pioneering counseling firms in this field, such as Sawyer Miller Associates (one of the firms that, over the past few years, has morphed into Weber Shandwick). And, while some see this as an unfortunate development, who can argue with the fact that it goes hand in hand with the growth of democracy? The need for such advice only exists where there is debate among political opponents, with resolution taking place at the ballot box. The clients of these firms (among them the Philippines, Colombia, Panama, Peru, Brazil, Turkey) are often ones that have sought to find their way in democracy after years under totalitarian systems of one sort or another, as well as very long-established democracies such as Britain, where the Prime Minister and leader of the Labour Party, Tony Blair, sought the strategic advice of George Stephanopoulos, a former chief spokesman for President Clinton, to complement that of his close adviser, Peter Mandelson (who subsequently had to resign his government position in disgrace).

None of the formidable barriers mentioned in this chapter have impeded the steady progress of public relations during the second half of the twentieth century. They have been dismantled by an increasingly well-educated world public with a thirst for information and material products. That thirst is being slaked by global media empires and producers of goods and services that use the proliferating new channels of communication.

Even the fear of propaganda and manipulation by hidden or famous persuaders has been countered by the recognition of the power of skilled communications to affect the hearts and minds of people and their voting or purchasing decisions. As the power of the professional communicator's skills is increasingly recognized, so more recruits are added, prestige is increased, new tools of measurement are being found. No longer does PR stand for "poor relation" among the professions.

CHAPTER 7

The Specialization of International Public Relations

Specialization, globalization and communications technology are currently the three most potent forces affecting the practice of international public relations.

Of these, specialization has had the longest history and the greatest impact over the past three decades.

Until the mid-1960s, public relations was a calling for generalists, whether they worked in-house at companies or in consultancies or agencies. As a youthful profession or craft, it also had to draw its recruits from other fields, mostly journalism, which at that time was also much more general than it is today. The business, arts, travel and other specialist sections in the newspapers of today are a relatively new invention. Journalists and PR people were expected to put their hand – and brain – to any task that came along.

The public relations officers (as they were mostly called) in most companies were expected to offer product publicity support on Monday, conduct interviews, write and lay out the employee newsletter on Tuesday, arrange a community sponsorship activity on Wednesday, write the chairman's statement for the annual report on Thursday and be ready on Friday to diffuse a crisis with consummate skill. (Crises always occur on Fridays, usually at about 5:00 p.m.) Over the weekend, he would be expected to study complicated reports from a management consultant, recommending a divisional reorganization. He needed to be ready on Monday with a plan to make the announcements internally and externally, and to prepare the executives involved with the presentation of their speeches. He would be expected to hone the key messages and to conduct media training.

The public relations executive at the consultancy or agency, meanwhile, would have to be able to take exactly the same week as his in-house opposite number in his stride. But he would also have to be knowledgeable and flexible enough to undertake the same functions for a variety of client organizations, ranging from pharmaceutical companies through producers of consumer products to banks and financial institutions or government departments.

It was clear this could not last. The huge horizon of public relations activity, which defies easy definition, demanded that it be broken down into manageable components. And in the intervening years this has happened with a vengeance.

From a situation in which almost every practitioner had started life in a job outside public relations, we have moved to a point where not only have some spent their entire working life in public relations, but some in their forties and fifties have spent it in a single specialty, often without even the opportunity to glimpse the wider world of their profession.

This is one of the conundrums facing public relations today. Many feel that the pressure of specialization detracts from the true contribution that public relations can make at the corporate level. Specialization results in too little broad perspective, too little general knowledge, too little awareness of the full range of shapes and dynamics that make up our societies.

And in the concerns about the narrow view of the universe that accompanies intense specialization, include a worry that too little attention is paid to international affairs.

I have to admit that one of the attractions of public relations to me when I started out was the opportunity to be involved in a huge range of industries and activities, and to draw on as many skills as I could possibly attain. No two days needed to be the same. The lessons of one project or assignment invariably found a useful application in another, and perhaps in a different industry. After 40 years in practice, it is this variety that still keeps me interested, challenged and learning.

On the other hand, the magnet of specialization is too strong to resist.

Why specialization?

Four factors are at work. The first is the increased recognition of the importance of public relations by different industries. This has meant the allocation of increasingly large budgets which, in turn, call for greater numbers of dedicated, qualified personnel.

The second factor is the accelerating complexity of almost every industry, as the knowledge base of science-driven fields of endeavor increases exponentially each year. The data that has to be mastered by anyone professing to be a communicator in any sector is enormous. Few are gifted enough to be truly able to work at the most detailed level in more than one industry. This factor has also made the practice of public relations itself, on behalf of any industry, more challenging in terms of the techniques and technology used.

The third factor is an increasingly educated and inquisitive consumer public served by a newly aggressive and growing media, which is itself structured on specialist lines.

The fourth force driving specialization has been the emergence of many industries and professions which traditionally had shunned communications. In some cases, as with law and medicine, self-imposed or common-law regulations forbade self-promotion. Many of those taboos have been torn down.

A careful look at the PR league tables shows that the engines of growth in recent years have been the boutique agencies which have offered specialist PR services of some kind. Even the major international full-service agencies mostly owe their successful growth to the performance of their individual specialist divisions.

Categories of specialization

What are these specialties, and how have they reshaped the public relations landscape?

There are three categories, and within each many specialties:

- *Industry, business or organization.* There are discrete PR specialties in Healthcare and Pharmaceutical Products, Consumer Products and Services, Financial Service Organizations, Technology, Defense, Professional Services and many more.
- *PR practice areas.* No matter what industry, there are PR specialties in Investor Relations, Public Affairs, Community Relations, Employee Communications, Sponsorship and Event Management.
- *Technical skills.* Within PR structures, there are specialist roles played by dedicated experts in publications, speechwriting, video production, media relations, CDrom and website development, and a number of other functions.

Just when you think you have grasped the full meaning of specialization, it becomes apparent that this is a continuous process of sub-division. Nowadays, even the specialties within specialties can support relatively large PR practices. An example can be found in the broad specialty of technology. There are individual PR practitioners who spend their entire working week narrowly focused on semi-conductors or systems software, of which they have to have extensive knowledge. These same people may not be able to work effectively in other branches of technology.

The movement toward specialization began in the mid-1960s with pharmaceuticals and with the investor relations branch of financial public relations, specialties that are still the most dynamic within PR. Technology began its dramatic growth two decades later.

These three specialties are also the most "portable" and international in the whole field of public relations, and so are of great interest and importance to the international practitioner.

I have not included one of the largest specialties – consumer products and services – because it constituted a major sector even in the earliest days of PR. It continues to be hugely important within PR as a whole, but having started on a high plateau, it has not demonstrated the exceptional growth of the other three specialties. It has, however, changed in the demands that it makes on practitioners, and this is discussed later in this chapter.

Pharmaceuticals

The description "ethical" for pharmaceuticals that were available to the public only with a doctor's prescription gives a hint about how the medical profession, producers and pharmacists viewed the broad industry group to which their fortunes were so closely tied. A stronger clue was the terminology usually applied to what are now known as over-the-counter drugs (OTCs), which were described either as "patent" or "proprietary" medicines.

In the first 50 years of the twentieth century, not only did doctors, as the sole source of prescriptions, control the sales of ethical drugs, they also controlled all information about these preparations. There was limited public awareness of available treatments. Physicians were apt to be testy when confronted by knowledgeable patients who might wish to discuss alternative forms of treatment. This was particularly true in the majority of countries where healthcare was socialized and the major "buyers" of prescription pharmaceuticals were governments.

The manufacturers of ethical pharmaceuticals were the self-same companies that made medicines that were sold over the counter with advertising and public relations support. They could see the power of communications to inform, educate and persuade the public in health-related matters.

No one ever dreamed that the day would arrive when prescription-only drugs would be advertised to the public in general print and TV media, as has been the case since the early 1990s in the USA (albeit under tight control).

Pharmaceutical companies turned in increasing numbers to public relations practitioners to step in and fill the informational and promotional gap to support what is now known as Direct To Consumer (DTC) marketing. In 2000 over $2.5 billion was spent on DTC advertising in America, an increase of 212 percent over five years, according to IMS.

We were entering an era of discovery of new life-saving or life-improving compounds for millions of sufferers, and even the birth of new sciences and production methods such as biotechnology. Pharmaceutical manufacturers wanted to tell the world. There were time and competitive pressures as well. The companies knew they had to make and grow their markets in time to achieve an adequate return on the investment in R&D during the 14-year life of their patents. If another manufacturer was on the same trail, it was important to establish a strong and secure market position which would be hard for the new rival to penetrate. The manufacturers could no longer leave this entirely in the hands of the medical profession, which was thought to move at a glacial pace.

Initial assignments were well within the scope of generalist PR practitioners. Then, the demands of parallel-track communications, both to and through the medical and pharmacy professions, as well as to the end user via the general media, called for more specialist PR knowledge. As the PR specialty developed, it attracted doctors, pharmacologists, pharmacists, chemists and other communicators with a special interest in and aptitude for these subjects. It has continued that way ever since and is now one of the two largest specialist sectors of public relations. The other is technology.

It has created its own sub-specialties which correspond directly with various medical specialties, such as cardiology, nephrology, oncology and sports medicine; health economics and politics; hospitals and other care-giving institutions; health professional groups; home delivery of health care; sub-divisions by gender, race, age; science writing; biotechnology; ethics; continuing medical education; meetings organization, and patient groups.

Pharmaceutical companies have also fueled the internationalization of public relations. Most of the leading companies have been active internationally for several decades and, almost without exception, their major products have worldwide application.

Although it is still exceptional for any new drug to be launched in all markets simultaneously, the data needed to support approval to market can increasingly be the same in several of the most advanced countries. Thus the rollout of a new preparation now usually takes place over a relatively short period. It is customary for pharmaceutical companies to develop the blueprint of a pre-marketing program, launch the campaign centrally, and then adapt and implement it locally in all key markets.

The movement toward specialization which is now deeply rooted in the USA and the UK is less pronounced in the smaller or newer markets for public relations. In many of these, the size of the business, the scarcity of qualified PR people and the continuing strict application of rules governing communications related to prescription drugs all work against the development of specialized PR practices on a comparable scale.

The size of the specialist market for healthcare public relations is evident in the growing annual figures recorded by the Council of PR firms (for the year 2000), as is shown below.

INDUSTRY SECTOR – HEALTHCARE

RANK	FIRM NAME	2000 FEES in US$
1	Ketchum, Inc.	42,092,000
2	Porter Novelli International	40,853,000
3	Edelman Public Relations Worldwide	38,883,571
4	Ogilvy Public Relations Worldwide	35,649,300
5	Fleishman-Hillard	35,080,000
6	Ruder Finn	32,100,000
7	Manning, Selvage & Lee	28,136,737
8	Burson-Marsteller	23,694,000
9	GCI Group/APCO Associates	21,459,204
10	Hill & Knowlton	20,775,000

Source: Council of PR Firms/PR Week

Chart 7.1

In the IPRA's Golden World Awards 2000, sponsored by Dai Nippon Printing Company, the Grand Prize winner was a healthcare program designed to influence the public as well as medical professionals. The program was titled "Two Against One."

"Two Against One"

Two Against One is a program tailored to reach an audience seldom noticed for its role in prostate cancer – the wives of patients – while at the same time building product awareness among doctors.

According to the American Cancer Society, more than 198,100 new cases of prostate cancer will be diagnosed in the United States in 2001 and nearly 31,500 men will die of the disease. While surgery and radiation are the most common treatments, the hormone therapy market in 1999 reached $1.05 billion in sales. For more than 10 years, two agents (TAP's Lupron and AstraZeneca's Zoladex) have dominated the hormone therapy market.

Two other pharmaceutical companies, Amgen and PRAECIS, are entering a generally satisfied market with entrenched competitors and their product Abarelix is the first urology product for either company. Since the FDA limits product-specific promotion during pre-approval, Amgen and PRAECIS made a commitment to launch a major, unbranded educational campaign. The goal of this campaign was to create visibility for the companies and lay the groundwork to establish the need for Abarelix. Working with the two companies was public relations agency Chandler Chicco.

Marketing research, conducted by Amgen and PRAECIS, showed that patients and physicians were concerned about the shortcomings of existing therapies (especially their side effects), communication issues and information needs. Amgen and PRAECIS believed the companies could address these concerns with an educational program thereby creating awareness for themselves in the prostate cancer community.

To further explore these research findings, a four-part Roper Starch survey was commissioned. It showed that men do not communicate as well as they should with their physicians. Given this, their wives/caregivers bridge the gap by playing a key role in their care. Physicians said they often get the "true story" of a patient's progress from his spouse and see wives playing a role in the treatment decision more often than men admit. Women report experiencing serious physical and emotional effects and altered lifestyles, including less sexual intimacy, due to their husbands' prostate cancer.

One-on-one interviews were conducted with urologists and patient advocacy leaders to glean insights from their day-to-day work. A literature search, media audit and review of website content conducted by Amgen, PRAECIS and CCA also validated the role of spouses. With this in mind, Amgen, PRAECIS and CCA engineered a program that would help wives of prostate cancer patients help themselves and their husbands to better understand the disease.

Additionally, research was conducted regarding celebrity spokespersons and a review of high-profile personalities with prostate cancer was prepared. New York Yankees manager Joe Torre and his wife Ali; Elizabeth Dole, wife of former US Senator Bob Dole; and "5th Dimension" singers Billy Davis, Jr. and wife Marilyn McCoo were recruited to discuss how as couples they successfully faced prostate cancer.

An advisory board of prominent urologists and oncologists was selected to guide the program and speak about the role of wives. The campaign team worked with partners, the American Foundation for Urologic Disease and cancer advocacy group US TOO! International to create written materials, speak about the need for spousal support and lend overall third-party credibility.

The program was strongly branded "Two Against One: Couples Battling Prostate Cancer," with a name and logo that were both trademarked. A 68-page booklet, *A Spouse's Guide to Coping with Prostate Cancer*, was created, including detailed information about what to expect when a loved one has been diagnosed with prostate cancer, personal reflections from Ali Torre and Elizabeth Dole, and a complete directory of prostate cancer-related organizations and resources.

A website, www.2against1.com, was developed to help guide families through the trauma of diagnosis, treatment and beyond. An educational video, "Not By Myself," featuring Billy Davis, Jr. and Marilyn McCoo, was also made available and a toll-free hotline was established for ordering materials and enrolling people to receive future offerings.

The national media launch of Two Against One was made during Prostate Cancer Awareness Week in September. Exclusive interviews with high-profile media outlets were pitched several weeks prior to ensure that the story was not lost among other prostate cancer awareness stories. In-studio interviews were secured on "Good Morning America," "The View," and "EXTRA!." The Torres participated in a satellite media tour reaching an audience of more than 7.5 million in 23 markets nationwide. A press kit, and video and radio news releases were distributed. Extensive follow-up ensued.

Placement highlights include an Associated Press article that appeared in 122 local newspapers and postings on 90 websites. Cover stories appeared in the two largest magazines for cancer patients, *Coping*, and *Cancer and You*, and in the consumer health magazine *Medizine* reaching 8 million people at pharmacies nationwide.

Leading up to the announcement, the team worked with the advisory board members to identify couples from their practices to participate in local interviews.

On the day of the announcement, more than 20,000 interested patients, spouses, advocacy partners and healthcare professionals called the hotline to learn more and order materials. As of December 31, 2000, more than 50,000 people had visited the website and/or called the toll-free number. Of these respondents 95 percent said they had heard about "Two Against One" from news stories.

Awareness among physicians of Amgen and PRAECIS' development of a new prostate cancer therapy has increased from a baseline of 0 percent in 1999 to 22 percent at the end of 2000.

Financial

The growth of financial public relations has been powered by a battery of forces combining to create a major practice area.

Increasing individual wealth in many countries has multiplied the number of individual share owners. Unit trusts and mutual funds have attracted huge sums of money from investors, allowing them the chance to participate in baskets of stocks of every kind. The media coverage of the performance of companies makes heroes (or villains) out of those who lead them and has captivated large audiences previously unmoved by the making of money or the movements of markets.

Internationalization of money markets and the world's major stock exchanges and the introduction of 24-hour trading in stock shares and bonds have supercharged the growth of international financial communications.

As if this were not enough, the fall of communism created millions of potential new capitalists. With the retreat of socialism came the worldwide fashion of privatization of utilities and other government or nationalized industries and services, an investment bonanza that made shareholders out of entire new population segments in many countries.

Increased wealth and wider share ownership demanded explosive growth in the financial services industry. Millions of people whose previous contact with financial matters had been through a bank account and one or two insurance policies were no longer content to leave their future prosperity in the hands of the old-fashioned bank manager. More and more took an interest in their savings, investments and insurance policies. They came into the market for home ownership. Credit and debit cards entered their lives.

Banks, payment services companies, insurance companies, brokerage houses and other financial institutions became major employers of PR executives and PR agencies.

The popularization of share ownership and use of the instruments marketed by financial services companies occurred at the same time as another phenomenon, which acted as a turbocharger to the growth of financial public relations practice – a tidal wave of mergers and acquisitions, through which huge industrial consolidations have taken place. Many of these were hotly contested, which meant that fulsome fees were generated by the PR firms that had established a sub-specialty in "M&A" (mergers and acquisitions) communications and were battle-ready to assist the predator or defending company.

When the current fashion of "divestiture" arrived as a counterpoint to the continuing merger mania, PR practitioners needed to explain the logic behind the decision to split a company into two or more parts. And then they had to convince investors of the potential value of the shares of each part. This has merely added another sub-specialty to the list of PR skills, and a new source of income besides.

Although both require a mastery of finance, public relations on behalf of financial institutions that sell products and services (insurance policies, mutual funds, mortgages, etc.) and investor relations are two quite different practices.

Internationally, investor relations (IR) as a general rule does not even report through the public relations channel to top management. Most public companies have vice presidents (or directors) of investor relations whose direct reporting line is to the chief financial officer, who in turn reports to the CEO. In only a few companies does the senior IR executive report to a chief communications officer.

IR in the USA even has its own professional organization, the National Institute of Investor Relations (NIRI). Similar organizations exist in other countries, operating outside the orbit of public relations organizations.

Like most other PR practitioners, beyond working with the media, IR specialists are heavily engaged in routine activities. Many of these are optional and just make good sense. Others are required by law or by rules of the regulating authorities. The USA, which probably requires the most disclosure of any country, is regulated by the Securities and Exchange Commission (SEC), which dictates what must be disclosed and when; it also investigates violations and imposes penalties on those who transgress. For instance, the SEC requires institutions that have $100 million or more in assets under management to file quarterly reports of their holdings. These filings are compiled and issued as public record, and are accessible through many databases.

IR practitioners can thank the tide of increasing regulation for expanding their career opportunities. When new disclosure requirements hit companies unfamiliar with the techniques of communicating information, this led to the creation of a major new area of PR practice.

Among the routine tasks undertaken by the head of investor relations are:

- production of the annual report. The most important document produced by any public company, this document must act as a brochure, resource guide and promotional vehicle with a life of 12 months.

Always in printed form, the reports of many companies now also have website and video versions;

- preparation of periodic interim reports, quarterly in the USA, semi-annually in many other countries, declaring financial results;
- a conference call to the analysts who follow the company's shares and to the media, within hours of the issue of financial results. Almost obligatory, this procedure allows the company to elaborate on the factors that contributed to the results and share expectations for the future;
- writing speeches the CEO and CFO will deliver to financial audiences and arranging one-to-one interviews with key journalists;
- organizing road shows, traveling presentations undertaken once a year or every two years. A team of senior company officers visits key cities in the home country in which there are important financial institutions or shareholders; less frequently, they take the show to foreign financial capitals. The events are orchestrated to reassure current stockholders and to attract new buyers.

For the IR specialist, there are two targets – the shareholder and those who might influence shareholder decisions. The problem is that many shareholders want to remain anonymous and their holdings are in the names of nominee accounts.

It is useful to know exactly who these people are in tranquil times. But it becomes vitally important in a contested acquisition, merger or other dispute.

Finding out the entire shareholder base is complicated and involves purchasing data from the specialist organizations known as proxy solicitors. They provide the names of all shareholders directly to the company in advance of the annual shareholder meeting. These firms send out, collect and tabulate the proxy votes for the meeting. Two leading proxy solicitation companies are D.F. King & Co. Inc. and Morrow & Co. Inc.

National depository companies where certificates are exchanged, such as Philadelphia Depository Trust Co. (Philadep) and The Depository Trust Company (DTC), are also repositories for stocks, bonds and other securities. Transfer agents, primarily commercial banks, keep the records and issue and destroy certificates.

In addition to these types of service firms, there are businesses that specialize in identifying and analyzing shareholders on a real-time basis. They utilize proprietary databases and sophisticated screening techniques to monitor changes in shareholder composition. This service is particularly important, for example, when a company needs to determine who is behind increased volume in share trading or unusual price movement. Among the leading firms that offer shareholder identification on a global basis are Corporate Investor Communications Inc., Carson Group, Technimetrics, D.F. King & Co. Inc., and First Chicago Trust Company.

Some of the largest IR/Financial PR firms are not included in the rankings of PR firms because they do not reveal their income. The total is impressive. Possibly the largest in the specialty is Kekst & Company, in the USA. And Brunswick is a formidable power in the UK, where it represents at least 25 companies of the FTSE Index. Through a series of acquisitions and mergers by Citigate, a new global player has been created under the name Incepta. Reporting $244 million in fees for the year 2000, this firm entered the rankings as the fifth largest of all global PR firms.

Technology

Anyone practicing public relations in the financial sector today will testify to the importance of technology as possibly the single most critical element in the economies of the developed world.

Technology stocks have, for some investors, even taken over as the barometer of performance of the stock market from the traditional baskets of blue chip shares such as the FTSE in the UK, the Dow Jones Index in the US, and the Hang Seng in Hong Kong.

For example, rumors early in 1997 that the long-running bull market would come to an end were based on the expectation that the sizzling demand for personal computers and their ancillary products had slowed down.

When category leader Microsoft produced results that were double the expectations of all experts, it was the trigger that enabled the entire US stock market to record one of its largest-ever daily increases.

The "bust" in technology stocks that began in 1999 and gathered steam, leading to the bursting of the dot.com bubble, had a ripple effect that was felt throughout the entire global economy. In 2001, every positive report from a major tech sector company was put under the microscope as a possible harbinger of a return to boom conditions for all shares.

This leadership among investments was the result of technology's explosive growth over three decades, with the arrival of Clive Sinclair in Britain and Steve Jobs, Paul Allen and Bill Gates in the USA.

The drivers of this phenomenon have been the Internet, the personal computer (PC), the digital revolution and the mobile phone and personal digital assistant (PDA). The significance of the Internet in the practice of international PR is dealt with in a separate chapter. The personal computer put at the fingertips of millions of individuals the information processing and communications capability that just a few years earlier had been available only to major corporations. Along with government departments, only they had the ability to invest in large mainframe machines housed in air-conditioned temples and tended by high priests who were the only people familiar with the binary codes needed to converse with the gods of calculus.

Bill "Microsoft" Gates' dream of a computer in every home is well on its way to becoming reality. And many of those terminals are connected to each other directly or through the Internet.

Technology advances arrived on cue, year after year. As machines became smaller as well as less expensive, they grew in power and range of functions.

All the while, other, related technologies blossomed to serve and augment the personal computer. In every phase of industry and the professions, in government, in retailing and banking, computing power combined with connectivity and the ability to store massive amounts of data.

Today's personal computers can design, control production and inventories, record, accept orders, buy raw materials, control deliveries and sales, audit performance, and undertake many other functions.

If money represents the building blocks of the new global economy, technology is the cement that will hold them together. These are the two most international specialties within the entire field of public relations. And according to the statistics of the Council of PR firms, in 2000 technology was by far the largest specialty within public relations.

Just like financial PR, technology communications is now made up of a mosaic of sub-specialties. The boutique agencies that were established less than a decade ago, along with specialist technology units at the major full-service agencies, have blossomed into powerhouses in their own right. They have divided into units dedicated to a large range of clients in sub-sectors of the information technology industry – among them, semi-conductors and microprocessors, business and personal software, Internet access, website development, PCs, servers, mainframes, supercomputers, telephony and wireless.

The pitch of complexity of each of these areas is such as to demand the full attention of highly qualified specialist teams of executives. Admittedly, a truly skilled PR executive should have the knack of communicating quite arcane concepts to the average, intelligent lay audience well enough to impart a good general understanding of the subject. But he first needs to be able to understand and communicate in the jargon and shorthand used by his peers in the industry – and the specialist media that serves it. At that level, the discussions will appear to be in an obscure foreign language to most members of the general public.

The worldwide ranking of the leading firms practicing technology communications is shown in chart 7.2.

The three cornerstones of internationalization and specialization of public relations – Healthcare, Financial and Technology – are followed by several other specialties based on industry, business or type of organization.

INDUSTRY SECTOR – TECHNOLOGY

RANK	FIRM NAME	2000 FEES IN US$
1	Fleishman-Hillard	109,551,000
2	Weber Shandwick Worldwide	88,223,281
3	Ogilvy Public Relations Worldwide	57,220,000
4	Edelman Public Relations Worldwide	56,522,835
5	Waggener Edstrom	56,163,310
6	Hill & Knowlton	54,350,000
7	Brodeur Worldwide	53,500,000
8	Porter Novelli International	53,396,000
9	Burson-Marsteller	43,742,000
10	BSMG Worldwide	35,900,046

Source: Council of PR Firms/PR Week

Chart 7.2

Consumer products and services

Do not be fooled into thinking that this specialty does not require a great deal of expertise and detailed knowledge. Today's consumers are better educated and more selective than ever. They have been bombarded with information about their consumer rights. Many say their purchasing decisions are affected by factors beyond the price, appearance and performance of a product or service.

For example, in food PR, it is not sufficient to promote a product using an appealing photograph and offering a recipe that works. Now editors and their readers will want details about the nutritional value of the item, its fat and calorie content. The PR practitioner also needs to know if any of the ingredients has been under suspicion as being a carcinogen.

The consumer will want to know about the safety of toys, the side-effects of over-the-counter medications, the chemicals used in gardening products, whether cosmetics have been tested on animals (such as the Draze test for eye make-up), or if packaging is recyclable.

In the broad consumer field there are PR specialties in: Food and Nutrition, Household Durables, Fashion and Beauty, Luxury Goods, the Home Office, Entertainment and the Arts, Personal Finance. Because of the size of the industries they encompass, some consumer sub-specialties deserve special mention.

Automobiles: Cars have been the driving force in many economies for so long that automobile PR has taken root as a well-defined specialty. It has for many years also been practiced both locally and internationally. Ford is in the vanguard of top companies with a truly global strategy. Automobile PR offers career scope for practitioners with similar aspirations. Anyone hoping to reach the senior-most position in an automobile-manufacturing company will have mastered the PR specialties of consumer product marketing, dealer communications, event planning and organization, and sponsorship and sports marketing. (Almost every car company is heavily involved in motor sport, as a marketing activity.)

Travel & Tourism and Hospitality: This is often considered a full-fledged specialty in its own right but I consider it to be a sub-specialty in consumer communications. It supports the employment of a huge number of PR practitioners and by definition it is international, calling for special skills in multi-country operations. At the heart of international T&T public relations lies "destination marketing," the campaigns undertaken by the governmental national tourist boards of the countries (or cities or resorts) for which tourism is a major foreign currency earner.

These budgets, many of which are eagerly sought by T&T specialist agencies, are large by industry standards. They are usually augmented by the process known as "matching funds," in which the government tourist authority will add one dollar to every dollar spent on approved activities by hotel and resort owners or state and city authorities. Other discrete branches of T&T PR involve work for Hotels; Restaurants; Carriers (airlines, railways, car rental, etc.); Cruise Lines; Theme Parks; Tour Operators and Travel Agencies; Payments Systems (Traveler's Checks, Credit Cards); and Computer Reservation Systems. More recently, a clearly defined practice area concentrating on the business traveler has emerged, as Airlines, Hotels, Car Rental Companies and Credit Card issuers have seen that it is the business traveler in a suit and not the tourist in shorts who delivers the most profit.

Consumer Technology: A recent development, this practice covers products based on increasingly sophisticated technology, and not confined to the home computer. It touches on every gadget in common use – cooking equipment, the telephone (both fixed line and wireless), home fax, the photographic camera and the entertainment center.

Government

Although there is now increased mobility between the public and private sectors in many countries, there are PR practitioners who choose to spend a lifetime's career in government service. This can be an attractive option for people wanting to practice internationally, if they can get a post in the foreign service or the ministry responsible for tourism. The former usually ensures intervals of postings as press attaché or counselor in embassies abroad. Legions of practitioners also work at the state, county or local governmental level, either as career civil servants or, in countries where that is the custom, as political appointees. Branches of government (such as the military, police forces and postal services) continue to employ large staffs engaged in communications.

Defense

There is a relatively small but highly skilled segment of PR practitioners who work in the defense sector, mostly for companies that manufacture aircraft, missiles, tanks, radar systems and similar products, whose only customers are governments.

Economic development and trade relations

A cursory look at *The Economist, Business Week, Industries Week* and similar publications will ensure that the eye spots several attractive, full- or double-page ad spreads extolling the benefits of investing in a particular country or state or development region. Such advertising has been one of the fastest growing categories in recent years, as emerging nations, developed nations and others undergoing industrial transformations have vied for the infusion of external investment to create jobs and build a modern industrial infrastructure. Educated, skilled labor, space, tax holidays/exemptions, subsidies – all were offered as enticements in an arena that is now extremely competitive.

Budgets for public relations professionals and firms specialized in economic development have been parallel to those for advertising and the work now represents a major practice area in our profession.

Not-for-profit organizations

Many PR practitioners have a vocation to work in non-profit organizations. These can range from long-established charitable organizations such as the International Red Cross (or Crescent) and their national namesakes, or scouting organizations, to the newer and more aggressive pressure groups, many of which have a single agenda, for example, Greenpeace in the environmental movement and People for the Ethical Treatment of Animals (PETA), a group seeking the abolition of animal testing. There are also numerous health – and illness – related groups, as well as those providing services to specific populations such as the homeless, children and battered women. Many of these organizations operate very locally, on a community basis, while others are global in their activities and reach, and some are both, such as food distribution agencies. This category also includes institutions such as museums, concert halls, schools and universities, for which the work of PR people is often divided between supporting fundraising efforts and attracting attendance and membership.

Professional services

Until recently, any form of promotional activity by the traditional professions was forbidden.

Lawyers, doctors, accountants, architects and pharmacists were strictly regulated by their own associations and tribunals that policed codes of conduct and imposed penalties and sanctions for infractions. Self-promotion was forbidden, carefully monitored and severely punished.

How times have changed in the past 25 years.

Now, in many countries, malpractice and divorce lawyers advertise for clients in TV commercials sandwiched between others for automobiles and dishwashing detergent.

Billboards proclaim the wonders achieved by plastic surgeons and penile prosthesis. International accounting firms' logos are seen at sponsored golf tournaments as well as in clever advertising, usually with the message, "we are clever."

Public relations techniques have proven to be a most potent weapon in the professional services' marketing armory. Among effective PR tools are straightforward publicity that produces media recognition for work done; case histories of successful client work; and speeches carefully honed for delivery at seminars where every delegate is a potential client.

Professional service organizations have quickly become masters of major creative PR initiatives. For example, Ernst & Young (E&Y) sought to support their goal of "getting in on the ground floor" with clients that have potential to grow big, by creating an "Entrepreneur of the Year" award. The 1996 E&Y Entrepreneur of the Year PR campaign was itself an award winner, taking a Golden World Award in the annual International Public Relations Association contest.

"Ernst & Young Entrepreneur of the Year"

Ernst & Young (E&Y), the professional services firm, wanted to reinforce awareness of its ability to help owner-managed, middle-market businesses in the US. With Edelman Public Relations Worldwide, the firm created the Entrepreneur of the Year Awards in 1994, to honor owner-managers of the country's fastest-growing entrepreneurial businesses, with revenues between $2 million and $250 million.

The program consisted of awards in 11 categories, for which contenders could be nominated by their employees, bankers, lawyers, and advertising and public relations advisers. Winners in 46 participating regions would be finalists for national awards, given later in the year during a conference and awards event in New York.

From the start, the program generated national attention. There were 1,000 nominations the first year, whose average annual revenue was $55 million. Business and trade media covered the regional and national winners.

With year-long publicity efforts, E&Y and Edelman were able to capture even better results and entries the following year, but they hit the jackpot in 1996 because they were challenged to come up with fresh ideas for an established program. In addition to persistent publicity efforts all year, they got mileage out of these elements:

- a new, 80-page *Entrepreneur of the Year Magazine* honoring award recipients and discussing how entrepreneurs shape the US economy, for distribution to prospective clients, elected officials, attendees at the final event and conference, and business and trade media;
- a four-page editorial inset in the Money section of *USA Today*;
- seven full-page advertisements in *USA Today* during the nomination–solicitation period;
- eleven 30-second video news releases on the national award recipient, sent to 700 television stations;

- a two-hour nationally syndicated radio program taped at the awards event for later broadcast by the WOR Radio network to its 100 stations nationwide;
- two high-profile national sponsors who lent their names to the program – *USA Today* and the Center for Entrepreneurial Leadership of the Ewing Marion Kaufmann Foundation.

As a result, the third year of the program delivered 3,500 nominations; the nominations were of higher quality, with award recipients averaging $125 million in annual revenues; 1,700 entrepreneurs and business leaders attended the culminating event; and the extensive media coverage included Cable News Network (CNN), CNBC, local television stations in major markets, *USA Today*, and regional and trade publications.

Trade associations

Many long-established companies gained their first experience with public relations through their membership in an industry organization or trade association. These were the vehicles for many years through which companies would make common cause to build markets for their products, so that they could focus on competitive activity to capture the biggest possible share of expanding markets.

Associations also acted as a single voice through which all members of an industry could represent their united views to government. While some trade associations still do undertake positive, proactive market-building programs, their PR personnel and agencies are generally more heavily engaged in defensive communications programs, issues management and educational efforts.

Today's wisdom among those who direct public relations programs at companies is that good news should be issued by the company but when there is bad news, the company should protect itself behind the defensive shield of the industry trade association. This attitude and policy have reduced the appeal of trade association PR jobs for many practitioners.

A relative of the traditional trade association has emerged as an important new player on the communications scene: the ad hoc coalition, or alliance, formed specifically to promote or fight legislation. If there is a long-term agenda, the life of a coalition may be long. Usually it ends its existence on the conclusion of the legislative process.

Business to business

The field of business to business communications is difficult to define because it spans a number of industries and, therefore, is not included in most of the PR rankings of specialist firms; it is the industries themselves that are deemed to be the specialist practice areas.

Nevertheless, communications on behalf of companies for which the end-consumer is another business have special characteristics. For one thing, there is usually nothing equivalent to a consumer supermarket or department store. Very often, buying decisions are not made by a single individual but by a group of people, all of whom have a say in the selection of the purchase.

Some business to business companies are: office equipment; raw materials needed for added value processing; industrial equipment; components; transport services; employment agencies; and consultancy services.

There are also business to business divisions of companies which sell directly to individual consumers for home use. One example is the telephone service. AT&T's Business Services division had sales of $26 billion in 1996 compared with the $24 billion recorded for private customers. Other illustrations are the catering divisions of food producers that predominantly sell to restaurants and hotels; the commercial and industrial divisions of manufacturers of cleaners and polishes; and the hospital and industrial products divisions of disposable paper products manufacturers.

In these companies, there is a clear distinction between consumer marketing and business to business PR techniques, though it can be argued that many of the same factors of quality, availability, price, brand name and value are at play.

The B to B – as it is increasingly known in jargon – public relations practitioner recognizes that he is supporting sales of "big ticket" items. It might be equipment costing thousands or, in the case of aircraft, millions of dollars in a single sale. Or it might be a contract for Kleenex at the Ford Motor company facilities, which will cumulatively involve an equally large amount. PR techniques to sell Kleenex to a large company will be different from those used to promote Kleenex to millions of consumers buying one or two boxes at a time.

The key messages in B to B PR must be relevant to the business buyer and are invariably concerned with cost, reliability in the case of equipment, service to ensure the minimum of down time, and, in some cases, the improvement of morale and productivity of the workplace. In many cases, B to B companies position themselves as the expert in a given field, seeking to elevate themselves from being a mere manufacturer of products. Office furniture producers depict themselves as office planners and leaders in ergonomics. Office equipment suppliers such as Xerox position themselves as expert consultants in workflow and document production.

Basic techniques of B to B public relations

The first step, as with any PR or marketing communications task, is Target Identification. The exercise, conducted in association with others engaged in the marketing and sales function, will yield three crucial sets of information: the most important industries that are potential buyers of your products or services; the principal qualities, and the usual process of influence and decision making.

With the target audiences identified, you will be able to build a relevant media database.

You will also be able to plan for a broad-scale series of news announcements with the widest possible outreach and highly focused activities such as the following:

- *Case histories.* Usually the most powerful and persuasive tool in this field, a detailed case study has multiple uses: an article in a trade journal, a newsletter to potential customers, an aid for the sales force. It is researched and produced in cooperation with a satisfied buyer/user of your product or service and should cover cost savings, efficiency and other benefits. If you identify several industries as the biggest users of your products, plan to issue one case study on a monthly basis, each time on a different industry, to ensure maximum exposure.
- *Seminars.* Plan events to which media and potential customers can be invited to discuss some "hot" topic, with keynote speakers as magnets and a display or exhibition that demonstrates the products in use.
- *Speaking platforms.* Arrange for senior members of your staff to speak at industry conferences organized by the target groups you have identified.
- *Surveys.* When conducted among people working in your targeted industry groups, surveys can unlock media coverage, provide substance for customer mailings and newsletters, and become the central topic for seminars.
- *Sponsorships.* Your research will show which sporting or arts events will be attended by your specific target groups, offering opportunities for those all-important face-to-face meetings.
- *Scholarly initiatives.* Fund an annual lecture or a professorial chair at a major college or university that undertakes work related to your field or to your key customer groups. This will enhance your company image.

The combination of some or all of these initiatives, if done well, can confer the reputation of authority and thought leadership that is a cornerstone of successful B to B marketing.

Specialties by practice

Specialization in PR occurs in practice areas as well as by industry category. Important practice areas are Public Affairs, which includes public policy, governmental relations and legislative affairs; Environmental Affairs; Crisis and Issues Management; Employee Communications; Investor Relations; Corporate Identity and Reputation; Sponsorship and Event Management. Such practices can span a wide range of industries and organizations but, increasingly, individuals and agencies conduct their practice in a single industry or a small number of related industries.

Some of these specialties are discussed in greater detail in other chapters of this book, for example:

Corporate Reputation stands at the apex of all communications activity and requires the greatest breadth of knowledge of all the public relations specialties and the ability to orchestrate them to the benefit of the corporation's standing with its key audiences.

Crisis and Issues Management is covered in the chapters on Issue Identification and Management and Crisis and Catastrophe Communications, chapters 8 and 9.

Litigation public relations is a new specialty that has grown very quickly in the past decade; it is a 'first cousin' of crisis management and can be seen at work in some of the case studies featured in chapter 9. In this arena, PR specialists work closely with not only their clients but also their legal counsel because an issue has escalated to the point where it is going to be litigated in court. While the task of the lawyers is to achieve a favorable result before judge and jury (if one is involved), the PR practitioner has the job of ensuring that his client gets the right verdict in the "court of public opinion." While an important goal in itself, public opinion can also influence the courtroom result.

Investor Relations is touched on in an earlier section of this chapter, under the umbrella of financial public relations, where it can equally be considered a sub-specialty.

Sponsorship and Event Management has its own chapter (11) titled "Sponsorship? Philanthropy? Or Promotion?," and Public Affairs is covered in chapter 10.

Employee communications

Anyone contemplating a career in this well-defined communications specialty should consult some of the many books that have been written on the subject.

I hold particular views about employee communications. First, I find it offensive to see "employees" listed among consumers, lawmakers and others in the Target Audiences section of many PR plans. The employees to me *are* the company and as such deserve privileged treatment. This means that, insofar as law and regulations allow, they should be the very first to know of any development that is going to affect the company – good or bad.

This should be enshrined in every communications plan.

In fact, in most companies, employee communications are the province of the personnel department, now usually referred to as the Human Resources (HR) department, whose very name suggests placing human beings in the same category as coal, steel, wheat or money – just one of the raw materials needed to feed the machinery of business. To serve the information needs of HR, public relations people become functional assistants who help draft messages, prepare videos, write speeches and, possibly, produce the employee newspaper or magazine. In truth, there should be exceptionally close cooperation between the two disciplines of internal and external communications in any organization, regardless of the management reporting lines.

Employees are influenced as much by what they read in the media about their company and its place in its market as by the echo they get from their friends and acquaintances.

And a company's external audiences are greatly influenced, especially at the local and regional level, by the attitude of the employees who are the first-line ambassadors for their employers. If employees are confident and persuaded of the correctness of their company's position, they will convey their attitude with strength to the external audiences.

Although good employee relations built upon consistent, truthful communications should be the aim of any organization at all times, they are especially important in this current business climate.

Change Management, usually a kindly euphemism for job reductions, involves a large measure of employee communications and the pace of change in most countries is breathtaking. With the USA in the lead, Europe has been following close behind. Japan and Korea are changing with the bursting of the "bubble economy" and even the hallowed concept of jobs for life is now being questioned.

Mergers and Acquisitions took place at unprecedented speed during the nineties, bringing change in their wake and exceptional challenges for those specializing in employee communications, as they seek to meld the different cultures, procedures and philosophies of two different merging companies. And the trend towards mergers and the creation of larger corporations is matched by the counter trend of divestiture and de-merger. One recent example was the "trivestiture" of AT&T, one of the world's largest corporations, into three companies: AT&T which continues to offer telephone and wireless communications service to 70,000,000 subscribers, Lucent Technologies which manufactures the equipment used in telephony, and NCR, maker of computers, scanners, automated teller machines (ATMs) and the card reading and pricing technology used in retail stores and supermarkets – the descendants of the original cash register made by the company more than 100 years ago. Another was the break-up of the Hanson Trust, the UK-based conglomerate, into four units and the similar break-up of ITT.

Diversity programs in America and many other countries with diverse workforces – by gender, race or religion – call for the most skillfully executed employee communications. In the USA particularly, the need is accentuated by the epidemic of law suits brought by employees who claim they have suffered discrimination in hiring and firing practices or have not had opportunity for promotion.

For the employee communications specialist and the Chief Communications Officer, it is now essential to learn how to manage within a changing economy and work environment and how to manage the change itself. These days, with constantly changing technology making certain jobs – and industries – outmoded overnight and a general shift from manufacturing to the service industries in the mature nations, the luxury of stability and security, mainstays of employee communication programs in the past, no longer applies. They must also learn how to balance the different messages directed at external audiences and those for internal consumption.

While the inflexible rule is that all messages must be truthful and cannot be altered (even though they may be slanted, or spun) for different target groups, those groups might react in widely differing ways.

Thus when a company announces significant staff reductions to keep costs under control, there is likely to be dismay and anger among employees, and joy in the investment communities of Wall Street, the City of London, Hong Kong, Tokyo and the world's other financial centers. When the payroll goes down, the share price goes up. At times such as these, intense, careful, caring and honest communication with employees is of vital importance.

Companies that have established systematic, regular vehicles for employee communication in normal times are usually better prepared to cope when crisis or change occurs. The messages might change but at least the channels of communication are in place. A sudden uncharacteristic burst of communication using previously unseen vehicles usually does nothing more than heighten the sense of alarm and disbelief in the internal audience.

What are these vehicles? Here is a list of some of the tried and true. Organizations need not use all of them. Only the first is important for *all*; one or two of the others should be used regularly and will quickly establish themselves as the accepted means of communication.

- *Personal contact* is the most important and original means of communication with employees. Every other form is a substitute seeking to replace the easygoing dialogue that takes place between the boss and the staff that is normal in start-up companies and small businesses. Take every opportunity (no, *make* every opportunity) for the management to meet employees face to face in walkabouts, "town hall" meetings, conferences and the like. Fight off pressures from stay-at-home managers to avoid and postpone meetings at which they will have direct contact with employees.
- *Video*. Use video for the employee annual report, and "state of the firm" messages sent out periodically. Video conferences are the next best thing to a personal visit.
- *News posters* are ideal for companies with multi-locations.
- *E-mail and Intranet* are fast becoming the means of communication in many companies. They have the advantage of reaching all locations worldwide at the same time.
- *Online chats* during which staff in many locations can put questions to the CEO are increasingly popular.
- *Parties* are great for team building.
- *Open days* when staff and their families can visit the offices, factory, research laboratories, etc. of the organization are a proven way of reinforcing the commitment of employees and their families and a chance for them to see other facets of the operation beyond their own departments.
- *Newsletters and house magazines* are the time-honored means of employee communication in most companies. They continue to be used nowadays for one reason: they work.
- *Hot lines*: Recorded latest company news for anyone who wants to dial a special freephone number.

Specialization by function

The final form of public relations specialization is found in the various functional skills called for in PR departments or agencies. They are the communications techniques and tools used by the international PR practitioner to implement his strategies and concepts. Because they have the capability of delivering messages and information in very targeted forms, the specialties can reach specifically identified audiences as well as the general public. Companies have organized to create and deliver these tools, directly for corporate communications departments or as subcontractors to PR agencies.

Functional specialties in constant use by PR practitioners are:

- Publications, print production, graphic design
- Computer graphics
- Interactive communications, website development
- Video and film production and distribution
- Research
- Media tour planning and booking
- Advertisement creation, copywriting, layout, media planning
- Advertorial production
- Conference and event planning and management
- Media training

CHAPTER 8

Issues Identification and Management

It is a source of wonderment to business leaders that companies held in high regard for their management, record of success and corporate citizenship can find themselves embroiled in highly publicized crises. The reputations of CEO and corporation so carefully nurtured are now suddenly imperiled and it all seems to come as a shocking surprise.

Globalization accentuates the potential for peril of a higher order, as issues manifest themselves in several countries at once and local conditions trigger problems not anticipated at headquarters. Crisis prevention is possible, and within the reach of the company public relations officer.

First, a simple definition of a crisis: It's an issue that has been poorly managed. On closer inspection, it becomes clear that, in the majority of such cases, there has been a trail of events or inaction over a period of several years or months, which has made the outcome almost a certainty. It should have been anything but a surprise to all who were close to the matter.

Foresee and forestall

An important part of the job specification of an organization's most senior public relations executive is to foresee and forestall any occurrence that could damage that organization's reputation, which he has been engaged to burnish.

Years of painstaking reputation-building can be wiped away in days or weeks if the company does not take early action to identify, intervene in and manage potentially damaging issues. It is just like a bank balance and the accumulation of capital, which take time and patience for most of us. Yet the savings account can quickly be wiped away by a risky investment on which our entire capital is wagered. It then becomes necessary to start the entire reputation-building task again, from the ground up – maybe from an even lower level, if credibility has been very severely damaged.

In the real world, unfortunately, it is often only when a crisis comes to trip up a company's management that thoughts turn to the measures that might have prevented the problem from reaching bursting point. Many are the corporate reputation management programs that were born in the furnace of post-crisis damage control.

The dynamics of issues management are not linear. They are circular and it is of little value to debate the chicken and egg problem of whether it takes a crisis to alert a company to the value of a disciplined issues management procedure or if the cycle begins with that procedure.

Cycle of action

The cycle of action with and without controls can be represented by a bisected circle in which proactive measures keep the company reputation well managed above the line and their absence sends it spinning into crisis below the line, as shown in chart 8.1 below:

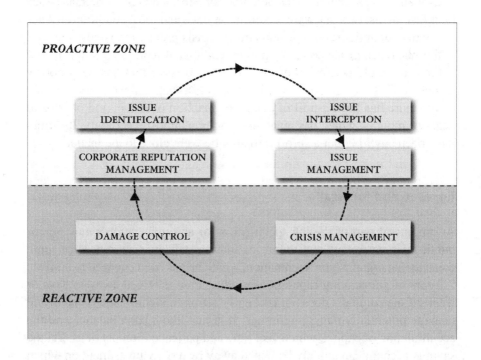

PROACTIVE ZONE

ISSUE IDENTIFICATION

ISSUE INTERCEPTION

CORPORATE REPUTATION MANAGEMENT

ISSUE MANAGEMENT

DAMAGE CONTROL

CRISIS MANAGEMENT

REACTIVE ZONE

Chart 8.1

Obviously, the corporate aim must be to avoid moving into the bottom half of the circle, which I have termed the "reactive zone" to indicate that events and opponents are dictating your responses. A more colorful and provocative description, which I have eschewed, might be the "danger zone."

Assuming that the process begins with the commitment of the organization to undertake a conscious effort to achieve a high corporate reputation, the strategies and proactive initiatives adopted to meet that goal must be accompanied by comparable measures to ensure that all those efforts are not brought to naught by an inability to foresee where there are serious weaknesses.

Analogies

Sporting analogies abound when this topic becomes the subject of discussion at management meetings. For example, a participant may announce that, "A sound defense is as important as a great offense," or, "Let's put up lots of runs on the scoreboard to make sure we are unbeatable when the other team goes in to bat."

But business life does not operate by the rules of sportsmanship even though sports increasingly operate by the rules of business.

Analogies are all well and good to establish a rough-hewn point. In the world of reputation management, however, the opposing team doesn't always have to equal the score to inflict serious damage to the reputation of an organization.

Perhaps the boxing arena offers the most useful analogy. One contestant can control a fight for eight rounds and be ahead on points, with the championship in his grasp, but lose it through disqualification for delivering a low blow; the rival did not have to build a comparable score with referee and judges. Many a reputation has been demolished through stupidity, hubris, overconfidence or the risky notion that rule breaking will not be noticed.

Identification

Whether it begins as part of a proactive strategy formulated in a period of calm, or in the aftermath of a bruising crisis, a systematic process of issues identification is an important function of management and the professional public relations executives involved. That process should lead directly to the establishment of issues management, intervention initiatives and management procedures, which in most cases should prevent the "explosion" that ends in a crisis.

The tools for identification exist. They are in daily use among enlightened corporations in various countries around the world. But in most cases the topics are dealt with on a country-by-country basis and little attention is given to those issues which play out on a global or, at least, multi-country stage. Later in this chapter, I will recommend a methodical approach to identification of such issues, but there are also basic professional behaviors that are a "must."

Follow the news

The simplest advice is often the best: Public relations professionals must be avid readers of newspapers and magazines, and followers of radio and television programs. To these traditional media must now be added the Internet which is, arguably, the most international of all.

News and feature pages, current affairs and discussion programs should be closely followed. A sense of the news of the future must be developed, an understanding that a story just at its beginning could have an impact on your organization's business.

Make sure to listen occasionally to talk radio and carefully read letters to the editor and op-eds, those articles that appear opposite the daily editorials, in which people with various viewpoints express their opinions.

You should not rest there. Delve into lighter media fare – fashion, home and gossip columns, and situation comedies on television. Here more than anywhere, you will learn what is most important to people today.

Just reflect on the demise of the communist regimes of Eastern Europe. One of the most potent influences in that development was the increasing ability of residents behind the so-called Iron Curtain to receive foreign TV broadcasts. But it was not the rhetoric of politicians or commentators that weighed most heavily in shaping opinions of the opposing ideologies of capitalism and communism. It was the style of life depicted in the soaps, sitcoms, mysteries, variety shows and dramas that showed people that there was another way of living, materialistic maybe, but also with freedom of expression and the opportunity to mock authority without fear of retribution. They wanted to try this style of living as an alternative to what they had known before.

Such attention to the media will give you a good grasp of the current political, social and fashion context in which your organization is operating. It will allow you to assess opportunities and alert you to threats.

Parochial media

As someone who is responsible for international public relations, you must carefully select your regular newspaper reading and TV watching so that they provide you with more than simply a parochial view. Most media is extremely parochial. As a rule, the larger and more self-sufficient a country, the more locally focused is its media. Many American companies have grown to great size without needing to export, and their world view has therefore been minimized. Even for the largest American corporations which have operations around the world, in 180 or more countries, the home market of the USA remains preeminent and that colors the outlook of management. Very few American companies have reached a point at which they derive more than 50 percent of their business from outside the USA. In turn, print and broadcast news media have reflected that inward look with modest foreign news and analysis.

On the other hand, in the smaller West European countries, corporate success requires global trading, companies are oriented to look beyond their national boundaries and the news media carry substantial international news. Consider Switzerland and Holland. Both these small countries are remarkable for the number of multinational corporations they have spawned. Yet, the "home" market for such companies' products is unlikely to exceed about ten percent. Knowledge of the world and overseas markets is an essential pre-requisite for anyone aspiring to a management position in these organizations. Media coverage of foreign affairs is correspondingly high in Swiss and Dutch media.

To round out your grasp of the issues making news around the globe, your reading list should include a well-written and eclectic weekly publication such as *The Economist*, and a couple of publications published domestically in the most important overseas markets for your organization. Listen to the BBC World Service and make sure you watch the news on CNN.

Surveys

The media is also an excellent resource to gain a more precise understanding of the issues of the day – and those of tomorrow.

Publishers, editors and TV program producers do not select topics for publication or airing merely on personal whim or instinct. They are guided by more formal research studies which tell them the topics of special concern to their readers and viewers at any given moment. So it is valuable to note the proportion of space or time devoted to various topics. The allocations will be instructive as to the topics of greatest interest to the public. While there are analytical services that will provide you with this data in certain countries, you can look in the media for more substantive information. Newspapers and magazines commission surveys on public attitudes and concerns, and publish the results. Often, these surveys set out to find out not only what views are held by the population but also the subjects that are of most concern to them.

The tempo of research invariably gathers pace during election seasons. The competing parties and the media seek to gauge the voters' priorities and views on a variety of matters, and cooperative research is commissioned from well-known research companies. Look carefully at this research, and tie it into your organization's areas of activity. You'll have more data than you can manage to interpret – and it is all free, if you know where and how to look.

The major research companies, among them Gallup, Opinion Research Corporation, Harris and Yankelovich, are eager publicity seekers and know that a sure-fire way to promote their names and services is to issue interesting research findings to the media. They go to great lengths to construct special research studies on current topics merely to engage the interest of editors. Editorial columns that contain data from these studies can be an invaluable free research resource.

Intelligent study of the media can, thus, provide you with rough bearings on a variety of attitudes you need to know, as you seek to zero in on those issues which might pose a threat to your organization. Possibly the information you glean will be sufficient for your purpose and you will have a very good idea not only of the issues of concern but also the ways in which they might be managed.

Risk management planning

But while sufficient for you personally, this data will almost certainly be insufficient for the senior management of your organization. This is especially the case if you feel certain issues are very serious and a significant budget, along with management time resources, needs to be allocated. Your management will almost certainly call for precise research data and a case strongly grounded in pragmatic business logic. Senior executives usually respond well to risk management planning. If you can clearly show the potential dangers involved in leaving an issue unmanaged, you will get the support and decision you need.

This is the time to consider commissioning a customized survey or participating in a standard caravan survey conducted regularly by one of the better research firms.

Every senior international public relations executive needs to be familiar with the multinational research firms, their services and their regular caravan or cooperative studies. No research firm provides a global research capability based on its own staffing resources. But a number of firms offer controlled multi-country surveys, tailor-made for individual clients. Some offer surveys conducted on an annual basis or some other regular frequency.

Action plan and budget

Once you have prepared the way by showing credible and relevant research to your management, demonstrating that a threat exists, you will need to develop a realistic scenario. The penalties of inaction need to be described in concrete, not emotional, terms. Along with revealing existing threats, the study you have commissioned might also have uncovered opportunities for far-sighted preventive issues management and for production-related moves. If your organization has been the target of environmentalists seeking to close down factories of the type used by one of your operating divisions until they meet certain pollution requirements, you must now work with colleagues to assess not merely the damage to the company's reputation but also the real costs involved in factory closure. Get as close as you can to a realistic dollar figure that your company would have to pay for closure of the facility for one, three or six months, while the necessary new equipment or controls are installed. This figure will be the starting point for the creation of the issue management budget. If you can persuade your management that the preventive course of action will cost only a small percentage of the "worst case" scenario, you are likely to get approval for your proposal. Your plan, and its attendant costs, should cover any modifications to the factory as well as the costs of the communications component of the issue management program.

Government legislative agenda

An essential component of any issue identification plan is the monitoring of the legislative agenda for the immediate and longer-term future of each government in your organization's most important regions of activity. Government in this instance means authorities at the local, national and supra-national level, the last being, for example, the European Union. Nowadays, many policies and measures affecting multinational businesses are made into law at the supra-national level.

Laws enacted by governments are important, but the regulations that follow, developed to interpret and enforce the intent of the laws, are always more important to business. They will dictate whether an organization has operated within or violated the law. Most problems arise in the fine print of regulations.

The legislative agenda is fairly easy to come by in democratic countries. Before elections, opposing political parties usually publish a manifesto which sets out their legislative priorities. When a government is formed, it, too, usually issues its agenda for each session of the parliament or congress. The full texts of manifestos can be obtained from the headquarters of the political parties, and the proposed legislative agenda is available at modest cost from the government publisher's office.

You can seek out reliable public affairs consultants who keep in close touch with political developments and undertake monitoring services on behalf of a variety of clients. They provide regular reports on changes in legislative priorities and also try to look ahead to the introduction of new bills that might affect your organization.

While some consultants and agencies confine their activities to monitoring, others offer services loosely described as lobbying, a process in which organizations can make sure their views are known and taken into account in the framing of new laws or regulations. (See chapter 10, Public Affairs.)

The Internet

The Internet has become a significant venue for issue identification and intervention. Its use for sharing and gathering information during times of crisis has increased in importance over the last two years, and it has become one of the most effective communications tools in the public relations professional's arsenal.

The Internet offers both new opportunities and challenges for communicating with and responding to an organization's publics. The dynamic nature of the medium makes it possible to share up-to-the-minute information instantly – and with little cost – to key audiences worldwide. The Internet also can pose challenges in the time of crisis or issue intervention, however, as it provides a global communications platform for adversaries and offers more information to which an organization must respond. It can precipitate a crisis. Anything can be said, with little – if any – recourse. In addition, competitors can also use the Internet to communicate and manipulate the management of the issue/crisis situation. The use of the Internet in the management of a global corporate reputation is covered more fully in chapter 12.

Critical Issues Analysis

Visualize yourself now as the repository of a vast amount of data culled from a careful daily study and analysis of the media. You have reports of legislative proposals from your key regions around the world. You have a good sense of the demands being made by single- and multi-topic pressure groups, and you are watching the latest hot topics being debated in chat groups on the Internet.

But the mass of material is confusing and hard to bring into focus for the preparation of an international public relations plan and budget.

A methodology which I have termed "Critical Issues Analysis" (CIA) offers an orderly process. Its purpose is to prioritize the issues which have found their way onto your list and identify those of particular concern in several countries. CIA will thus deliver a prioritized shortlist of issues that are critical globally and allow you to develop centrally funded intervention and management strategies.

This is a vital preparatory stage in your PR planning process. It is relatively simple to do and it has the merit of involving executives – and therefore creating allies – in many countries and in different departments. Engaging in the process will pay huge dividends when you put forward your final public relations plan for approval; you will get the support and buy-in you need.

Here is how Critical Issues Analysis works.

STEP 1: List all the issues that you and your consultants around the world have identified as being sensitive for your organization. Do not be surprised if your first list has more than 50 issues, some of them closely related, one to the other.

STEP 2: Sort the issues into groups under a series of subject headings. Examples might be:

Social
Environmental
Personnel/human relations
Competition
Safety
Potentially harmful product ingredients

Shorten the list to a total of ten subjects by combining similar issues into one.

STEP 3: Check the wording of each issue to ensure it will be easily understood by someone unfamiliar with the topic. Avoid jargon – it does not travel.

STEP 4: Make a list of senior public affairs and public relations executives in your organization's regional and national subsidiaries and affiliates. Add some names from among the top rank of executives in line operations and the office of the Chief Legal Officer. Add up to five names from among your most senior regional external consultants. By now, you will have a research universe of 20 or more names. Try not to have more than 25 names in total, as you embark on the next step.

STEP 5: Compose a letter to members of the research panel, asking each person to review the list of issues very carefully. Then ask the interviewees to rank each issue, on a scale of one to ten, one indicating that the issue is of minimal importance and ten signaling a hot-button issue needing maximum and urgent attention. Leave room for each respondent to add an important issue that might have been missed, or to comment on issues that he believes are cool now but have the potential to become hot in a year or two. It is the purpose of this exercise, after all, to identify those issues that are gathering speed and support. The letter should stress the importance of the exercise for the organization as a whole. It is usually a good idea to send it out over the signature of the CEO, to signal its priority.

STEP 6: Analyze the results by adding the scores given to each issue and review the comments added by the respondents. You will find that the issues divide themselves into four distinct categories:

- *Global*: Four to seven issues will be ranked high by all or a large majority of respondents, indicating a global threat. These are likely to have an average score in excess of seven.
- *Multi-country*: One or two issues are significant across several countries in a region.
- *Isolated*: Some issues score nine or ten in one or two markets.
- *Minimal*: Some issues are of minimal concern to all respondents (average score below four).

The comments may point to issues that are on the rise and thus will need more attention in your planning for the future.

The CIA should be conducted annually, as an essential preliminary to the development of the public relations and issues management plan. Those issues which achieve a high global score should be studied closely. Each should have a special mini-issue management plan written for it, and global financial and personnel resources should be applied. Issues that are significant in a particular region can be dealt with by a regional team and with a regional budget. Resources and guidance from corporate headquarters should be made available if needed. Similarly, single-country issues, even if they are serious, should be dealt with at the local level. However, it is possible that the country unit concerned lacks experience and resources. In such cases, global headquarters should assist in the form of strategic and program development, possibly assigning one or more executives on loan.

The methodical approach of Corporate Issues Analysis will provide a solid basis for the issues management recommendations you make to your CEO. Involve a representative selection of executives from within your organization as participants in the process, to ensure enthusiastic and committed implementation of the program.

Non-governmental organizations (NGOs)

One of the most important influences on your organization's reputation – and indeed on the way it conducts its business – will come from one or more of the non-governmental organizations pressuring for change to take place. The identification of the NGOs, local, regional and global, that have agendas that will affect your organization is a vital part of the process of issue identification, intervention and management. NGOs and their supporters cannot be dismissed as irrelevant and little more than a nuisance. They have humbled great corporations (Shell, Coca-Cola, Nike, Wal-Mart, Nestlé to name just a few) using nimble and communications-savvy tactics at major world meetings of the WTO, G7, IMF and World Bank. Such actions have brought home the fact that those organizations represent many people who have great concerns about the impact of globalization on their lives.

"Business now has to recognize," says Jonathan Wootliff, Managing Director of Stakeholder Strategies at Edelman Public Relations Worldwide, that: "NGOs (a.k.a. 'watchdogs' or advocacy groups) have become the new sophisticated communicators and perceived instigators of change in the global marketplace. However, what defines an NGO is incredibly broad. Some are pro-industry; others more cautious. Still others can find no redeeming qualities at all in multinational corporations or global free trade. Despite great differences of size, scope and approach among NGOs, according to a study conducted in the USA, Europe and Australia, NGOs are no longer perceived as small bands of activists but rather as the new 'super brands,' surpassing the stature of major corporations, government bodies and even the media among consumers." (See chart 8.2.)

Predicts Professor Robert M. Worcester, chairman of UK-based research firm, MORI, "Given the power of communications and the strengthening of the NGOs, the picture over the next decade will increasingly be:

- Young against old
- Poor against rich
- Rural against urban
- Scientists against the people
- Producers against consumers
- The people against the institutions
- Local government against central government
- Globalised against the globalisers
- Everybody against big business."

TRUST INDEX

Respondents were asked: How much do you trust the company or organization to do what is right?
1 = No Trust   9 = High end of Trust

Top 4 Box (6–9)	USA %	Australia %	Europe %
Government in general	27	30	36
Media in general	20	18	23
Business in general	44	38	32
NGOs or non-governmental organizations in general	36	53	48
Exxon or Esso	31	16	17
Nike	40	30	25
Greenpeace	40	69	65
WTO or the World Trade Organization	25	29	27
Monsanto	24#	12#	6#
Amnesty International	36#	80	75
Ford Motor Company	43	46	26
Sierra Club*	40#	72	2#
World Wildlife Fund	46#	70	63
Microsoft	61	34	44

(Base = 300)
*Asked as Sierra Club in all markets but Australia (Australian Conservation Organization)
#Never Heard Of over 15 percent

Source: StrategyOne and Edelman Public Relations Worldwide

Chart 8.2

Against this contentious background it is clear that there are many opportunities for trying mutually beneficial partnerships between industry and NGOs while maintaining a stout defense of a well-thought out policy.

1. *Adapt the obvious techniques.* Be clear in communications. Do not use corporate speak.
2. *Take an external view.* Adopt the charm of the selfless crusaders. Focus on the external issues that are impacting your publics.
3. *Build bridges with the NGOs.* Watchdog organizations will often embrace the company that sincerely looks to put dollars and resources behind their cause. This is a measuring stick for NGOs and considered a success.
4. *Be provocative.* Business does not need to be boring to be serious.
5. *Track the NGOs who are tracking you.*
6. *Stay above the "minimal level" of acceptable behavior.*
7. *Start at home.* Engage your employees and your local communities. Change begins at home.
8. *Make corporate responsibility a part of your strategy.*
9. *Be prepared to fight.* NGOs do not always have ownership of the high ground. Arm yourself with expertise and third-party support in the event that you have a clear conscience on the issue at hand.

CHAPTER 9

Crisis and Catastrophe Communications

There are ten kinds of crisis. Four of them are slow-burning issues, which can be detected and managed with the identification and intervention techniques discussed in the previous chapter:

- Litigation
- Product Liability
- Action by Pressure Groups
- Labor Disputes

The other six kinds of crisis usually come as surprises, even though most of them are potential hazards for all businesses. In all cases, advance preparation can limit the damage from such crises and ensure a prompt and effective response when they occur:

- Exposé or Whistle Blowing
- Hostile Takeover Bid
- Disclosure or Revelation
- Disaster/Accident/Explosion/Oil Spills
- Production Mistake, Product Recall
- Terrorism, Tampering, Extortion

Ten golden rules

Whether a slow-burning issue finally bursts into flames or a completely unforeseen catastrophe takes place, there are Ten Golden Rules to observe in times of crisis:

1. The CEO takes charge

The chief executive officer must be informed of any *major* crisis *immediately*, wherever he is and whatever the time. The ultimate impact of the crisis on the company's reputation and bottom line is shaped in the first few hours after a "surprise" crisis occurs. Of course, Murphy's Law dictates that most crises occur on the evening before the start of a long weekend and the CEO has just boarded a 14-hour intercontinental flight. In such cases, his second-in-command must be told and he should assume responsibility.

The need for CEO involvement might appear obvious but it is not the rule in most companies, which pay dearly in the long run. When companies become bureaucratic and grow out of touch with their consumers and other audiences, they also tend to build walls around the senior management team and, in particular, the chief executive officer. He is shielded from activists, shareholders, customers and the general public. The media is seldom, if ever, provided open access.

In such companies, there is no recognition of the rule that it is vital for the CEO to take personal charge of every significant crisis and to go to the site of the crisis as fast as possible.

The importance of this rule prompts me to propose a new Law of Crisis Management: "The negative reputation impact of a crisis is directly proportionate to the length of time it takes for the CEO to assume control and reach the scene." The underpinning of this law is solid.

■ Fritz Gerber, shortly after being elected chairman and CEO of Hoffman-La Roche, in addition to his role as chief of Zurich Insurance, arrived at the scene of a factory accident at a company unit in France within 14 hours of its occurrence. There were several fatalities, but his prompt action and presence ensured that there was minimal negative publicity and no lasting hostility. Compare this with an earlier company accident that occurred at the Seveso, Italy, plant of Hoffman-La Roche's subsidiary Icmesa, before Gerber took over. A hexachlorophene production unit exploded, sending a cloud of dioxin into the air. Neither the chairman, Dr. Adolf Jann, nor any senior executive of Hoffman-La Roche, visited the site, in fear of being jailed by distraught Italian authorities, and Seveso became the symbol of industrial catastrophes for at least a decade within Europe. It was the subject of some 60 books, countless articles and TV documentaries. In fact, no deaths or serious long-term ill effects have been proven to have been the direct result of the explosion. Some believe the biggest casualties of the Seveso affair were Hoffman-La Roche's reputation and its bank balance, because millions were paid out to assuage the concerns of an anxious group of citizens and their local government.

■ There have been many fatal air crashes, notwithstanding the fact that air is statistically safer than travel by land or water. One crash remains fresh in the memory of most people in Europe and America – that of Pan Am 103, which was brought down by a terrorist bomb over the village of Lockerbie in Scotland, on December 21, 1988. The chairman of Pan Am did not visit the site or the hospital to which injured survivors had been sent. It was left to the Queen of England to travel to Lockerbie, to offer sympathy and visit the injured in hospital. Pan Am is pursued to this day by a group of parents of children killed in the crash; the airline never recovered financially from the disaster and went into bankruptcy. In contrast Nicki Lauda was on the scene of a fatal crash of a Lauda Air 767 in Thailand and Michael Bishop, CEO of British Midland, was at the site of a British Midland 737 crash at Kegworth within hours. Many credit Lauda's visit as critical to saving his airline.

■ Of all the many disastrous oil spills that have caused severe environmental damage, the most notorious is the *Exxon Valdez* spill in Prudhoe Bay, Alaska, in 1989. Probably no worse in reality than other, bigger spills, it is the emblem of how to superimpose a public relations debacle onto an environmental catastrophe. *Exxon Valdez* remains imprinted on the memory for the way in which communications in the first hours after the spill were bungled and because Exxon's chairman and CEO did not deign to visit the affected area.

■ An explosion that killed more than 2,000 people at a chemical plant in Bhopal, India, in 1984, has gone on record as one of the worst peacetime disasters in this century. Yet the financial and reputation consequences for Union Carbide, the ultimate owner of the plant, were softened by the prompt and brave action of Warren M. Anderson, the CEO. Within hours, he flew to India to be among the victims, to start an investigation, open a fund for those affected, consult with the authorities and make sure emergency relief services were operating efficiently. It surely needed courage to resist the temptation to say that the company operating the Bhopal plant was an autonomous subsidiary and to confront the prospect of being arrested and jailed. Instead, this single action did much to maintain Union Carbide's reputation, when many of the circumstances of the explosion seemed to point to quite inadequate management oversight of equipment and safety measures in the manufacturing process at the local facility.

■ Speed to the scene of the outrage at the World Trade Center in New York and the Pentagon in Washington, D.C. by national and civic leaders in the USA on September 11, 2001, has been the subject of much media comment, particularly outside the USA. Mayor Rudi Giuliani's immediate arrival on the scene and his regular and open communication have received universal plaudits. President George W. Bush, it seems, must have had to assert himself over the protective instincts of his advisers and security men and had to rally the nation after a slow start. He was able to do so with the country seeking strong leadership. Very soon his approval rating rose to record levels; Mayor Giuliani was voted *Time* magazine's Man of the Year, 2001.

Before becoming too critical of corporate leaders who did not act – and travel – promptly, one should understand the powerful corporate dynamics that might have worked against their direct involvement. In many major bureaucratic corporations, there are legions of executives who see their roles as shields for their senior management. They talk about "crisis containment," a valid policy, but only when directed by the CEO himself, in which the first battles are fought by the lower ranks. Such executives prevent travel by the CEO by saying, "Your place as captain is here on the bridge of the ship, directing operations. How can you do that if you are at the scene of the battle?"

Ploys like these ought not to work with high-caliber CEOs, who trust their own judgment and reject late, staff-screened data that may minimize the damage that a catastrophe might cause.

The top-flight CEO will know instantly what to do. If he has the advice of a strong, honest public relations adviser, all the better. Job number one will be to get to the scene of the disaster where a command post can be set up. The CEO should never be seen in a TV interview in a wood-paneled office, behind a large desk, while television news crews are showing pictures of the injured or body bags containing the fatalities.

Having taken charge, the CEO's next step is to execute Golden Rule No. 2:

2. Issue holding statement within two hours

Two hours is the maximum length of time that should pass before you issue a statement summarizing the facts of the matter as far as they are known. Stick to the facts and do not elaborate or try to interpret them. In the case of an oil spill, air or rail crash, explosion or other accident, the media will begin its coverage immediately. Every minute you delay with your statement means reporters must find alternative "experts" to explain the cause. Corporate and industry enemies will be eager to step in and give their views. Speculation far from the truth might well take hold in the public mind and become the reality before you even start to communicate.

I cannot move on without citing the famous quotation of Winston Churchill that acts as a caution to all public relations practitioners: "A rumor can be half way round the world before the truth has time to get its trousers on." It is amazing to realize that this was said years before satellite TV and the Internet, although that powerful often-overlooked medium, radio, had been in existence for several years.

The initial statement should be open, sympathetic toward any victims, but brief. It is perfectly acceptable to state that the cause of the problem is not known, along with giving assurances that everything is being done to find out. The statement should end with the time and place of the next update to the media, setting the scene for a regular dialogue during the crisis period.

3. Create a crisis task force

In any significant crisis, the CEO should nominate a special task force early. The task-force leader should be a senior executive of the company, who will be able to take on some of the time-consuming communication duties that will emerge as the crisis evolves. The task force should consist of a legal representative, a communications officer and the technical specialists appropriate to the accident.

Members of the task force should be assigned full time in the heat of the crisis, with counsel and support from a specialist PR agency team. The secondary effects of a crisis can be extremely damaging and the huge time demands it creates distract the company and its executives from their true purpose. The company must field two teams, defense and offense, at the same time. The role of the communications officer is to ensure that the media and other audiences who have a right or a need to know are kept informed at regular intervals.

In some catastrophes, a secondary crisis is created as a result of inadequate communications to specific groups. In the 1996 case of TWA 800, when a Boeing exploded in midair and crashed in New York's Long Island Sound without any survivors, media coverage turned at one stage, from the investigation of the cause of the crash and the location and identification of the bodies, to complaints from relatives of the passengers who said they were being given inadequate information and were being poorly treated by TWA.

4. Establish a press office within six hours

The task force communications officer should set up a fully staffed and equipped press office within six hours of the first news of the crisis. It should be separate, with phone and fax numbers different from those in the regular company press office. All incoming calls from media inquiring about the crisis must be routed to this center. All other staff should be told they should not speak to the media.

The staffing of the news bureau/press office should be sufficient to cope with the intensity of media interest. On-site skills should include:

- Ability to create and update a special "crisis news" page on the company website.
- Capacity to log all media inquiries and organize them by topic so that Q&A templates can be prepared.
- Specialist ability to deal with the requirements of the electronic media. The designated professional should also be responsible for the preparation and dissemination of company-produced video B-roll and video news releases.
- Support-staff capability to undertake time-consuming administrative tasks involved in disseminating statements, calling back all media who have made requests for specific kinds of information when it becomes available, and all the other detail work that is vital to establishing an effective two-way channel.

The communications officer must also make sure that, if any potentially damaging evidence emerges, he is the one to inform the media, however distasteful or unwelcome the task. The result will be much less damaging than if the facts come to light from another source.

5. Arrange brief media training refresher course

Although the CEO and other senior executives have probably undertaken media training previously, it is a "must" to arrange a short refresher course – even if only for an hour or two – to remind your spokespersons of the tenets of a successful interview and to rehearse them on the key messages to be communicated, along with answers to likely questions.

6. Call on civic and other government leaders for help

In cases of loss of life, property and similar dangerous situations, do not try to fight the crisis alone. Call on civic, police and other appropriate leaders for help. Not only will this help to mitigate the disaster more quickly, it will make the impact of the crisis a shared problem. Often companies are the co-victims in an "act of God" crisis but all too often they get positioned as blameworthy (or at least suspect) while others suffer.

7. Announce establishment of a disaster fund within 24 hours

The victims of some disasters are faced with immediate, unusual expenses for medical treatment, travel and shelter, and often have no money to cover these costs. Many companies involved in crises suffer additional reputation damage because it takes a long time to establish a fund to deal with victims' costs. Even when a fund has been set up, it can take years for the money to be released to those in need. Damage from the crisis can be reduced by the creation of an emergency crisis fund to take care of immediate expenses – without red tape – of those people who have suffered. Prompt action in disbursing the money when it is actually needed creates goodwill that will surely be reflected in the company's reputation and the financial settlements that are ultimately made.

8. Institute daily news conferences

Establish a routine in the immediate aftermath of a crisis that reflects the news-gathering needs of the media but also allows the press center to operate efficiently. By scheduling a daily news conference to provide progress reports at a time that fits in with deadlines, press officers can respond publicly to a variety of media inquiries and extend an invitation to participate in the next press briefing when there will be a Q&A session. This system ensures that *all* media are equally well served and no favorites are given exclusive treatment, something that would be guaranteed to alienate the majority of reporters.

9. Communicate proactively

In the pressure of a crisis situation, it is easy to become reactive under the onslaught of media attention and questioning. Yet it is vital for successful crisis management that you take control and communicate proactively. Do not wait for questions to be asked. In addition to the daily news conference, make sure you release regular news bulletins – by fax, video news release, web page and all the other means at your disposal. Report what you have found out about the cause of the crisis, what the company is doing to put things right, how it is helping those affected, and steps being taken to prevent future occurrences.

10. Survey public opinion

Do not fly blind in a crisis. Opinions may vary among senior management as to the extent of public awareness of the crisis and its effect on your company's reputation. The impact of the crisis will also vary widely in different parts of the world. You should know at intervals how your response to the crisis is being viewed by employees and audiences key to your business, for example, opinion leaders and members of the public.

So one early step should be the commissioning of a series of surveys which will give you the information you need. The feedback will help you to adjust your communications strategies and will also tell you where the crisis has had the most impact. Although the Internet and satellite television transmission mean that news gets around the world in an instant, it does not follow that all parts of the world and local media will be interested in your crisis. Most media is extremely parochial and, unless there is a direct, local connection, will not report even on significant events taking place far away. The Seveso hexachlorophene plant explosion was a top news item in Europe for a decade, but it went unnoticed in the USA. Similarly, Shell's Brent Spar Oil Rig brouhaha with Greenpeace was headline news and high on the political agenda throughout Europe for several months, and was followed with interest in certain other countries. However, in the USA and Latin America, the media focus was on other problems nearer to home and if anyone there had heard of Brent Spar, it was unlikely to be damaging to Shell Oil's reputation.

Catastrophes and emergencies are not exclusively reserved for poorly managed and ill-prepared companies. They can affect all.

Being prepared

The company that systematically identifies issues early on, then manages them purposefully, will dramatically reduce the potential of being surprised by a crisis. If that company prepares itself to expect the unexpected, it will be at the ready to face a crisis when it does occur.

Finally, if the ten golden rules are followed, the company will control damage to its reputation and set the stage for a strong recovery program.

Crises are among the best-documented specialties of public relations, perhaps because they so often capture the headlines, much to the chagrin of the organizations concerned. The most useful way to illustrate various types of crisis is through cases covering both slow-burning issues and surprises. You will, however, never have heard about some of the most adroitly handled crises precisely because they attracted little attention in the media. The companies involved are not usually eager to publicize the steps they took to manage the crisis because it would work against the achievement of the goal: containment of the problem to the most limited audience possible.

For the sake of illustrating crisis management, following are some landmark cases. In order to make space for new case studies, some of those featured in the first edition of this book have been excluded. They can be found at <www.palgrave.com>

"Nestlé boycott"

When a British journalist suggested publicly in 1974 that hard-selling manufacturers of powdered infant formula were contributing to the deaths of Third World infants, he found a ready audience among a new breed of activists – anti-business groups, religious organizations, champions of Third World concerns and an end to world hunger, and feminists. The product, he said, encouraged poor, illiterate mothers to give up breast feeding in favor of the heavily advertised powder. They often diluted it excessively to make it go further and used dirty water and unsanitary procedures – all of which led to deadly digestive disorders and malnutrition in their babies. The author recognized that some mothers were malnourished themselves and could not breast feed adequately, while others had to take employment to support their families and had to use supplements to breast milk.

Even though several infant formula manufacturers operated in the Third World, the booklet the author had written was soon reprinted without the qualifications and with the title, *The Baby Killers*, by the Swiss activist Third World Working Group. In quick succession, these developments occurred: Nestlé sued for libel in the Swiss courts, wrongly assuming that a legal victory would resolve the problems of public perception. The result was that the assertions made in the book received a second, unexpected burst of publicity as evidence was given during the hearings. And although the judge found that Nestlé had indeed been libeled, technically, he awarded Nestlé a derisory ½ cent in damages, the lowest amount possible, and accompanied it with a lengthy judicial statement that made it clear he felt the company morally and ethically guilty.

One result was that INFACT, the Infant Formula Action Coalition, was established in the USA, focusing primarily on Nestlé and organizing a world boycott of Nestlé products, with such slogans as "Crunch Nestlé Quick," punning on the brand names of Nestlé chocolate products.

Religious coalition

Boycott leaders were not concerned that the US Nestlé company did not sell infant formula. They were soon joined by The World Council of Churches, national Protestant and Catholic institutions and local churches, teachers' unions and other labor groups, and Hollywood celebrities. Soon media attention turned to other major manufacturers of infant formula: Glaxo in the UK and Ross Laboratories (subsidiary of Abbott Laboratories), Bristol-Myers, and Wyeth Laboratories in the USA, along with a producer based in Holland.

But the main media spotlight remained focused on the Swiss company. Nestlé at its headquarters in Switzerland became the leader of an industry group that took an uncompromising position, emphasizing that its advertising always stressed that breast milk is best; powdered formula actually saved infants' lives; local sales people were vital educators of mothers on infant care; distribution of samples to new mothers through hospitals was generous and educational rather than a marketing ploy; and government authorities welcomed the manufacturers' activities. The industry alliance was ICIFI, the International Council of the Infant Formula Industry.

The media had a field day, locally, nationally and internationally, especially if a celebrity joined the ranks of the boycotters. Publicity-savvy groups often called press conferences to announce they had uncovered another piece of evidence about Nestlé's aggressive marketing in a Third World country, where tactics were used that were even outside the company's long-standing sales and marketing guidelines.

It should be specially noted by those who work in decentralized multinational organizations that the "violations" uncovered by the coalition were in most cases the work of sales agents who did not even belong to Nestlé and a few that arose from the activities of "rogue," distant local subsidiaries. Thus, a fine company, practicing the virtues of empowering local management and agents to operate entrepreneurially and independently, paid a high price for their mistakes or excesses. In the matter of corporate reputation, a company is as strong as its weakest link.

At headquarters in Vevey, Switzerland, and at Nestlé USA, executives insisted the boycott was having no impact on sales. The US company designated senior staffers from several unrelated departments to constitute truth squads that were trained to face off with adversaries in venues across the country.

Edelman Public Relations was hired in the US and London, to work with Nestlé USA and the international formula manufacturers' organization to correct misinformation in media coverage. The mission also included educating groups within the adversary coalitions about Nestlé's historic efforts to improve Third World nutrition through research, and a charge to effect a positive outcome to the landmark World Health Organization conference convened in Geneva in 1979 to act on the problem.

A code of infant formula marketing practices emerged from the conference that many members of the industry saw as unnecessarily crippling, but least damaging to Nestlé and its major share of the market. Nestlé reorganized itself, ostensibly to face the challenges of changing late-century markets.

While the boycott seemed relatively ineffectual financially, it branded Nestlé as part of what activists of the day saw as a big-business global collusion to abuse helpless people in order to make higher profits. A venerable company's reputation had been damaged. Nestlé had, early on, delivered an inconsistent corporate response. It had deployed overly conservative tactics. It had sought technical legal redress in a matter where the only judgment of importance would be made in the court of public opinion. Its claims of a good record in nutrition-related advertising, education and research had a skeptical reception. Cultural differences got in the way, as when Swiss managers could not understand why their American counterparts could not control the media better.

Now, nearly 20 years after the publication of *The Baby Killers*, the infant formula debate continues and attitudes toward Nestlé and the role it played linger. However, the topic has left the front pages for the most part.

"Coca-Cola"

Although a leading Belgian newspaper wrote in July 2001 that Coca-Cola in Belgium had fully recovered from its 1999 crisis, the company is still living with the profound effects of the much-publicized tainting scare. Douglas Ivester, CEO at the time, resigned; the share price tumbled and has never regained its normal high standing; and the entire marketing and communications strategy has been turned on its head and now operates under the mantra "think local, act local," introduced by the CEO who succeeded Ivester, Australian Douglas Daft.

The most thorough analysis of this case has been conducted by Maureen Taylor, assistant professor in the Department of Communications at Rutgers University, New Jersey, whose scholarly paper (*Public Relations Review*, September 22, 2000) examines how cultural and societal variations affect the communication between international organizations and the publics in the host nations.

The Tainting Crisis

On June 14, 1999, school children in Belgium reported feeling ill after drinking Coca-Cola soft drinks. The Belgian government immediately ordered

Coca-Cola Belgium to recall the product. The company complied with the order, but maintained that independent laboratory tests did not show any harmful substances in their products. On June 15, the nations of Spain and France accused the soft drink maker of selling tainted products.

Two possible explanations exist for the poisoning incident. First, some tests found that the outside of cans had been in contact with a fungicide that had been applied to the wooden pallets that were used in the shipping process. A second plausible explanation identified very low quality levels of carbon dioxide in the "fizz" in the bottles made at the Coca-Cola Belgium factory. This low quality "fizz" may have made the children ill.

Coca-Cola's public relations strategy originally discounted the claims of tainting in its products. The company did not accept any responsibility for the incident, and the organization even suggested that the people who had fallen ill were part of a mass hysteria. Coca-Cola did, however, agree to pull the drinks from the shelves. The public relations response has been considered "a waffle," "foot dragging," "a poor attempt at damage control," and "ducking away from a health scare." Nine days had passed before the chief executive officer of the organization acknowledged the problem. CEO M. Douglas Ivester finally flew over to the region and offered a free can of coke to consumers to win back their loyalty. Coca-Cola also promised to pay more attention to the bottling process and hinted that "we let the consumer down."

There were many key publics that needed Coca-Cola's attention during the first week of the crisis. Stakeholders in each nation included consumers, government leaders, and shareholders. Belgium was located at the epicenter of the crisis. Belgium's key trading and cultural neighbors include France and Spain to the south and Sweden, Norway, and Denmark to the north.

Coca-Cola's slow response affected the levels of trust of consumers who were once loyal to the Coca-Cola brand. Over 200 people fell ill after drinking Coke products, and many felt betrayed when the company refused to believe their claims of illness. Belgian, French, and Spanish consumers not only stopped drinking traditional Coke products, but also stopped buying related Coca-Cola brand products, such as Fanta, Nestea, and Coca-Cola Light. Given the competitiveness of the soft drink industry, Coca-Cola needed to strengthen consumer loyalty, not discourage it.

The Belgian government was a key public that was all but ignored during the crisis. If Coca-Cola had conducted research into the current events of Belgian health issues, the organization would have learned that the Belgian government had recently been scandalized over a livestock feed scare. During the spring of 1999, the government of Belgium was publicly humiliated in front of its European Union member states after a contaminated feed scandal resulted in several resignations of high-level Belgian officials. The Coca-Cola tainting scare was badly timed for both common citizens and policymakers in Western Europe. The Belgian government sought to use Coca-Cola as an example because government officials did not want to be accused again of not protecting the public interest.

The governments of Spain and France were also displeased with Coca-Cola. Coca-Cola's claims that its products were safe angered these two national governments by challenging their authority.

France, a nation that dislikes the entry of any global products into its culture, was directly affected by the tainting. During the summer of 1999, consumers in France reported illness at the same time as the Belgian school children. Indeed, although the majority of the illnesses were in Belgium, the factory where the Coca-Cola products were made was located in Dunkirk, France. In an attempt to minimize uncertainty, the French government closed down the Dunkirk manufacturing plant. Public discussion centered on public distrust of multinational companies selling their products in France and blamed multinationals for causing economic problems for national brands.

Officials in Spain also reacted strongly to the tainting crisis in Belgium. Ironically, most Coca-Cola products that are sold in Spain are manufactured in Spain by Coca-Cola España. There was little risk to Spanish consumers from the Belgian tainting; yet the Health Ministry pulled all imported bottles of Coca-Cola, regardless of nation of origin, and the consumer public stopped buying all related Coca-Cola products.

It was Coca-Cola's CEO's absence, in both comment and presence, that directly affronted the nations affected during this crisis. Coke was not condemned so much for the tainting situation, but was criticized because the company remained silent for over a week after the first illnesses. On June 22, 1999, nine days after the scare, Coca-Cola finally issued a public apology. In an open letter to Belgian consumers, CEO Ivester finally apologized for any inconvenience and discomfort associated with the scare. The company pledged to deliver high-quality products in the future. This tainting crisis has been considered the worst health scare in Coke's 113-year history and a public relations disaster.

The summer tainting case is over now. Coca-Cola continues to fight to regain market share and rebuild relationships with its European publics. Improved quality controls are now in place, and the company is spending millions trying to rebuild its relationships with its publics. Public relations efforts include "road shows and beach parties, rock concerts and free handouts to refurbish the European image of Coca-Cola, the world's most famous brand, and new advertising campaigns depict Coca-Cola as a 'local' brand, along with the creation of new local brands developed to appeal to individual markets."

Marketing efforts have also changed. Coca-Cola has a new business strategy that attempts to improve its understanding of the unique cultural and economic issues in many nations of the world. Coca-Cola's previous one product, one global strategy, will now be modified under new CEO Daft. In an interview with the *New York Times*, Daft summed up the Belgian situation: "Maybe there was no one there who understood the environment. Or, if we had people who understood the environment, we didn't listen to them."

Coke is listening now.

"Shell/Brent Spar"

Doing proper research and conforming to the law don't guarantee that a corporate decision will go down well, especially if there are environmental implications. Shell/UK learned that lesson when the company decided to dump a redundant oil storage platform in the North Sea in 1993. All requisite technical and environmental research had been done. British and international law had been followed. But Shell was not mindful of geography that gave neighboring countries a stake in the decision, and certainly the company was not sensitive either to popular sentiment or to the power of Greenpeace, the international environmental protest group that would eventually become the winning David to Shell's Goliath.

Shell was still reeling from damaged reputation and lost business, even after an admission from Greenpeace that it had not told the truth when it published certain "facts" about Brent Spar which sparked an international public and political outcry.

After 20 years of operation, Shell's Brent Spar oil rig in the North Sea was to be decommissioned in 1993 and dumped at sea. Multi-million-dollar research on the science of deep-sea dumping had been conducted and the plan met the requirements of international law.

Then, Greenpeace issued a report on the dangers of sea dumping, and, despite the fact that the British Energy Ministry had approved the plan, Greenpeace activists occupied the rig and began a sophisticated communications campaign from there.

Boycott

Greenpeace also triggered antagonism to Shell in Germany, which considered the North Sea a "German Sea." A powerful boycott against Shell gas stations started in that country, and some stations were fire-bombed. Shell evicted Greenpeace from the rig, only to have it retaken. UK Prime Minister John

Major defended Shell in Parliament, but Chancellor Helmut Kohl, under severe pressure from Germany's "greens," asked Major to withdraw the dumping permit.

International conferences, including the Oslo–Paris Convention of North Sea Nations and the European Parliament, took up the issue. The bifurcated history of European borders gave voice to Iceland, Norway, Sweden, Denmark, the Netherlands and Belgium, which, in addition to Britain and Germany, felt some ownership of the North Sea. Shell had neither consulted them nor taken into account the ferocity of animal welfare concerns among their citizenry, quite the equal to Germany's and the UK's.

Three years after decommissioning Brent Spar, Shell abandoned the deep-sea dumping plan but the fallout was ultimately much more damaging to Shell than just the rig disposal about-face. Consumers, shareholders and the media across the globe were exposed to the long fight and lost faith in the venerable company. The consumer boycott in Germany cost Shell 30 percent of its sales there and sales even plummeted at gas stations in Shell's home country of the Netherlands. Intracompany warfare ensued between Shell/UK and Shell/Germany.

"Eco-terrorism" as a strategy and "shock news" as a tactic had been tested and validated on the battlefield, as for example when a helicopter piloted by a woman tried to land Greenpeace protesters on the rig's deck and Shell used high-power water cannon to fend it off under the glare of bright lights focused on the scene for the benefit of the TV cameras. Pictures were beamed by satellite around the world and Greenpeace emerged eminently victorious.

Photo opportunities

"The Brent Spar shows that high profile cases, properly framed and easily explained, can ignite widespread public interest, especially if the news media get plenty of good photo opportunities," said the *Wall Street Journal/Europe*. the *Financial Times* advised that "Brent Spar means that businesses must include public opinion in environmental plans." A former Greenpeace board member commented, "Greenpeace now has a fleet of ships running around the oceans looking for something to do." A Greenpeace spokesperson promised, "The battle continues. Brent Spar is only one example. Four hundred other rigs are likely to be dumped into the North Sea."

Recovery program

To repair the damage to its corporate reputation in the 1990s due to the Brent Spar controversy as well as its much-criticized actions to protect its oil drilling operations in Nigeria, Shell International embarked on a global Corporate Identity (CI) program intended to highlight its commitment to sustainable development and to reporting that commitment to its stakeholder groups.

Shell International and its lead communications consultancy, Fishburn Hedges, developed a program to help Shell defend its reputation and promote a more positive image of the group in the 140 countries in which it operates. Regional workshops were held on each continent for external affairs and brand executives to brief them on the strategy, receive input and comment and make any changes necessary before launch. Ahead of the launch, full briefing packs were sent out, and features appeared in Shell's main internal news media, *Shell World*, its global magazine, and Shell Business Television, its satellite television channel.

In June 2000, a major new charity, The Shell Foundation, was set up, with initial funds of $30 million earmarked for sustainable energy and other social investment projects worldwide. The Shell Report, a yearly investigation of group performance from an economic, environmental and social perspective, is now in its third year and is widely acknowledged as an example of best-practice in the field of corporate reporting.

Research was conducted at the end of 2000 among global special publics around 14 agreed reputational metrics to assess increased levels of awareness and engagement, and how well Shell's CI program rated against the key drivers of company reputation. The research, in over 40 countries, found that the campaign has penetrated 60 percent of the target audience, and that overall favorability of opinion has improved.

More detailed findings have shown that of those who were exposed to the campaign; 88 percent think the content is relevant; 75 percent think Shell lives up to its business principles; 75 percent find the Shell Reports credible; 80 percent think that the PR-driven advertising makes a positive contribution to Shell's reputation; and 21 percent wish to receive more information.

"The sweatshop scandal"

Child labor had been used in developing countries for decades to manufacture products for American consumption, and the issue had surfaced now and then, in attacks on corporations by labor and human rights activists. Rather than read those attacks as warnings of a potentially, reputation-damaging crisis, most American business was largely unconcerned, protected by industry lobbyists and public inertia.

When publicity-driven attacks targeted cultural and commercial icons in 1996, accusations of sweatshop operations against Wal-Mart and Nike made page one and network newscasts. The faces on the issue were now those of Kathie Lee Gifford, the American television talk show celebrity with a successful line of clothing at Wal-Mart stores, and Michael Jordan, the Chicago Bulls basketball hero who lent his name to Nike's Air Jordans. Other retailers and manufacturers soon were swept up in the crisis – Liz Claiborne, J.C. Penney, Talbot's, Kmart. Congress held hearings at which media-savvy activists testified; the US Labor Department and the White House were interested, too.

The issue is another example of the power of pressure groups with the media and, in particular, one battle in a long war being fought by organized labor.

Corporate response changed day by day, company to company – even though there had been plenty of warning to prepare issue management plans.

Complex problem

Child labor in the manufacture of name-label clothes was a complex problem. Opponents said that working children were deprived of education and innocent childhood, they took jobs adults might otherwise have, and American manufacturers were depriving higher-paid American workers of jobs. On the other hand, some economists and governments of developing nations contended that if the children were not working on American products, they would not be in school but rather working for lower wages making goods for domestic consumption; families in poverty would be deprived of the children's meager wages; and the issue was a cover for American labor protectionism. Pulling out American contracts would not resolve problems of economic standards, education and social reform, many said. Nonetheless, after she was personally attacked by a labor activist testifying before Congress, Kathie Lee Gifford wept on her syndicated television show at the suggestion that she would sanction unfit conditions for child workers in order to turn a profit. Then, both she and her partner, Wal-Mart, complained the attack was unfair and they were being picked on because the clothing line was successful, making them victims of pot shots.

Though the initial charge had to do with children in a plant in Honduras, it later included workers in a New York sweatshop. Kathy Lee's sports commentator husband, Frank, visited the New York shop and gave envelopes containing $300 each, in cash, to a dozen workers after the *New York Daily News* reported that they were getting less than the minimum wage and had not been paid for months. Statements from Wal-Mart were bland, corporate, unsympathetic. The Giffords hired public relations counsel Howard J. Rubenstein Associates. They later blamed labor groups for bringing attention to the issue and the media for promoting it.

Wal-Mart announced upgraded inspections of foreign plants through an independent monitoring company and Gifford promised to hire her own outside auditor.

"Nike's 'Heart of Darkness'"

In November, 1997, the *New York Times* reported on a leaked, confidential Ernst & Young labor and environmental audit conducted for Nike on one of its factories in Vietnam. The report, which outlined dismal labor and environmental practices, generated a series of scathing articles and columns on the business pages and sports pages of newspapers across the USA and around the world. NGO, Working Assets Citizen Action, picked up on the story and generated 33,000 letters to Nike CEO Phil Knight, urging him to pay workers a living wage and to implement a comprehensive third-party monitoring system. Later, ESPN ran an hour-long documentary on unsafe and unjust working conditions inside Nike and Reebok factories in Vietnam.

Pressure was brought upon Nike by student groups and NGOs such as Global Exchange and Vietnam Labor Watch, demanding that universities doing business with Nike hold it to higher standards. Michael Moore's documentary film, *The Big One*, featured the situation in an embarrassing light for Nike. Nike's sales figures and stock price suffered.

The response of Nike and Michael Jordan to similar attacks, by the Made in the USA Foundation, took a different tone and tactic. From the start, Jordan referred questions about the sneakers and their manufacture to Nike. The company pointed to product labels to show manufacturing was in Taiwan, not Indonesia as charged, and gave out data on its wages – twice the minimum in most of the countries where it operated. It also showed the code of conduct all its production subcontractors must sign, covering wages, overtime, safety and other standards.

In mid-1998, Nike announced its pledge to end child labor, follow US occupational health and safety standards, and allow NGOs to participate in the monitoring of its Asian factories. The company also publicly stated that the conditions in its factories needed to be drastically improved. Nike is now one of the most visible actors in all issues related to corporate social responsibility, but the path taken to this point involved costs to its financial bottom lines, as well as its brand equity.

"Attack challenged"

An attack was made on Kmart and actress Jaclyn Smith, whose clothing collection the store chain carries. Claims that the clothes were made by abused, low-paid teenagers in a Honduras factory were challenged by the company and the Honduran Embassy in Washington.

Many other apparel companies took another look at their policies and controls over suppliers. A very few had anticipated the potential disaster years earlier, for example Levi Strauss & Co., with its strict labor initiatives, and assessments of human rights conditions and political stability in countries where it does business. Philips Van Heusen had created a code for contractors and had been conducting surprise inspections.

The American public, however, had become sensitized. Polling cited by the Institute for Policy Studies in Washington showed that 84 percent of US consumers said they would pay more for products manufactured overseas if they could be sure the goods were made in decent working conditions.

A newsmaking children's letter-writing crusade to companies such as Guess, Inc., manufacturers of jeans, and The Walt Disney Co., as well as to members of the US Congress, was triggered by electronic mail messages, magazine articles and television programs on child labor. Manufacturers, while denying the allegations, also contended that unions and labor activists had stirred up students, from grade school through college, to garner public support for unionizing efforts and campaigns to protect American workers.

Support has been growing in the US and other countries for an international "made without child labor" label.

Early in 1997, major sporting goods manufacturers and child advocacy groups joined in a plan to eliminate the employment of children to stitch soccer balls in Pakistan, which produces 75 percent of the world's hand-stitched soccer balls. The plan focused on a $1 million fund to pay for independent monitors to inspect ball-making operations and a manufacturers' pledge not to sell balls made by children.

Progressing from corporate indolence to media sensation, the foreign child labor issue had triggered action and a change in public values. The cost to corporate reputations has yet to be measured.

"Reason for hope: Companies and NGOs build a better banana"

Chiquita Brands International and the Rainforest Alliance provide an apt example of how companies and NGOs can find common ground, initiate true partnership, and create a win–win for both the company's business imperatives, as well as the NGO's civil society goals.

The Rainforest Alliance, an NGO certifier of agriculture and timber products, began the Better Banana Project (BBP) in 1991 in an effort to transform business and land use practices as well as consumer behavior. Together with a network of conservation organizations in Latin America, they develop and certify the use of best practices that protect water quality, worker health and safety, wildlife habitat and rainforests.

Better Banana Project standards for farm assessment and certification are based on these nine principles:

- Ecosystem Conservation
- Wildlife Conservation
- Fair Treatment and Good Conditions for Workers
- Good Community Relations
- Minimal, Strictly Managed Use of Agrichemicals
- Integrated Management of Waste
- Conservation of Water Resources
- Soil Conservation
- Environmental Planning and Monitoring

Because of its scientifically valid and increasingly rigorous performance standards, independent verification by local conservation organizations, and continuous re-certification, the BBP establishes clear performance standards that significantly exceed those of other standards currently in use in the banana industry.

In 1996, Chiquita announced its intention to begin compliance with the Better Banana Project's guidelines. Prior to adopting the Rainforest Alliance's Better Banana Project, Chiquita commissioned another environmental NGO, Conservation International, to conduct a review of the program to verify the scientific and environmental validity of the standards. Following a six-month field study, Conservation International concluded that the Rainforest Alliance program "is an innovative system that looks for environmental improvement ... serves as a guide for the establishment of environmental measures, and promotes gradual changes in land use and practices ..."

In late 2000, Chiquita announced that it had achieved a major milestone in its work with the BBP – the certification of 100 percent of its owned banana farms in Latin America. Chiquita has achieved certification on more than 71,000 acres (29,000 hectares) of its 127 company-owned farms in Colombia, Costa Rica, Guatemala, Honduras and Panama. An additional 30 percent of independent farms supplying bananas to the company have also been certified.

Thus far, Chiquita is the only global banana company to have undertaken to meet Better Banana Project's guidelines. However, the company's actions influenced many independent producers who sell their fruit to Chiquita to follow these same standards. To date, over 30 percent of these producers' farms have achieved the Rainforest Alliance's Better Banana Project certification.

"The mad cow disease feeding frenzy"

Mishandled communications by a government can create a global crisis. That was the case in 1996, when the British government did not anticipate the panic that would be created domestically and internationally by its lackadaisical treatment of a scientific study suggesting a possible link between a serious disease in cows and a similar one in humans.

In what came to be known widely as the "mad cow" problem, Britain's Ministry of Agriculture, Fisheries and Food released a report citing strong evidence that there was a connection between Bovine Spongiform Encephalopathy (BSE), a brain disease, and the human version, Creutzfeld-Jakob Disease, a deadly illness which also affects the brain. The announcement of a "very worrying" link came after ten years of government denial that BSE posed any health risk to human beings, an embarrassing reversal. Making matters worse, the government did not put the new information in perspective for the general public.

There was no word that more study was necessary, or that the risk was minimal because bovine organs and spinal material, affected by the disease, are not allowed in foods, or that added measures had been in place for years to prevent the disease's spread.

Hungry for a sensational story, the media focused on the fact that some scientists had conjectured that every cow in the country – 11 million animals – might have to be put to death and that 500,000 people could die of the disease.

Commission astonished

Restaurants closed. Schools no longer served beef. France, Belgium, the Netherlands, Portugal and Sweden joined the United States in keeping English beef out – the US having taken that stand seven years earlier. The UK Meat and Livestock Commission was astonished it had received no prior warning of the study, and it hired Lowe Bell Communications to help handle the crisis. Others in private industry did their best to allay consumer fears. For example, McDonald's put out the word that its hamburgers were made of top-quality prime beef, containing no risk-carrying carcasses.

Despite the facts that there continued to be no proof that mad cow disease can go from cattle to humans, and that there was no evidence of the variant form of Creutzfeld-Jakob disease in the US, the American beef industry moved swiftly and dramatically. The National Cattleman's Beef Association joined with the American Sheep Industry Association, because sheep carry a similar disease and sheep offal is used to feed cows. The two groups linked up with the National Milk Producers Federation, the American Veterinary

Medical Association, the American Association of Bovine Practitioners and the American Association of Veterinary Medical Colleges, in a collaboration to ensure that feed for cows did not include protein derived from cows and sheep. The coalition supported US Food and Drug Administration (FDA) regulations on this prohibition and pressed for the Department of Agriculture to step up its oversight activities and conduct research and education programs. Reassuringly, the group said a ten-year government study of BSE had found no evidence of the illness in American cattle and the new actions were preventive.

Subsequently, the FDA proposed a ban that would start in 1997 of the use of any tissue from ruminant animals, such as cattle, sheep and goats, in making animal feed.

On balance, the efforts to respond to the crisis in Britain were too little, too late; substantial harm had been done to the credibility of the government and the beef industry.

"Pepsi syringe scare"

When corporate and product reputations are of the highest order, the buffeting of crises is diminished. That was the case with Pepsi-Cola Company when incidents of tampering with Diet Pepsi cans began being reported in June 1993. A high degree of consumer trust combined with decisive company action to end, within a week, what could have been a global disaster involving a high-volume, high-visibility product.

Initially, a Seattle television station reported that someone had discovered a hypodermic syringe in a can of Diet Pepsi. Subsequent, similar reports led to a Food and Drug Administration (FDA) regional advisory that consumers empty the contents of their Diet Pepsi cans into a glass before drinking. The events made national news and within hours, other regions of the country were reporting more incidents. The traditionally high sales volume during the July 4th Independence Day holiday was threatened.

Fortunately, crisis management and response guidelines had been in place at Pepsi, and periodically tested and revised, for ten years. Pepsi officials knew that effective communication is the key to crisis resolution and they went into action on Day One of the syringe scare. The Seattle bottler initiated an investigation and responded readily to the media and the public. A crisis team worked to reassure consumers of Pepsi product safety and leveraged trust in the 95-year-old Pepsi trademark. The driving theme was that a planned tampering involving syringes could not logically take place in current product manufacturing practices and a recall would not solve the problem. The company communicated early and often with media and all audiences, and worked with the FDA to investigate how syringes could have found their way into Pepsi cans. Audiences included media, regulatory officials, bottlers, shareholders, employees and customers such as retail stores, restaurants and Pepsi sales outlets.

At first, the agenda was to understand the problem, rule out sabotage, provide on-site interviews in Seattle and media access to the high-tech plant there, and issue company press releases assuring the public that Pepsi would discover the answer.

Vicious cycle

The FDA quickly found a "vicious cycle of media reports begetting copycat complaints." Pepsi's crisis team created video news releases, press releases, consumer talking points, bottler advisories, employee bulletins, trade letters, graphics and interview opportunities, particularly aimed at reaching audiences that could help Pepsi and the FDA bring the scare to an end. Recognizing that television would reach the widest audiences quickly, Pepsi and media consultant Robert Chang produced compelling video footage, showing the speed and safety of the manufacturing process and the illogicality of the complaints simultaneously occurring in different locations.

Pepsi CEO Craig Wetherup appeared on major network news programs to reassure viewers that the tampering could not be happening in Pepsi plants. Some 70 media and consumer specialists, aided by volunteers, staffed phones. Advisories were faxed twice daily to 400 bottling plants and additional Pepsi staff counseled bottlers and field personnel on local issues. FDA national and local officials were crisis counselors to the company and focused on finding the cause of the tampering claims, while Pepsi concentrated on demonstrating that its package and process were tamper-proof.

Having suffered $25 million in lost sales, Pepsi ultimately bounced back and ended its summer season with record sales. Even more important, the company documented consumer confidence. At the peak of the crisis, attitude and awareness surveys showed 94 percent of consumers believed Pepsi was handling it responsibly; 75 percent said they felt better about Pepsi products because of the way the company had responded. The cooperation of the FDA and among bottlers and customers in resisting demand for a national recall of Pepsi products was unprecedented. In editorials, the news media questioned their role in escalating consumer and business fear of unsubstantiated product tampering. Even the US House of Representatives took note, with an entry in the Congressional Record praising Pepsi for quick and decisive action to end the national scare.

"The first Internet-age crisis – Pentium chip"

An industry-wide crisis of credibility threatened when a single prominent manufacturer dug in its heels about a product malfunction and the news went out on the Internet. The protagonists were no less than the computer industry and Intel with its new, vaunted Pentium chip, in what *Fortune* magazine called "a brouhaha that always was more about PR than actual product problems." The handling of this crisis was an unusual PR fumble for Intel, which was voted third most admired company in the USA in *Fortune* magazine's 1997 ranking.

In mid-1994, a mathematics professor found computing problems occurred with his Pentium-equipped computer. Intel told him he was one of some 2 million Pentium users who had reported the same "obscure" problem, a response the professor and his friends posted on the Internet, reaching 20 to 30 million people globally. The problem initiated use of the Internet as a crisis-publicity tool, in advance of media coverage. Intel told customers who requested a replacement chip that they had to prove they needed one. Massive advertising for the Pentium chip stayed on track. The company had calculated that the problem would affect a spreadsheet user once every 27,000 years, and this did not justify a consumer alert or product recall.

IBM stops shipments

But by the end of the year, IBM, concerned for its customers, announced it had decided to stop shipments of its high-powered PCs equipped with the flawed Pentium chip and said that Intel had severely underestimated the chip's potential for error. That decision was front-page news. Some observers cynically said this was an IBM PR offensive, not justified by the mere 5 percent of its computers carrying Pentium chips but rather boosting IBM's future competition with Intel in the chip business. Intel executives were mostly unresponsive to media calls. One apologist said the company was not accustomed to dealing with end-users.

Pentium's largest client, Dell Computer, made no public announcement but dealt directly with Intel and customers to remedy the problem. Dell knew affected customers would be those doing sophisticated calculations and statistics.

With unhappy computer users growing in number and its lesson brutally learned, Intel in late December said it would replace the flawed Pentium chip for anyone who wanted one, without questions asked. In full-page newspaper ads, the company apologized for its bland handling of consumer complaints. But a great deal of damage had already been done, not just to Intel's reputation but to the credibility of the entire computer industry. Consultants, computer columnists and business reporters were advising companies and individuals to put off buying Pentium-equipped computers until corrected chips became available. It was expected that, henceforth, new computer technology would be more thoroughly tested and therefore introduced more slowly. The heart of the damage could have been prevented, through candor, generous handling of consumer complaints and quick response to the media.

Takeovers and mergers

It is not hard to identify companies that are ripe for acquisition. Indeed, the financial writers in the business press periodically publish lists of such companies in different fields. There are any number of reasons why a company should be included: It might have large assets but low earnings. It might be too small to compete with its larger rivals. It might have an alternative product pipeline which the predator company wants or feels it can develop more successfully. The geographical strength of the target company may prove a good fit. There are many more reasons.

Likely target companies can and should be aware of the likelihood of a bid and should plan accordingly. Nonetheless, the announcement of a takeover bid often comes as a surprise, with the target company ill-prepared to repel the advances.

Even if the eventual acquisition of the company is a foregone conclusion, a strong defense can influence the price that is paid and even the ultimate merger partner.

Today, it is increasingly the case that non-financial considerations can play a major role in making or breaking a political merger, a fertile field in which the public relations practitioner can play a key role. Anti-trust and defense factors often weigh heavily in the matter.

And then, of course, there is chauvinism. A recent example played itself out in France, the country of Chauvin, a Napoleonic veteran 200 years ago.

"France/Thomson"

No one had predicted the strength of popular negative feeling in France, about selling off a state-owned electronics company, a division of which would have ended up in South Korean hands.

As part of a privatization plan and an effort to reduce its military-industrial complex, France had decided in 1996 to sell Thomson S.A. to Lagardere Group, a French company mostly interested in the military component of Thomson. Lagardere planned to spin off the consumer division of Thomson to Daewoo Electronics Company of South Korea.

Thomson was heavily indebted and had already eaten up substantial French government resources. It was not lean enough to compete with American companies. Still, the French people were prouder of it and more attached to it than government leaders had anticipated. A furious protest to the proposed sale ensued, ultimately halting it.

The *New York Times* captured the problem in its reporting: "... The terms of the sale to Lagardere had set off a storm of protest by the opposition Socialist Party and labor unions, who denounced the idea of giving away part of the national patrimony in the name of market efficiency – and to foreigners, to boot ...

"But the main thing against it was the national mood in France, where 'globalization' and 'market efficiency' are becoming dirty words as government austerity policies aimed at making France more fit for international competition have helped keep unemployment at 12.6 percent of the labor force."

Insult

Anti-Asian sentiment was an undercurrent, topped by the added insult that the valuation of the company was set at a token figure of one franc.

Officially, the government ended the episode by saying that final approval of the sale had been withheld out of concern about transferring advanced technology to a foreign country. The promise of a substantial infusion of funds and job creation by both Lagardere and Daewoo had not reversed popular sentiment. It is probable that both acted too little and too late to explain the benefits of the plan.

Once the sale cancellation was made public, the French government announced intentions to privatize Thomson in two stages, starting with the defense business, the multimedia one later.

Characterizing the episode as symptomatic of a failing government, *The Economist* concluded: "France's leaders have a straightforward choice: to encourage the largely healthy revolution that is already beginning to refashion French commerce, or to resist it – and watch it happen anyway."

"British Airways 'World's Biggest Offer'"

It is not sufficient to prepare for and manage a crisis when it hits. Forward planning requires that there be a "recovery" plan in place to rebuild the business that might have been badly damaged by a catastrophe. It does not matter whether the cause was human error, engineering failure or "act of God," as the insurance companies categorize events over which you have no control.

Companies that operate globally feel the impact whenever there are tumultuous world events.

The repercussions are especially dramatic for the travel and tourism industry, as British Airways and other airlines learned in 1986, immediately following the bombing of Libya and the Chernobyl reactor explosion. Four years later, the passengers, crew and ground staff of a British Airways (BA) flight landing in Kuwait were detained as "guests" of the Iraqi government, during the Gulf War. A recession was already under way and air travel had been substantially reduced. News of the Kuwait incident appeared on television and in newspapers, precipitating further losses.

Early on in the Gulf War British Airways recognized that there was little they could do to encourage air travel while hostilities continued. However, they did create a "recovery task force" which spent three months planning a high-profile campaign to "jump start" air travel once again after the war ended. There was a big gap to make up because business had dropped by 30 percent. The model for action already existed. It had been created in response to the 1986 losses. Then, the "Go for it America" campaign had sent 5,000 lucky travelers on cost-free sprees from the USA to Great Britain. This earlier success prompted BA to create "The World's Biggest Offer" in 1990, a $100 million promotion "to get the world flying again."

"Every seat free"

Working again with Edelman Public Relations Worldwide, BA announced that on April 23, every seat in its system would be free. People holding tickets would fly free and other seats would be raffled through a coupon entry, for a total of 50,000 free seats. As in the earlier program, the new campaign would include special offers from hotels, car rental companies, restaurants, theaters and stores.

The global campaign, masterminded in London, required secrecy until launch day and was coordinated among BA's in-house PR managers and 42 consultancies. The tactics had to be replicated throughout the world and all press materials were localized and translated.

Announcement press conferences around the globe were held simultaneously. The entry and selection process was then monitored for anecdotes with publicity potential.

On April 23, dubbed "Up and Away Day," bobbies, bagpipers and other costumed characters were in 62 airports in BA gateway cities, and 435 previously pitched reporters, photographers and broadcast crews from 60 countries covered the winners' trips to London. Photo opportunities were set up with the British Prime Minister and Transport Minister.

The complex effort yielded major print and television coverage, including all national TV networks in the US. Worldwide, some 500 million people read about the campaign and 200 million saw it on television. There had been a grand total of 5.7 million entries and BA was able to add millions of qualified names with travel preferences to its database. Recovery from the travel slump was complete within 120 days. Every major travel market in the world was stimulated.

"Ford/Firestone"

Jessica LeAnn Taylor, a 14-year-old cheerleader, was driving with friends to a football game in Mexia, Texas, one October afternoon in 1998, when their Ford Explorer flipped after its rear left Firestone tire shredded at 70 miles per hour. Jessica died.

What has been called "one of the greatest crisis communications breakdowns of our time" followed.

Three years after Jessica's death, at the end of 2001, the crisis was still far from over. There had resulted 270 more deaths and 800 injuries from thousands of Firestone tire-related accidents. Most of them had been installed in Explorers, America's favorite sport utility vehicle.

Ten million tires were recalled by Firestone in moves a year apart. Ford replaced 13 million Firestone tires, which included some in the second Firestone recall.

The essential problem was that the Firestone Wilderness AT and ATX tires produced before May 1998 and used as standard equipment by Ford on its best-selling Explorer SUVs could cause higher stress at the edge of the steel belt and lead to a tread separation. The tire failures occurred mostly in hot-weather states, especially Texas, and usually in the summer.

After cooperating on a federal investigation initially, Ford and Firestone split apart in Congressional hearings during which officials of each company blamed the other for the problems. Successive hostile moves by the protagonists sustained the crisis. Ford's CEO at the time, Jacques Nasser, told Congress that Ford had to "pry" warranty claims data from Firestone. After weeks of silence from Firestone's Japanese parent company, Bridgestone, Firestone's CEO John Lampe blamed Ford and Explorer owners for not keeping tire pressure up.

Ford shared with federal regulators – and without Firestone's knowledge – data showing that Firestone tires on Explorers had higher rates of problems than tires made by other manufacturers. Firestone posted information on its website showing its calculations that Explorers had been in tire-related crashes up to ten times more often than other vehicles equipped with the same tires and that those crashes had been more severe. Firestone's CEO read about Ford sharing information with federal regulators in a newspaper article and called Ford's CEO, who did not return the call. Firestone announced it had stopped selling tires to Ford just days before Ford announced that it would replace 13 million more Firestone tires on its Explorer SUVs. Ford publicized its decision to equip new Explorers with Michelin or Goodyear tires.

Firestone made a settlement that could add up to $51.5 million to avert consumer-protection lawsuits by states. There are still lawsuits on three continents. Firestone started helping state attorneys general to investigate Ford's role in the accidents. Bridgestone suffered an 80 percent drop in profits in 2001 as a result of the Firestone recalls and related costs.

Ford Explorer sales were down 22 percent in the first five months of 2001. Ford has spent millions to settle lawsuits – the details are under wraps – and about $3.5 billion on costs related to replacing tires in 2001.

The 95-year relationship between Ford and Firestone ended. It had started in 1906 when Henry Ford ordered 2,000 of Harvey Firestone's tires, and it was reinforced in 1947 with the marriage of Martha Firestone and William Clay Ford. The rift seemed permanent until, toward the end of 2001, there were reports that the two companies were meeting to try to restore ties. The attempt at reconciliation did not necessarily reflect an emotional ping between the two long-time buddies but rather was an effort to present a united front against damage claims. The *Wall Street Journal* said, "The conflict between the auto maker and tire supplier has been a boon to plaintiffs' lawyers."

At the end of November 2001, a federal judge in Indianapolis granted class-action status to plaintiffs seeking compensation for economic losses connected to Explorers and Firestone tires mounted on them. The decision broadly defined classes of people who would now be entitled to initiate class-action litigation, and it was viewed as potentially affecting millions of plaintiffs.

The two companies, it was reported at the time of that decision, had already spent billions of dollars recalling and replacing tires during the previous 15 months. They also faced hundreds of personal injury lawsuits brought on behalf of victims of deadly accidents with Firestone-equipped Explorers of earlier generations.

Throughout the three-year crisis, broad-scale, global coverage was assured every time either company made a move or there was a new development.

For example, the press paid attention when Ford-Venezuela was accused of hiding information about fatal accidents involving Ford Explorers. The allegations were that Ford had discarded reports that the Explorer's shock absorbers were too soft for Venezuela's terrain and the tires were experiencing tread separation.

The crisis was ultimately a significant component in the downfall and ousting of Ford CEO Jacques Nasser, who was also undone by internal strife and poor financial results.

An item that summed it all up appeared in mid 2001 in the trade publication, *Modern Tire Dealer* magazine, pitting one CEO against the other, in a "he said ... he said" set of quotes.

HE SAID
FIRESTONE CEO
JOHN LAMPE

ON THE NEW TIRE RECALL
"Our tires are safe. When we have a problem, we admit it and we fix it. We've proven that. The issue is the safety of the Explorer."

ON FORD'S MOTIVES
"We believe you are attempting to divert scrutiny of your vehicle by casting doubt on the quality of Firestone Tires."

ON CORPORATE DUTY
"People will know that we took a moral and ethical stand. I hope that's the message that comes out of this."

HE SAID
FORD PRESIDENT & CEO
JACQUES NASSER

ON THE NEW TIRE RECALL
"We simply do not have enough confidence in the future performance of these tires keeping our customers safe."

ON FORD'S MOTIVES
"We had to be certain that the tires on our vehicles were as safe as possible for our customers. Pure and simple."

ON CORPORATE DUTY
"Based on the information that we now have, we feel it is our responsibility to act immediately. This is what we said we would do."

New advertising campaigns by the two companies in 2001 moved in distinctly different directions. Firestone, in its largest campaign ever, reassured customers that the company was committed to "making it right" in tire design and manufacturing. The campaign featured Firestone chairman and CEO Lampe, counteracting earlier criticism that the company had not been forthcoming. To reach women, who had been found less trustful of Firestone after the recalls than men, Firestone television commercials were scheduled for morning and evening news programs and news magazines rather than sports and racecar programs. A second wave of advertising reverted somewhat to the company's more traditional ground: endorsements by racecar drivers, recommending proper tire maintenance.

Millions of tire gauges were given away as part of Firestone's consumer outreach. Firestone also established tough internal quality-control and safety-tracking processes, the kind that some observers said had been set up by other tire manufacturers long before.

The Ford advertising campaign, on the other hand, focused on the new Explorer 2002, which, the company said, had been redesigned before the tire recalls began. The new SUV featured independent suspension, a longer wheelbase and a wider stance intended to add stability and reduce the potential for rollover accidents. But safety issues were not the focus of Ford advertising. Rather, the vehicle was positioned as enabling customers to collect enriching life experiences, such as fishing and hiking. Ford research showed that potential buyers of Explorers had few concerns as long as there were no Firestone tires on the vehicle. The company could afford to avoid the safety issue.

CEO Nasser did not appear in Ford's television commercials. His role in earlier commercials had been criticized because of his Australian accent. Ford fought the drop in Explorer sales with deals and rebates, free oil-change coupons and lots of communication with customers.

Observers of the far-from-over corporate reputation disaster cited some of the protagonists' corporate errors:

- Lack of communication and clear decision making at the highest levels of management
- Disregard for the power of public opinion
- Corporate denial, finger-pointing and arrogance instead of willingness to address consumer concerns
- Uncontrolled messages and media access to executives

Concluded one communications sage: "Surviving a crisis is often determined more by management's response than by the crisis itself."

CHAPTER 10

Public Affairs

It is fashionable nowadays among many people in communications to describe their work broadly as Public Affairs, implying that public relations is a branch of that umbrella activity, rather than the opposite. I will not debate here the appropriate terminology because so many words have been spoken or written on that subject elsewhere. Suffice to say that for our purposes we will take the term "public affairs" to mean that part of the communications activity that is directed toward government representatives at local, national and supranational level. These representatives may be elected legislators or the civil servants whose translation of laws into a host of regulations can often have more impact than the laws themselves.

Examples of how decisions by regulators can derail corporate ambitions and plans are the blocking of the plan for an alliance between British Airways and American Airlines and a proposed merger of United Airlines and US Airways by the US Federal Trade Commission and the veto of GE's plan to merge with Honeywell by the Competition Commission of the European Union.

Public Affairs is sometimes loosely referred to as Lobbying, but we should be more precise. While many activities covered by a public affairs executive can be described as lobbying with a small "l," Lobbying with a capital "L" has traditionally had a particular and regulated meaning in the USA and in Great Britain.

"A Lobbyist" deals directly with lawmakers, regulators and their various committees. The very word "lobbyist" arises because the practitioner hangs around the lobbies of Congress and the Senate, or the Houses of Parliament in Britain, hoping to waylay lawmakers as they move to and from their chambers.

But the distinctions are becoming blurred.

US lobbying

The majority of mainstream public relations firms in the USA do not undertake lobbying as described above. It is the province of law firms, individuals and highly specialized companies offering management consultancy, including integrated PR & PA services. As a matter of comparison, it is interesting to notice that public affairs and specifically lobbying with the European institutions is not subject to strict regulation. This may change since the current code of ethics regarding EU lobbying is being revised.

Many individuals who run the representative offices of companies close to the centers of government are informally or formally registered as lobbyists under the appropriate local code.

But, in the USA, the code was substantially tightened when Congress passed the Lobbying Disclosure Act (LDA), which took effect in January 1997, and reformed laws that had been in effect since 1946. It eliminated the distinction between the small "l" and capital "L" lobbyist in the USA, as far as the letter of the law is concerned, although in PR circles the distinction remains as a way to distinguish between the activities of individuals and firms practicing the different kinds of public affairs.

The LDA said a company's public relations agency rather than the company itself might qualify as lobbyists and be required to register with Congress and the Justice Department. "Many public relations activities that no one would previously have dreamed of calling 'lobbying' now fall under that category," warned attorney Thomas P. Steindler of McDermott, Will & Energy (Washington, D.C.), an expert on the new requirements. "As always in law, ignorance is no excuse, and noncompliance can be costly, with civil penalties amounting to as much as $50,000," he said after the Act's passage.

The new rules also say that client companies or their agencies cannot pick up a restaurant tab when they're with members of the House of Representatives or their staff members.

On the Senate side, the new rules allow you to pay for meals of Senators or their staffers, if the meals cost less than $50 (with a $100 annual limit). "I foresee a rise in the number of chats taking place at hot-dog stands," joked Steindler, referring to the fact that meals valued at less than $10 do not count toward the $100 annual limit.

As newly defined in the LDA, a "lobbyist" is any individual who is paid by a third party to make more than one "lobbying contact." A lobbying contact is an oral or written communication to a vast range of specific individuals (or specific job titles) in the Executive and Legislative branches of the Federal Government. These are "covered" individuals. Which brings us to the question of what constitutes "lobbying activities"? Lobbying activities are lobbying contacts and efforts in support of such contacts, including preparation and planning activities, research and other background work that is intended at the time it is performed for use in contacts, and coordination with the lobbying activities of others.

For the first time, the definition of "lobbying activities" covers research and other background work, as long as it is prepared for a lobbying purpose. Therefore, if you or your PR agency prepare an issue brief for a member of Congress or staffer, or you have an informal meeting for that purpose, it would be treated as a lobbying activity. So, you are required to register. There's a loophole: "Under the new law, not just your actions but your intentions matter: Preparation of a study for some purpose other than lobbying would not be considered a lobbying activity – even if the study were later to be used in the course of lobbying activities," said Steindler.

What about the definition of "lobbying contact"? It refers to any oral or written communication to a covered official that is made on behalf of a client and relates to formulation/adoption of Federal legislation or a Federal rule, regulation, Executive Order, or any other program/policy/position of the US Government; administration/execution of a Federal program or policy; nomination or confirmation for a position subject to confirmation by the Senate.

Exemptions to the definition of lobbying contact include communications made in a speech, article, publication, or other material distributed to the public through radio, television or other medium of mass communication; testimony presented to a committee or task force of Congress; and comments filed in the course of a public proceeding or in response to a Federal Register notice.

Aides included

One of the most dramatic changes from the 1946 law relates to the definition of a "covered official." These are members of Congress, and, for the first time, congressional staffers. The 1946 law covered only members, not their aides.

"Inclusion of congressional staffers is a tip-off to the intent of those who drafted the new legislation," said Tom Steindler. "They know that 90 percent of lobbying gets done at the staff level, and they wanted to make sure that the real movers and shakers were covered by the law."

The new LDA is cross-referenced with reporting requirements under the Foreign Agents Registration Act (FARA), which covers work done for foreign entities, foreign governments and/or foreign political parties.

Anyone required to register under the LDA as or on behalf of a foreign commercial entity is exempt from registering under FARA. And anyone required to file under FARA as or on behalf of a foreign government and/or foreign political party is exempt from registering under the LDA.

It is vital for non-US PR executives to understand FARA. Many foreign organizations prefer not to believe that it exists. It is dangerous to take this view. Penalties for willful violation can be a fine of up to $10,000 or imprisonment for up to five years.

Virtually all representations of foreign governments and foreign political parties require registration under FARA, even if the representation does not involve traditional lobbying and is confined to public relations, investment and trade promotion, tourism promotion, or the like.

There is a gray area in which work for a foreign corporation can involve the political or public interests of a foreign country. Examples include promotion of the sale in the US of so-called "political" products, which have included Cuban sugar, coffee from certain South American countries, and textiles from Japan.

If in doubt, the rule is register or seek advice from legal counsel.

FARA

FARA is strict in its requirements. Agencies must file before beginning registrable work for a client and in any event within ten days of signing a contract. And the contract itself, along with the financial terms, has to be submitted and immediately becomes open to public view. Naive governments are sometimes shocked when they hear that not only their PR strategies and tactics are available to all, including their political opponents at home, but the cost as well. The lesson is to be prudent in the detailed action program that is disclosed in the written contract.

Disclosure is not a one-time event. FARA calls for a report of all activities and payments every six months. The reports require a detailed, itemized statement for every news release issued, every meeting held and more besides.

Not only must meticulous reports be prepared and submitted within 48 hours of a news release but all written materials must be labeled with a statement declaring that the PR firm is registered at a specific federal court. Labels all basically must follow the wording of the example shown below, used by my own firm in its work for the Government of Egypt.

"This material is prepared, edited, issued or circulated by Edelman Public Relations Worldwide, 1500 Broadway, New York, NY 10036, which is registered with the Department of Justice, Washington, DC, under the Foreign Agents Registration Act as an agent of The Egypt Ministry of Foreign Affairs. This material is filed with the Department of Justice where the required registration statement is available for public inspection. Registration does not indicate approval of the contents of the material by the United States Government."

Additionally, a FARA label or its equivalent must appear at the beginning of any motion picture film or videotape distributed on behalf of a registered client.

Few countries have regulations as stringent as the USA but all have their own rules and customs. It behooves the international PR practitioner to familiarize himself with those that apply in all markets of importance to his organization.

Obviously relationships with government are more important for some companies than others. Defense contractors, oil and mining companies, utilities and others that rely on their ability to use natural – and national – resources, along with other heavily regulated organizations such as airlines, and radio and television companies, are all dependent on government decisions that can deliver or cost huge amounts of money to the income statements.

Trade associations and public affairs

Because many of the issues arising at the governmental level affect all companies in a particular industry, trade associations, described more fully earlier as a PR specialty, are the mechanism by which many companies handle a large number of their public affairs issues. In Washington today, no fewer than 1,830 trade associations have their headquarters or a satellite office engaged in government relations. In Brussels, headquarters of the supra-national European Commission, there are offices with "lobbyists" representing 40 different branches of agriculture in France alone. It is estimated that there are around 5,000 "lobbyists" in Brussels. This number will increase over the next five years with the European Union enlarging from 15 to 28 or 30 Member States, as a result of the accession negotiations currently under way with several Central and Eastern European countries.

And for many companies, governments are the largest buyers of their products or services.

There is not a single organization that does not have some reason to think about and act on a public affairs policy. From the day doors are opened for business – and even before – there are numerous contacts with various forms of government. Permission to locate the business at your selected site is probably the first contact, followed by dealing with local ordinances, and labor practice laws, and paying local and federal taxes. All these issues affect General Motors as well as the sole proprietor of a PR counseling practice that operates from a home office. Although Public Affairs is largely practiced at the local level, every public relations practitioner aspiring to an international career needs an understanding of the different government structures in important markets, as well as of the customary ways of dealing with officials in a variety of countries.

"Tenneco Report"

An excellent example of a public affairs campaign that achieved total success in a notoriously difficult market – Japan – was the "Tenneco Report," winner of the overall prize in the 1997 Golden World Awards of the IPRA.

Tenneco Automotive, a major US auto-parts manufacturer, had made little progress over 20 years in selling its shock absorbers in Japan. In 1994, it had only a 3.5 percent share of shock-absorber sales in the after-market there. After hiring Inoue Public Relations to help turn the situation around, extensive research was conducted, which disclosed that:

- Japanese legislation over 40 years had established standards for car safety, maintenance and the inspection system that protected the domestic after-market, with no room for imported parts.
- Domestically manufactured auto parts were labeled "genuine OE (original equipment) parts" but imported parts were handicapped by being labeled "non-OE parts."
- Most certified auto-repair shops were controlled by top Japanese auto makers, who had relationships with domestic parts manufacturers.
- Operators of repair shops were conservative by nature, resisting change.
- Imported parts were made more expensive by Japan's complex distribution system.

The research findings were compiled in "The Tenneco Report," which would become pivotal throughout the campaign.

Tenneco's objectives were to secure de-regulation of the Japanese auto-parts after-market, find new business partners for distribution of Tenneco products, and create new demand by re-educating Japanese car owners regarding purchase of shock absorbers.

Among the critical audiences to reach were key ministries in the Japanese government, industry groups such as the Japan Auto Parts Industry Association, car shops, prospective new distribution channels such as gas stations, and industry experts. Media targets were newspapers, news agencies, business and trade press, TV stations and the foreign press.

The Tenneco Report was initially delivered to the US Department of Commerce and the US Trade Representative office; then it went to the White House. In Japan, it was given to high-ranking officials in the Ministry of Trade and Industry (MITI) and Ministry of Transport (MOT), and the American Embassy, with unofficial briefings for the ministries.

On October 1, 1994, President Clinton declared US intentions to apply trade sanctions to Japan as a result of the auto-parts after-market situation.

Behind-the-scenes discussions with both governments continued, focused on the Tenneco Report. Off-the-record briefings were conducted for major Japanese newspapers and TV stations, which had previously depended on the Japanese government for their information.

Negotiations between the US Trade Representative and the Japanese government stalled just before a June 28, 1995, deadline, and the US threatened to enforce sanctions. Media coverage of the negotiations, informed by the Tenneco briefings, had a major impact on public opinion, which put pressure on the Japanese government to settle.

With de-regulation under way, Tenneco successfully negotiated distribution partnerships with Toyota Motors, Autobacs, an auto-parts 380-store chain, and Japan Energy, one of the country's major oil companies with 6,400 "JOMO" gas stations.

A press conference to launch the sale of Tenneco shock absorbers was held at a JOMO gas station, a "first" in Japan. It was covered by more than 100 Japanese and foreign journalists.

Armed with an information update, Tenneco Inc. chairman and CEO Dana Mead met with high-ranking Japanese officials to get their support for further opening of the auto-parts after-market.

Throughout the campaign, extensive and quality coverage was generated as a result of one-on-one interviews and mailings of press releases. *Nihon Keizai Shimbun*, equivalent to the *Financial Times* or the *Wall Street Journal*, published a special report after a settlement was reached in Geneva between Japan and the US; it revealed the existence of the Tenneco Report and its influence on the talks.

The most important results were:

- fast action by the Japanese Ministry of Transport to exclude shock absorbers from the list of auto parts requiring inspection, which made possible the sale of the products at locations not certified as inspection stations;
- instructions sent by MITI to distributors, telling them not to discriminate against foreign-made products;
- instructions from the Ministry of Transport to auto-repair shops not to discriminate and to allow consumers to select the shock absorbers they wanted.

Sales of Tenneco shock absorbers increased more than 40 percent in Japan from 1995 to 1996. President Clinton, in an April, 1996, White House press conference marking the successful end of US–Japan auto negotiations, honored the achievements of Tenneco in Japan.

New genre of public affairs

With the liberalizing of world trade, the reduction of tariff barriers and the formation of regional trading groups, a more integrated international genre of public affairs is growing up.

Some individuals have special knowledge of particular institutions, such as the Commission, Parliament and Council of Ministers of the European Union; others have a deep expertise on global or multi-country institutions, such as the United Nations, the Organization for Economic Co-operation and Development and the World Trade Organization.

Increasingly, issues are being decided at the supra-national level that were once resolved at the national level, whether a charge of illegal "dumping" of cheap goods in a market or a dispute over access to a particular market (such as the case between Kodak and Fuji Film).

Practitioners who once were used to dealing effectively at the national level now have to enhance their understanding of what it takes to win when matters are adjudicated at the international level.

Many of the issues-resolution techniques commonly used in the USA are gradually being adopted in locally customized format in many other countries. (In fact, there is a minor industry growing up in which experts in this area devote much of their time to transferring their knowledge to institutions in other countries eager to adopt the American methods.) One such method, coalition or alliance building, has been briefly mentioned in the section on trade associations.

Coalitions and alliances play a powerful role in times of change, especially when legislation or a ruling by a government department has a major impact – for good or ill – on a particular group of organizations. Some examples are:

- an alliance formed by American Airlines, United Airlines and Delta Airlines to fight the proposed strategic alliance that British Airways and US Air were seeking to establish;
- an alliance established between the normally deadly rivals United Parcel Service and Fedex to prevent negative, misleading television advertising from the United States Postal Service;
- the Coalition of Long Distance Carriers (CLDC), a group of long distance telephone companies, led by AT&T, MCI and Sprint, to ensure that the major Telecom Act which was going through Congress in 1995 and 1996 was not unduly favorable to the local Bell operating companies as a result of their immense lobbying power and resources.

Similar alliances have been formed in Europe in fast-changing de-regulated markets such as energy, telecommunications and postal services.

Grassroots campaigns

Healthcare reform ... most favored trade status for China ... telephone de-regulation ... tax reform ... mining law reform ... utility de-regulation ... the North American Free Trade Agreement ... These major legislative initiatives, as singular issues, could not be more different, yet they have one thing in common – they either passed or failed because of public opinion shaped by effective, well-organized grassroots lobbying campaigns. For years, these issues languished in the legislative arena. They were finally acted upon and resolved once the public weighed in.

Although grassroots activism, in a much simpler form than is common today, has a long and proud tradition in American politics, there is no doubt that it has become a very sophisticated and integral part of the American political process.

Environmental and labor groups gave life to the modern grassroots campaign. Today, however, corporations and coalitions of different organizations are embracing the practice. Indeed, any organization that intends to influence the lawmaking process needs to incorporate grassroots lobbying in its plan because it is a primary weapon in the legislative arsenal.

How does a grassroots campaign differ from public relations when it comes to influencing public policy? Whereas a public relations program generally consists of one organization getting out a message through the use of media relations activities, grassroots lobbying campaigns are marked by the organized, systematic implementation of a wide-ranging series of "political-campaign-style" activities undertaken by a large number of people. All of the communications actions are geared to ensuring a certain legislative outcome. Messages are sent directly to lawmakers as well as delivered through the news media. If one is looking for a simple definition, a grassroots campaign may be described as "any technique that provides the 'folks back home' with information designed to stimulate communications" by letters, telegrams, e-mail, and meetings (*The Lobbying Handbook*, John L. Zorack, 1990).

The grassroots campaign, because it is organized like a political campaign, covers four phases: identification, education, mobilization and activation of an "interested public." The tools or vehicles used to deliver messages for the purpose of impacting legislation include personal letters, mailgrams, telephone calls, personal contacts and special events designed to attract media coverage.

Why does grassroots campaigning work? It matters to a politician what people back home think, since they control the electoral fate of the official.

Among the first highly visible and successful grassroots campaigns in America was one that was conducted by the banks and brokerage houses in 1985. These corporate entities used grassroots efforts to defeat legislation that would have required them to withhold a percentage of their customers' interest and dividends for taxation.

Getting involved in a campaign for a cause is an exciting way to participate in the civic process and exercise your right to be heard on issues that are important to you. Also, it is rewarding to know that for each person who steps into the arena and gets involved, democracy grows healthier.

Environmental affairs

Environmental communications are either considered a full-fledged specialty, a part of consumer communications or integral to public affairs.

Interest in environmental issues is spread across business and consumer constituencies. Manufacturers face laws and challenges regarding plant siting, recycling and chemical disposal. Consumers take up the causes of forest preservation and keeping carcinogens out of everyday products, nuclear contamination and air and water quality.

The twinning of environmental communications with public affairs is because governments, at the national or local level, are decisive institutions in matters of the environment. Lawmakers can vote to implement recycling projects, for example, that will cost millions or close down plants in violation of emissions laws, and thus possibly eliminate jobs in the short term for a perceived long-term economic and social advantage. Or they can frustrate the attempts of environmentalists, represented by well-organized pressure groups, to enact protective legislation.

The field is an important one for communications professionals. A number of specialist practices experienced in and knowledgeable about environmental affairs have established themselves in several countries, including the US, the UK, Germany and France.

GE–Honeywell merger

GE's appeal is still before the Supreme Court of Justice of the European Union but nobody expects the rejection of the deal by the EU Competition Commission, under which GE hoped to acquire Honeywell, to be reversed. Too much will have changed at the two companies over the many months before that verdict is in.

The case is destined to be the subject of close scrutiny and study by many professions: business consultants and managers, lawyers, politicians, regulators and perhaps sociologists. It has many points of interest and lessons for public relations professionals, especially those specializing in international public policy issues.

The case attracted special attention for several reasons. GE is the world's largest industrial company and the merger with Honeywell would be the largest combination ever of two industrial companies. Jack Welch, the long time CEO of GE, had achieved iconic status as a business manager and was viewed as being the most successful of his generation. In recent years under his tenure GE had been at or near the top of many "Most Admired" company lists. What's more, he had agreed to postpone his much-publicized retirement to see the deal to its conclusion, making it the crowning achievement of an illustrious career. Finally, the origin of the story gave special spice. In October 2000, Mr. Welch chanced on the information that United Technologies Corporation (UTC) was about to announce a $40 billion bid for Honeywell. Within 48 hours he had the GE Board's approval to announce an offer valued at $45 billion in GE stock. Here were all the elements of a thriller – with an all-star cast.

Statistics suggested that there should be no insurmountable barrier to the merger on anti-trust grounds. After all, only two percent of the hundreds of applications made each year are denied.

The story of how GE joined that two percent is a powerful drama, including rival groups, strong personalities, miscalculations and misunderstandings, and the suggestion of hubris on the part of GE. At the heart of GE's failure was an inability to recognize and adapt to the different approaches towards anti-trust decision making in the USA and Europe. Ironically, it was another American company, Honeywell's jilted suitor, UTC, which played the most pivotal role in the EC's decision.

Since 1990 the European Commission, the executive arm of the 15-nation European Union, has had jurisdiction over all mergers of firms with combined revenues of $4.2 billion, of which $212 million must be in Europe. GE/Honeywell was well within these guidelines when the two companies announced their plans; GE alone employed 85,000 people and generated $25 billion in revenue in Europe during the year 2000.

For many years since a cooperation agreement was signed in 1991, the ways in which the world's two leading industrial powers, the USA and the EU, have approached anti-trust matters have been converging. The rulings in respect of the AOL/Time Warner merger were very similar in America and Europe, with the green light being given overall but a requirement for the disposal of EMI as a condition in each region.

Disapproval of mergers is rare on both sides of the Atlantic. But each side has rejected a few proposed combinations that had been approved by the other. The EU had no problem with the proposed alliance of United Airlines and US Airways but the Department of Justice rejected it in America because the combined airline would have too great a dominance on certain routes. The merger of MCI Worldcom and Sprint received the blessing of the US authorities but was turned down in Europe.

From these cases there should have been amber lights flashing for GE and Honeywell. History illustrated that along with the more global aspects of mergers, each authority examines the case as it might affect competition in its national markets or even local markets within the region and countries concerned.

In comments I have heard from both Mr. Welch of GE and Mr. Mario Monti, the European Commissioner for Competition, neither expects the GE/Honeywell decision to become a full-blooded spat with tit for tat between the USA and Europe – as much as the media has been savoring the prospect. In fact, both believe that the real outcome will be more positive – an even closer harmonization of the approaches of both trading blocs (and others around the world). The reason is obvious: mergers, especially cross-border alliances, are the cause and result of globalization. Business leaders need to know with a predictable degree of certainty whether their proposed alliances will be approved or not. To do this, all must operate by the same rulebook. At a breakfast meeting I attended with Mr. Monti, he said he thought it most unlikely, however, that there would ever be a "global" authority responsible for anti-trust matters.

So what did GE do wrong?

They got off on the wrong foot in Europe because of the long delay between the GE/Honeywell filing for permission with the Department of Justice in America and the EU. "This did not help," says Mr. Monti, although he dismisses any suggestion that the EU's decision was in any way the result of pique. Many Eurocrats did however draw the conclusion that GE's strategy was to get a green light by the hometown referee and that the EU would come in line later on.

Mr. Monti points out that the delay caused real problems because the EU laws on the timing of each phase of an investigation are very clear. The result of GE's tardiness in making its application to the EU had a knock-on effect in giving the EU too little time to make its official inquiries. Incidentally, it also gave the prime opponent of the deal, UTC, plenty of time to gear up its lobbying and communications strategy with the advantage of first strike in this market. At a critical juncture GE entered the "quiet period" in which it was barred from contacts with the European Commission (EC).

UTC had appointed a top US economist, Robert Reynolds, to prepare arguments that would convince the EC to turn down the deal and Mark Leddy, UTC's top anti-trust lawyer, chose Polish-born economist Janusz Ordover to convey messages and market facts to the Commission. Both worked closely with law firm Cleary, Gottlieb's Washington and Brussels offices in an integrated communications and lobbying effort. This in turn attracted other like-minded companies, in particular British aero engine maker Rolls Royce, into augmenting the voices raising concern about the alliance. In contrast, GE used two different law firms in Washington and Brussels, which many believed caused significant delays in finalizing the notification to the Commission.

The GE case confirmed that the EU Commission has some criteria which go well beyond the legal arguments on which US decisions are founded. These same criteria had been seen before in Mr. Monti's veto of the all-European Volvo–Scania Truck merger. He himself declared in New York that "mergers in this period of globalization need to have public policy elements integrated that are not damaging to the civil society."

When eventually GE and Honeywell were in a position to make a strong case for the benefits of the merger and to assuage the fears of regulators and the public, the decision deadline was approaching. If sentiment up to this point seemed to be going against an approval of the merger with conditions that might be acceptable to GE's Welch, the death blow came when the process was politicized.

Time Magazine in an article of July 16, 2001 titled, "How Jack Fell Down," wrote: "Welch placed a call to Andrew Card, chief of staff to President Bush, who was about to sit down with European leaders in Goteborg, Sweden. As the GE boss recounted the conversation to *Time*, he told Card that he would appreciate 'whatever help you can give us.' In the formal meetings in Sweden, GE never came up. But on June 15, in Warsaw, Bush said he was 'concerned' that the Europeans had rejected the merger. Monti was furious – not with Bush, he told *Time*, but with those who had sought the President's help. Three days later Monti said he 'deplore[d] attempts to ... trigger political intervention.' And though the case dragged on for two more weeks, the deal was dying a slow death."

Eric Vaes, chairman of Edelman Public Relations Worldwide's European Public Affairs practice says there are many lessons to be learned from GE's experience: "A personal approach is critical and successful lobbying is a matter of trust, something that can only be built up over a matter of years. Then there is the need for respect for cultural sensitivities which in the case of Europe is a kaleidoscope of the sensitivities of several nations. Early and careful preparation of your case and analysis and refutation of the arguments of your opponents are essential; in this you should use the opportunity to give the EU Commission pre-notification in the strictest confidence. This will tip you off to prevailing attitudes and concerns and allow you to prepare your case in good time. Make sure to identify all your supporters and those of like mind who can be organized into an unofficial coalition of support. Finally, make sure that all communications initiatives are prepared early and in the closest of cooperation with the lawyers and lobbyists. There can be only one message for the media, the lawmakers and the regulators. Explain the benefits of the merger beyond the fact that it is legal – say how it will be good for business, the nations and localities, for employment and for civil society at large."

Postscript: For those interested in the subtleties of merger investigations by anti-trust authorities Mr. Monti has suggested that on rare occasions the conditions imposed for approval of a merger application by the authority have been a welcome relief to one or both of the CEOs involved. He says that during the detailed review that is undertaken by officials, the two sides get to know each other much better than during the short acquaintance gained while hammering out the terms of the deal. They do not always like what they see and get a sinking feeling that they might not have chosen an ideal partner. Given time, market conditions also change, making the rationale for the merger less convincing. And during the detailed investigation, each partner gets to know much more about the financial position, pipeline of new products and other information about their intended partner than is usually to be found from even the most diligently conducted due diligence. With a twinkle in his eye, Mr. Monti suggests that when some companies retreat from deals stating that the conditions imposed by the authorities were too onerous, those conditions may actually have come as a godsend to the parties involved. "We have to realize," he says, "that sometimes we are going to be placed in the convenient role of scapegoat."

CHAPTER 11

Sponsorship? Philanthropy? Or Promotion?

The finest athletes who competed in the ancient Olympic Games in Greece were celebrated heroes whose company was sought by the most influential figures in the democracy at that time.

Nero and other Roman emperors two millennia ago arranged spectacular events in arenas such as the Colosseum in Rome where gladiators fought each other and wild animals as well.

The Popes in Rome and families such as the Borgias and the Medicis provided encouragement, subsidies and shelter to a host of Renaissance artists such as Leonardo da Vinci, Michelangelo and Benvenuto Cellini as a memorial to their power, wealth and good taste, and in so doing gave the world lasting treasures of inestimable value.

Emperors, kings, princes and archbishops in Europe and elsewhere maintained orchestras, theatrical troupes and composers. We must thank them for Monteverdi, Vivaldi, Bach and Mozart.

More recently, communism created its own state patronage system, in which athletes were provided sinecures in the military so that they could practice and win gold medals in world championship events and Olympiads. In the arts and entertainment, the same regimes patronized the arts through such institutions as the Bolshoi Ballet and the Moscow State Circus as a way of maintaining the prestige of the state.

Yet many of us persist in seeing the huge growth in sponsorship and event management as a recent phenomenon rather than evolution in which industry and commerce have taken over the role of patron or sponsor from the ecclesiastical hierarchy, the aristocracy or ruling totalitarian party. It is a role that has been played through the centuries by whichever group was most powerful and rich.

Sponsorship (I will use that word with a small "s" to embrace all the activities described in this chapter; a capital "S" when applied specifically to the more narrowly defined underwriting of particular events) is of vital importance to anyone aspiring to practice international public relations.

It is one of the few activities that can eliminate boundaries and borders when it is well understood and practiced with skill.

According to the international CORPerceptions research regularly conducted by ORC (Opinion Research Corporation), those companies engaged in sponsorship of major world class events such as the Olympics or the World Cup achieve higher favorable ratings than non-sponsors. It is apparent that in certain countries more kudos is given to these major sponsors than in others.

Dr. Jim Fink of ORC interprets this phenomenon thus: "People are impressed by companies that are major sponsors of worldwide events. Not only do they assume they have the money to buy the rights, but somehow they feel they have been selected for this position of honor from among their competitors. In several eastern countries where the notion of 'face' is of the highest importance, to be an Olympic sponsor ensures you the highest level of 'face'. It signals that your company has arrived at the pinnacle of its industry."

Moreover, to be a top-tier sponsor of the Olympic Games or World Cup immediately classifies your organization as global. There would be little point in paying the extremely high entrance fee for the worldwide rights (US$55 million for the most recent pair of summer/winter Games) unless you operate in all the world's markets. The names of recent top-tier sponsors of the two premier events underline this assertion.

For the World Cup in 2002, being held in Korea and Japan, the official partners are McDonald's, MasterCard, Philips, Yahoo!, Adidas, Budweiser, Fuji Xerox, Gillette, FujiFilm, JVC, Toshiba, Avaya, Hyundai, Coca-Cola and KT/NTT.

For the Olympics in Salt Lake City (2002) and Athens (2004), the prime worldwide TOP V Partner categories have been claimed by Coca-Cola, John Hancock, Kodak, McDonald's, Panasonic, Samsung, Schlumberger-Sema, Sports Illustrated/Time Inc., Visa, and Xerox, as shown on the Olympics website. Also shown are sponsors of other levels who may be entitled to use the Olympic rings in their promotional materials.

But the major world championship events are not the only avenue for international companies with smaller purses – or incompatible goals – to include sponsorship as a key element in the communications strategy.

As an international public relations executive, you will be one of several people within your organization who may have a hand in selecting sponsorships. If publicity is the most important aim of the sponsorship, your opinion will carry much weight, but that is not always the case. The important thing to keep in mind as you analyze the options and make your selections for recommendation is that you must stay in control of the process. The road to selection and, after selection, management and exploitation of the sponsorship, offers many enticing detours, hairpin bends and landslides to block your progress, but few road signs.

The first problem you will encounter in most companies that are quite new to sponsorship is that there is a lack of understanding on the part of many senior executives as to the purpose and definition of sponsorship. It has been my experience that, depending on where you are in the world, the concept of sponsorship varies and can range from philanthropy to sales promotion.

I have been asked by certain companies to recommend "philanthropic action programs" which turn out, on closer questioning, to be requests for event sponsorships that will gain wider recognition for the company or brand name. And, vice versa.

It must be stressed that the various forms and gradations of sponsorship do not make one better or more important than another. Each has its place, value and particular strengths, which can help an organization achieve its goals. It is, however, of crucial importance to determine at the outset what those goals are, and which of the many forms of sponsorship is most likely to be right for your needs.

The second roadblock you will almost certainly encounter is the "CEO's pet." It can be intransigent and you may have to work around it or accommodate it. The CEO's pet may be a particular sport, branch of the arts or community or charitable activity. The CEO might see it as the most deserving of your company's support and even believe that it is the ideal vehicle to be the centerpiece of company sponsorship strategy. That might well be the case, but the chances are that there will be better ways of spending your sponsorship money. It will be up to you to navigate between the personal desires of your leader and the evidence produced by your investigations and analysis of the available opportunities. You will want as scientific a methodology as possible for identifying and prioritizing candidates for sponsorship. It allows for a rational discussion rather than a fight among a number of favorite events or causes, each with its own supporter.

The third hazard is the slick salesmanship of the organizations that own events or represent athletes and artists. You are likely to receive a torrent of applications for support from a range of agents, suggesting that you must not miss the once-in-a-lifetime opportunity to ensure your company is featured on the sleeve of an aspiring Formula 1 Grand Prix driver or a team that is about to be formed, or to support an attempt by someone wanting to make the first journey to the South Pole on roller blades.

Make sure you resist, at least until you have formulated your own sponsorship policy, decided how much you can afford and are completely ready to make a selection from several possible candidates.

Before you start this process, it is important to establish internally the role and goals of the activity to be planned. It will save misunderstandings and harsh post mortems.

Get clear what is expected by the key group of decision makers in your organization. You might find that one board member is expecting an activity that is quite altruistic and another something that will demonstrably improve the bottom line. Others will be in between. It is useful to list out for your interviews internally the range covered, as follows:

Pure philanthropy

This is the anonymous donation of money to charities, specifically nominated or via a distribution committee. The donor does not wish to have his name disclosed or to have any credit. This kind of donation is declining and now represents a mere 3 percent of charitable giving in the USA. A *New York Times* reporter said that the pressure to publicize the names of donors is not coming from donors themselves, many of whom are publicity shy, but from the recipients, such as hospitals and universities. They have discovered that the way to attract contributions is to publicize major gifts received from prominent people; this sets up a "top that" kind of competition among the rich, which swells the coffers of the luckier institutions. A less cynical view is that, when identified, major donors become leaders and role models in fundraising campaigns. The result? "To those that have, shall be given."

Posthumous philanthropy

Beware of the creation of a major trust fund by individuals who have accumulated exceptional wealth during their lifetime by methods that some might consider to have been excessively harsh and callous and, on occasion, unethical. Cynics dub this "conscience money." The trusts may be set up late in life or willed upon death. Some prominent trusts which have attracted notice because their independent boards have sometimes given money to causes and institutions that would have been anathema to the donor are the Ford Foundation, the Carnegie Foundation and the Rockefeller Foundation.

Smart philanthropy

There is, of course, truly altruistic posthumous philanthropy, too. This is a term used by companies that want to build a bridge between charitable giving and self-interest. In essence, this means they want to donate money (or services, or something else of value) to charitable causes that are strongly related, if possible, to their business and its goals. It is perhaps a new variant on the saying "charity begins at home." It can mean that there is some direct payback, not always in monetary terms; or it can mean that the organization is in a special position because of its own know-how or resources to offer help unavailable from any other sources.

"Exxon Mobil"

Long before its merger with Exxon, Mobil was a company that had been practicing smart philanthropy for decades, and long before the term itself was first used. But this element must be seen for what it is, one arrow in a quiver full of many forms of philanthropy.

To name just a few of Mobil's initiatives: Masterpiece Theater, a weekly TV broadcast of British drama on America's Public Broadcasting System which attracts a huge audience; annual publication of the Mobil Travel Guides, now a self-standing business in its own right with the guides established as the "bible" from which travelers and diners in the USA should pick places to stay and to eat; USA Track and Field Athletic Championships.

But it is in Mobil's sponsorship of carefully chosen arts and cultural projects that the keen observer can see just how smart Mobil's philanthropy can be. The company's selection of the subjects for sponsorship is anything but random. Each relates directly to a topic or region of interest to Mobil, often a place where it has important activities. It has sought to merge the interests and benefits to the communities in which it operates along with a public service and self-interest. Examples are:

- Treasures of Ancient Nigeria: This exhibition of the remarkable bronze sculptures created in the Kingdom of Benin (province of Nigeria) was shown at the Royal Academy in London, the Metropolitan Museum of Art in New York and other major art venues. Mobil's initiative was appreciated by Nigeria's government as a valuable way of depicting the evolution of Nigeria's civilization and helped cement relations with this important source of oil production.
- Painters of the American West: The oil-well-owning Anschutz family of Denver had accumulated the USA's finest collection of "Western art" – paintings by such well-known artists as Remington. Mobil curated and exhibited a selection of these paintings at the Institute of Contemporary Arts in London with an opening ceremony performed

by Prince Philip, Duke of Edinburgh. The show later toured to other venues. Shortly thereafter, it was announced that Mobil had acquired several oil wells from Anschutz.

- Patterns of the Hebrides: This was an exhibition commissioned from the photographer Gus Wylie at the time that Mobil was undertaking explorations in the North Sea and there was great concern for the environment by residents of the Hebrides and environmentalists at large. Gus Wylie's commission was to record on film the life and scenery before and after the completion of explorations and the laying of pipes. This would show Mobil's concern to return the islands to their natural state, and the desired result was achieved. The exhibition, which toured, was opened in London by the Minister for Scottish Affairs.

"Telecom"

Another example of smart philanthropy is the creation of a consortium of major companies in the telecommunications industry to fund the attendance of representatives of less developed and newly developing countries at Telecom '95. The world's largest trade show and symposium, held every four years, Telecom in 1991 had raised eyebrows in many parts of the world for its display of opulence. One exhibitor's booth was an architectural wonder costing over $3 million. Critics said the event was becoming a rich man's club and was not affordable by many of the poorer nations.

The organizer of Telecom is the International Telecommunication Union (ITU), whose membership consists of 184 states and organizations from around the world. It is responsible for regulating, standardizing and developing telecommunications globally, as well as promoting a harmonious environment conducive to effective use of telecommunications products and services worldwide.

Formally affiliated with the United Nations, ITU has as one of its objectives to close the telecommunications gap between developed and developing countries. ITU decided to ensure that Telecom '95 would be open to the less developed and newly developing countries where the need for technological and infrastructure advance was greatest.

Financial contributions were solicited from 13 of the world's most prominent telecom companies – Alcatel, Cable & Wireless College, Ericsson, IBM, MCI Communications Corporation, Motorola, NEC, Northern Telecom, Nynex, Philips, Siemens, Telebras and TIA/USA. ITU created the Programme for Development with its mainstay a two-and-one-half day workshop for Least Developed Countries (LDCs) and Low Income Countries (LICs). This was the first such workshop and the first time giants of the fiercely competitive global telecommunications industry collaborated on such a joint project.

Though the telecommunications development gap between the affluent countries and the developing world has narrowed in recent years – LDCs and LICs account for more than 77 percent of the world's populations, but only 5 percent of the world's telephone lines – more than two-thirds of households around the world still have no basic telephone service.

According to the United Nations, the number of LDCs has increased from 25 in 1971 to 48 in 1994, and that figure was expected to reach 52 by 1999. Of the present 48 LDCs worldwide, 30 are in Africa, 13 in Asia-Pacific, 4 in the Arab Region and 1 in the Americas.

Titled "Human Resources and Technology," the workshop focused on these two areas of crucial importance for nations seeking to improve their telecommunication facilities and enhance their ability to operate efficiently in the rapidly changing telecommunications environment.

And, as the 200 delegates planned to upgrade their national telecom systems, you can be certain the 13 sponsor companies, all of them equipment suppliers, would be reminding them of their support for and participation in the ITU initiative. Smart philanthropy.

"United Parcel Service"

United Parcel Service is an example of an organization that seeks to use its special knowledge, resources and skills in its philanthropic outreach, rather than indiscriminately doling out contributions to a variety of causes, however noble. The UPS Foundation, the company's philanthropic arm, analyzes several charitable needs and agencies serving them, and then selects those which it feels it is in a unique position to help.

Throughout its 95-year history, UPS has been committed to community service. It has stated the commitment in its Corporate Mission Statement, in a subsection that specifically addresses "Communities." UPS spreads the word, both internally and externally, that a fundamental element of its mission is to "build on the legacy of our company reputation as a responsible corporate citizen whose well-being is in the public interest and whose people are respected for their performance and integrity."

In 1988, the UPS Foundation reviewed research available at the time in an effort to help UPS better target philanthropic efforts. Illiteracy and hunger were identified as the two most urgent social challenges. UPS adopted these issues, contributing money and manpower through national and regional outreach efforts. For example, in 1988, UPS developed the Prepared and

Perishable Food Rescue Program (PPFRP), which supports the growth and development of hunger relief programs. The company developed a technical services manual for new program start-ups and helped form FoodChain, a network of PPFRPs for shared information and resources. The precept was this: There are areas of the USA where food is scarce. There are other areas where there is an overabundance of food. UPS was able to use its unrivaled knowledge of transport and distribution systems to help the excess food get to the areas of need.

In 1989, UPS developed an adult literacy award program, which provides grants to programs that have proven effective in increasing basic literacy skills in the areas that the organizations serve. UPS expanded its literacy outreach to include education initiatives, including "school to work" and "welfare to work" initiatives in states where UPS has a strong presence, including Georgia, Kentucky, Illinois and Pennsylvania.

While UPS has strong relationships with national non-profit organizations such as the United Way and provides funding through the UPS Corporate Grants program, much of its charitable giving focuses on the individual UPS regions and programs developed by UPS. The primary focus for UPS is to support organizations in areas where UPS employees live and work. Each UPS region and district is responsible for making small contributions to local organizations, through the Corporate Charitable Contributions program.

In addition, UPS relies on one of its largest resources – its employees – to identify worthwhile local charities to receive grants and other donations. Through the UPS Region/District Grant Program, established in 1984, employees in each of the UPS domestic, Americas and Canada regions, the Corporate Office, the Air Group and Information Services recommend local non-profit organizations to receive grants of $100,000, $50,000 or $25,000.

Apart from monetary contributions, UPS's single largest contribution to non-profit organizations is its manpower. UPS is one of the largest employers in the US. Thousands of its employees have been giving back to the community – building and painting houses, cleaning up parks, teaching computer classes and hosting reading hours. So, in 1993, UPS organized this widespread network of volunteers into what is now the UPS Neighbor to Neighbor program. The goal was to increase the number of UPS employees who volunteer, and diversify their options. And, no dollar amount can be placed on the service that they provide.

Community philanthropy

Giving in the community where they operate is natural for companies that were founded and have grown and prospered for many years in a particular place. As growth takes place, the city or town grows and the bonds between the company and the community strengthen. Often, that is the origin of schools, libraries, parks, buildings, streets, theaters, clubs and pools made possible by philanthropic support from the major local business enterprises.

Now, multinational companies, which are by definition also multilocal, need to approach the question of community philanthropy in a systematic fashion, as UPS has done in the way described earlier. Most consider it a very important element in establishing the newcomer company as one which intends to be a good corporate citizen and contribute to the community in which it is setting down roots.

The best policy is to take your time, study the balance of local politics on the one hand and make a careful list of the needs of the community on the other. Note those community activities that are already "owned" by other sponsors and discard them as prospects. Select one or two activities or needs which will gain the most credit among the local people. Has there been a long-term need for a swimming pool? A youth club? A day care center? Read the local press, talk to local people, listen to the debates at the local town hall meetings and pick the causes to support that will do the most good and enhance your reputation as a valued local citizen.

Community philanthropy is not just a question of giving cash. Equally important can be the personal commitment on the part of staff members or the donation of equipment or resources. An excellent and bold example of a multilocal community philanthropic initiative was that taken by AT&T in 1997 when it announced AT&T CARES, the most recent addition to its community service programs. This initiative encourages AT&T's 127,000 employees worldwide to devote one paid workday per year to their communities. According to the Points of Light Foundation, AT&T CARES is the largest publicly announced corporate volunteer program. It was launched in 16 states and Washington, D.C., where AT&T volunteers helped a national charity, Second Harvest, collect food and set up a warehouse for its annual Thanksgiving Day food drive. It is estimated that AT&T CARES represented a 1997 donation of one million hours, valued at approximately $20 million.

A complementary AT&T CARES grants program, initiated in 1994, reinforces employees' volunteer work. When an employee gives at least 50 hours of service annually to a non-profit group, he can request a $250 AT&T CARES grant, and when four or more employees volunteer at the same organization, they can combine their requests for a maximum grant award of $2,500. "By giving our time and money, we demonstrate not only our commitment, but also our conviction," says Marcy Chapin, the AT&T Foundation's vice president of community service programs. For example, Jenna McCaffrey and 20 AT&T colleagues, who are literacy coaches for academically at-risk elementary school students in Chicago's inner city, helped keep the tutoring project alive through an AT&T CARES grant.

Another AT&T initiative is the AT&T Learning Network, started in 1995, the most comprehensive technology donation ever made by an American company. It offered to connect all of the 110,000 US elementary and secondary schools to the Internet by the year 2000 and, in doing so, foster family involvement in education, provide professional development opportunities for teachers, and integrate technology training into the preparation of new teachers.

This scheme attracted a wave of favorable publicity in the national and international media. It has also created the framework for 127,000 opportunities to create good will at the local level – in addition to media stories – as each of AT&T's employees dedicates his charity day during each year.

The topic of community philanthropy is one of special importance to the international PR practitioner because customs vary from country to country. For most Japanese companies, corporate philanthropy was puzzling because it was not practiced in the same way as has become customary in the USA and other Western democracies. Industry and commerce were seen to be intruding in the province of government agencies, the family and other societal organisms. For some time, this impeded the readiness of communities in other lands to accept Japanese companies as they established overseas branch operations, and that surely hampered the smooth path to growth and success.

After a while, Japanese, Korean and other Asian companies recognized philanthropy as part of the way of business life in their new markets and manufacturing locations and, as might be expected, they studied the topic very carefully. They sought and paid for the advice of philanthropic experts and public relations professionals on the correct way to begin. Now, even though the notion of corporate philanthropy is still foreign to them and is not practiced in the same way in the home market, Japanese and other Asian companies are among the most significant donors in the Western world.

Cause-related marketing

Cause-related marketing stands at the halfway mark between philanthropy and sales promotion. This is the means by which companies can tie charitable giving to sales. In the broadest sense, cause-related marketing can be used to describe the activities of companies which are identified with certain causes or aspirations and which they promote to the public along with their products. A good example is The Body Shop, which achieved a worldwide reputation as an activist organization on behalf of the developing world and its peoples.

Through its buying policies and the way it made donations to less developed countries, as well as through its stated aims to be environmentally responsible, The Body Shop attracted a huge customer base among people who felt they were supporting these causes indirectly through their purchases. However, The Body Shop is also a cautionary tale of the man-traps and pitfalls awaiting companies with golden reputations. There are those who will not rest until they can show that the god others worship has feet of clay.

"The Body Shop"

The worldwide effect of a single negative thrust was demonstrated dramatically in the mid-1990s when the image of The Body Shop as an environmentally friendly and socially conscious cosmetics enterprise was shattered by an article in *Business Ethics*, a small Minneapolis journal. It laid out alleged details of corporate hypocrisy and exaggeration in the autumn of 1994, two years after a television documentary had charged the popular company with false claims about its position against animal testing.

In short order, publications all over the world reported contentions that The Body Shop, with 1,366 retail outlets worldwide, was actually just like its competitors; though highly regarded for being environmentally concerned, using pure materials of exotic origins and engaging in public-spirited programs, it was now accused of having exaggerated its claims, used chemicals tested on animals, bought very little or no natural materials from Third World countries, and done little charitable giving. Disgruntled former employees and franchisees came forward with more allegations of an "inside/outside" strategy: they said founder/CEO Anita Roddick, an iconoclastic marketing whiz, publicly attacked the so-called monsters of the cosmetics industry who continued to test product safety on laboratory animals, while at the same time her company used ingredients that had been animal-tested, and that she had admitted privately that such tests were essential.

The company's stock plunged. Senior staff members left, complaining of organizational problems. Overly fast expansion in the United States lost money. Anita Roddick and her husband, Gordon, co-founder and chairman, failed in their attempt to borrow money to take the company private and then turn it over to a non-profit foundation that would use profits to finance good works. Massive reorganization ensued, along with the hiring of Hill and Knowlton Public Relations.

Deep into its makeover, the company commissioned an independent audit which concluded that The Body Shop *had* maintained a strong social responsibility record and it refuted most of the criticism in the damning

Business Ethics article. The study found, however, that the company's relationships with its external audiences had been poorly managed, particularly with shareholders and media, and it criticized response to customer and franchisee complaints as well as exaggeration in its communications materials about the environmental aspects of its products.

The global franchise corporation, which had started in 1976 in a tiny shop in Brighton and which had gone public in 1984, saw its stock ride high in 1992 but drop by 65 percent four years later. The Body Shop reorganized in 1999, creating a regional management structure, selling its Littlehampton manufacturing sites and appointing a new executive board of directors. When Body Shop stores opened in South Africa in 2001, there were more than 1,900 around the world. In March 2001, retail sales worldwide were £691.4 million.

Social activism was sustained with the launch of the Body Shop Human Rights Award in 2000 and the Community Trade program in 26 countries in 2001.

"'Dolphin Safe' tuna"

The StarKist subsidiary of Heinz decided to end a consumer boycott of its canned tuna products by environmentalists by becoming the first company of its kind to establish a "Dolphin Safe" policy. This meant only buying products from fishing fleets that used nets that did not trap dolphins along with the tuna.

StarKist immediately won the loyalty of millions of people who had for long been identified with this cause. The results could be seen in an immediate surge of StarKist brand share against its rivals.

But the most obvious and measurable cause-related marketing programs directly link sales and philanthropy. Although it is commonly assumed that this is a technique that has only emerged over the past two decades, it has in fact been practiced for a long time by many corporations and other organizations.

"Conservation coin"

A fine example of cause-related marketing was a collaboration in the early 1970s between Spink, the famous London auction house specializing in numismatic coins, the Royal Mint and the World Wildlife Fund. This alliance created the World Wildlife Conservation Coin Collection, a series of coins issued by the 24 countries where a variety of creatures were threatened with extinction. Each country issued four coins, all of which were marketed on a worldwide basis to numismatic coin collectors. Care was taken to ensure the design of each coin was superb and the striking and polishing of each coin was to the highest standards, using the correct weights of gold and silver. In the sales literature, advertising and the public relations launch, it was made clear that a fixed proportion of the receipts from sales would go to help save the wildlife that was in peril. Buyers could, through their choices, indicate the animals they wanted saved because the person buying, for example, the four coins issued by Kenya, would be assured that his donation would go to that country.

"Statue of Liberty"

Jerry Welsh, when he was an executive at American Express, became the father of modern-day cause-related marketing, and Amex is a consistent and successful practitioner of the technique. The most famous example of the genre was the campaign to restore the Statue of Liberty, which was to celebrate its centennial in 1986 but had suffered structurally and decoratively. In short, "the lady," as the statue is affectionately known, needed a face lift, along with some even more radical reconstructive surgery. With no city, state or federal government eager to underwrite what was going to be an exceptionally costly undertaking, along came American Express as a white knight and savior of the statue that symbolizes the nation. How? The company pledged that it would donate one cent on every dollar for purchases charged to American Express cards, a dollar for every new card approved during the campaign period and a dollar for every $500 travel package purchased, toward the Statue of Liberty renovation fund. At the end of the promotion Amex handed over a check for $1.7 million. They also undertook a major advertising and marketing campaign which helped attract other support for the renovation. Not only did American Express's sales volume increase, its reputation took a huge boost in America as a grateful nation celebrated the centennial. All the power of a skillful Amex PR Department was deployed to make sure it was so.

More recently, American Express has had another cause. Charge Against Hunger is a campaign in which a percentage of all purchases made with the American Express family of cards is donated to charities devoted to feeding the hungry and homeless. Communications messages to members who use their charge cards for accommodation in hotels and splendid meals in restaurants make them easy prey for the promotion.

But American Express's larger rival in the payments system business, Visa, is also a major factor – internationally – in cause-related marketing, using its prime position as a "TOP" (The Olympic Partnership) Worldwide sponsor of the Olympic Games as its key into this arena. "Pull for the Team" is an ingenious campaign that can be customized for use by Visa in every nation which participates in the Olympic Games. In this scheme, Visa pledges that a percentage of all charges billed to the Visa card at certain periods will be placed in a fund to help support the training and attendance of athletes of the nations concerned. As Summer and Winter Games approach and Olympic fervor becomes feverish, Visa benefits because people do their best to ensure their favorite athletes get a shot at winning gold.

Sponsorship

In the whole complex, costly and difficult-to-measure field of sponsorship, there is one rule to keep firmly fixed in mind from the outset, even at the evaluation stage of the various opportunities. It is the Iceberg Rule: The visible cost of the project is ALWAYS less than one-third of the total final cost of a successful sponsorship.

A large number of new sponsors enter the field either not knowing this rule, or, having heard of it, believing that it only applies to sponsors other than themselves. They are wrong. The rule has no exceptions.

The visible part of the sponsorship is the price publicized by those who "own" an event, athlete, exhibition or team. In the case of the Olympic Games, the published cost of the highest level of Worldwide Sponsor was last recorded at US$55 million for a pair of games (Winter and Summer). But this merely represented the amount payable to the International Olympic Committee to obtain the rights to that title. To be sure, the purchase of those rights also came with attractive-sounding benefits, such as the right to use the Olympic rings in advertising and promotions, some free seats at the events and special rights to provide customer hospitality in the venues of the games.

But, in truth, the $55 million is a relatively small down payment, an entrance fee that opens up the chance for the sponsor to pay millions more to gain any real benefit from that down payment. Advertising, employee communications, sales promotion, public relations campaigns, all necessary to put the spotlight on an Olympic or any other sponsorship, always come extra.

Sponsorship selection

With sponsorship costs as high as they are, it is essential to select the right event, person or team to sponsor. This is where an objective scoring system pays huge dividends, especially because everyone believes they instinctively know the right choice – theirs.

The selection process you adopt – and there are many available – should start with a statement of the goal of the sponsorship. The goal of "creating wider awareness" of a corporate or brand name might call for a different vehicle from that which might meet the goal of "directly increasing sales and distribution" of a product or family of products.

The former goal will lead you to select an event which will attract a high level of media attention and will carry your name along with it. The second suggests a less widely publicized event but one where there are opportunities for offering hospitality to key distributors, or programs that allow for tie-ins at the retail level.

The other key consideration is the matching of the event with the brand or corporate identity strategy. There is little value in a sponsorship that has high visibility but has an irrelevant or unfortunate connection to the sponsoring company or brand.

"Visa Olympics of the Imagination"

An interesting example of a sponsorship within a sponsorship that helped reinforce brand identity is Visa's Olympics of the Imagination. This was created to offset an aggressive and sharp advertising strategy with a project that was warm, human and in the spirit of the Olympics, even though the Games had become overly commercialized and crowded with sponsors by the 1990s. In planning its agenda for the 1994 Games in Lillehammer, Norway, Visa International, the official worldwide payment system for the International Olympic Committee since 1986, needed to capitalize on its sponsorship in a way that would be global, good for business and sensitive to public perceptions.

The company had already initiated an association with art and culture during previous Olympic Games, by commissioning Olympic-themed art works from five prominent European artists. For 1994, Visa wanted to open the door to wider publicity opportunities, reflect the Olympic founding principle that sports should be blended with art, culture and education to enhance people's lives, and take note of the 100th anniversary of the International Olympic Committee.

Thus was born the award-winning Visa Olympics of the Imagination, developed with Edelman Public Relations Worldwide. An invitation would be issued to talented, artistic youth in many countries, to submit images they thought represented the Olympics 100 years ahead in 2094. Ultimately, Norway, Canada and the United States were chosen as venues for the competition that would produce 25 young winners who would attend the Lillehammer Games and whose art works would be exhibited there.

It was most important that the program would be internationally implemented but adapted to local market needs. The campaigns in the USA, Canada and Norway were anything but the same.

In the USA, daily newspapers in ten major markets partnered the campaign by advertising the contest and printing entry forms, distributing posters and 50,000 Olympics information kits to schools, judging entries and honoring the winners at special events and in more advertising.

Publicity came in three waves: the kick-off and call for entries, announcing the winners, and covering their departure for Norway.

The Norwegian program partner was Sparbanken Nor, one of the country's largest banks and an Olympic sponsor, which promoted the art competition and offered entry materials in its branches. The Oslo International Children's Art Museum participated in the judging and was the site of the press conference to announce the winners.

In Canada, Visa partnered the Canadian Olympic Association (COA), in cooperation with the ten provincial and two territorial departments of education, enabling the Visa program materials to be inserted in school packets distributed by the COA. Canadian school rules restricting commercial programs made this partnership critical and enabled the Visa of the Imagination contest to be positioned as an integral part of the Olympic Resource Kit distributed in 15,000 private and public elementary schools.

In addition to the publicity and attention Visa gained in the three countries, significant visibility was garnered at Lillehammer, through the centrally situated, high-traffic exhibit of the 25 winners' entries and related VIP events. The invitational opening of the art exhibit and dinner drew the highest-level Olympic officials. The winners were invited to participate in the opening ceremonies of the Games. Members of the Canadian Bobsled Team, the US Ski Team and the Norwegian Cross Country Ski Team came to the exhibition tent to have their portraits painted by the young artists.

Upon its conclusion, the Visa program had generated stories read, heard or seen by 300 million people globally, always with a positive portrayal of the company. More than 7,000 youths had submitted art works and the winners were a compelling group who were naturals for publicity efforts. Visitors to the art exhibit at Lillehammer numbered more than 100,000. About 125,000 special-edition postcard reproductions of the art works were distributed, in two or three languages, as invitations and announcements.

The 1994 Visa Olympics of the Imagination won a Golden World Award from the International Public Relations Association, a Big Apple Award from the Public Relations Society of America/NY Chapter, and a Creativity in Public Relations Award from the publication *Inside PR*.

Two years later, for the Centennial Atlanta Games, the well-tested program expanded to 20 countries, including South Africa, Japan, Israel, Australia, the Netherlands, Canada and the USA. It had a site on the Internet, international distribution of point-of-sale materials through Visa merchants and banks, strong media partnership and coverage in the USA, and school materials in nine languages going to 50,000 schools worldwide.

Visa Olympics of the Imagination has continued as an element of the company's Olympic sponsorship at Sydney (2000) and Salt Lake City (2002).

Process

For the international PR practitioner, the selection process is all the more complex with a matrix of different cultures, sporting interests and local managements all making a choice, or even choices, very hard. This is where a disciplined selection process pays the most dividends. A good process will help you decide whether you will get greater benefit from investing in one of the multi-million-dollar global sponsorships available, such as the Olympics or the Soccer World Cup; or from a mosaic of smaller local sponsorships. The attractions of each approach (and some major sponsors with plenty to spend take both roads) are easy to see. A company that was an important and thoughtful early sponsor on a multinational basis was Gillette. It saw very early – in the 1960s – that sports sponsorship was an effective and powerful promotional weapon, and it was the first commercial sponsor of cricket in England.

The Gillette Cup, started in 1963, was not only the first commercialization of the game but the birth of a new form of the game, one-day competitions, a development that has since ensured the continued success of cricket as a spectator sport in the new commercial age.

This sponsorship was not a random selection. To be sure, for the modern television era, cricket needed a new injection of money, promotion and the creation of a new, less lengthy format than the usual three-, five- or six-day matches. Gillette was there to help and to gain the benefits. But this was just one example of a worldwide sponsorship policy in which the company had set its own rule: It would sponsor the national sport of each country where it conducted a sizable business, thus demonstrating its local corporate citizenship and also winning over local customers for its products. The Baseball World Series in the USA, Gillette Cup Cricket in England, Pelota in Spain and other similar sponsorships combined into a coherent global sponsorship policy.

For the international company, it is important to involve regional and local managements in the selection and planning process of any sponsorship. Early participation pays dividends later on, in the form of enthusiastic implementation of the agreed programs.

It might also help to reshape the global sponsorship policy. Many companies now have several levels of sponsorship ranging from the mega global effort (such as the Olympics) to subsidies for small local events.

Multilayered sponsorships

Rank Xerox was an early and clever exponent of the multilayered sponsorship policy. At the national level in major markets, such as the UK, they would select one or more high-profile events to sponsor. At one time it was the Slazenger Golf Tournament, which offered a combination of awareness through name association in media advertising, posters and public relations as well as superb hospitality opportunities for their major customers.

At the same time, the Rank Xerox headquarters required each of its regional units in the United Kingdom to allocate a certain sum of money for local sponsorships. It also required a report and rationale for the selection of the events and the plans for maximizing the return on investment in the sponsorship through ads, PR, etc.

Each regional unit picked events that were very local and important to the communities in which they operated – the Scottish Opera was one selection for the Scottish Region – so that the company became a welcome member of the local business circles in each of the principal cities where their customers were situated. Guidelines were given and experiences were exchanged, but there was no requirement for the money to be directed to any particular sport or branch of the arts. The only requirement was that the money allocated should be spent, and spent wisely.

Sponsorship criteria

For any major international corporation to plan, manage and implement an effective global sponsorship program, there needs to be a common commitment to work within an agreed set of criteria. Here is a suggested list.

Every sponsorship activity *must*:

- Express agreed brand or corporate values
- Approach audience targeting systematically

- Create an opportunity for direct contact with specific audience groups
- Have sufficient impact on a wide scale in order to be visible to individuals not directly engaged with the sponsorship activity
- Demonstrate synergy across all operating regions/countries
- Show the company's edge against its competitors. For this, the company must have the broadest possible exclusivity within its product/industry category and be able to play an active part in the development of the sponsored activity. This means influencing and approving the way your organization's involvement is presented and communicated
- Allow your products, services and technology to play an active part in the development of sponsored activity and offer a contribution or benefit to the sponsored party
- Be exploited actively and aggressively in order to extend the value of the sponsorship package

Make a 'no go' list of events that might be offensive or controversial because they might be considered discriminatory, violent, immoral, unethical, antagonistic or environmentally harmful. Do not sponsor religious groups or political organizations, issues or activities, with the exception of those issues or organizations that are indisputably humanitarian or directly related to your business activities.

Evaluation scoring systems

There are many evaluation scoring systems to help the potential sponsor weigh the competing offerings. You can also make up your own system with weightings that are highly relevant to your particular case. I show here the proprietary system developed by Edelman over several years of involvement in this special field. It rates six potential elements of a successful sales promotion/public relations program, as viewed from the PR perspective.

Post-event evaluation process

As important as the pre-evaluation process is the post-event evaluation.

I suggest you use the same format as for the Edelman M.U.S.T. S.ystem – just to make sure the musts were not "maybes."

In addition, qualitative and quantitative research should be undertaken.

Table 11.1 EDELMAN 100-POINT M.U.S.T.S.ystem[SM]

Edelman M.U.S.T. S.ystem Element	Scoring	Score (100 point max. total)

Media Appeal
Does the program generate news about the company, brand, retailers, etc.?
  – Nationally: consumer; trade/business media
  – Locally: consumer; trade/business media
	20 points	

User Friendliness
Is the program flexible and easy to implement?
Does it encourage participation among:
  – Consumers
  – Trade
  – Salesforce
	15 points	

Sales Appeal
Does it reach out and "sell" the brand in a unique way?
Does it differentiate the brand from the competition among:
  – Consumers
  – Salesforce
  – Brand Management
  – Trade
	20 points	

Thematic Applications Does it identify the brand "spirit"? Does it make participants feel good about being involved?	15 points	
Special Event Potential Does it offer opportunities that increase reach; impact; duration in market?	15 points	
Bonus Points Does it offer extra benefits such as brand imagery? Does it elevate brand from clutter?	(+/–)15 Points	
TOTAL SCORE (100 points maximum)		

EDELMAN 100-POINT M.U.S.T.S.ystem Measurement Standard

Superior Program	95–100
Excellent	90–94
Good	85–89
Fair	76–84
Don't Bother	75 or less

Quantitative:

- How many people were aware of your sponsoring involvement? This measurement will be gleaned from audience ratings (if broadcast), gate/attendance ratings (if an exhibit/exhibition), entry numbers (if a competition), clip numbers (if magazine based), etc.
- Cost per thousand. This measurement will be determined by calculating the overall cost of the sponsorship program for each thousand individuals reached.
- Optionally, try to calculate the level of increased business which will have been directly influenced by the sponsorship.

Qualitative:

- Through focus groups, establish the match between audience expectation, lifestyles, or mindset and the sponsorship personality; rate positive feedback from the demographic and psychographic groups of importance to you.
- Through telephone interviews, establish awareness and favorability of the sponsorship program with specific audience groups (consumers, channels, operators, business partners), as well as with employees.

CHAPTER 12

The Internet: Medium, Message, PR Tool, Manager

Among the huge changes that have taken place in international communications since the first edition of this book, the rise of the Internet can make claim to be the most significant. Today it is an integral part of almost everything we do.

First, it is a medium of extraordinary power, one that puts the public relations person in direct dialog with his target, without the filter of a third party. This is known as disintermediation and is a phenomenon that radically changes how PR people work. Second, it is the message in the McLuhan sense of "the medium is the message." The very fact that important information is carried, perhaps for the first time, on the Internet itself communicates something to the recipient. Third, it is a PR tool of extraordinary flexibility and power in the hands of a skilled communications professional. Finally, it is a back office manager that has changed the way PR people work with each other, clients work with agencies, how we monitor the media, how we maintain our databases, aspire to knowledge management and report our results.

As with all powerful weapons, the Internet can be used for good or evil – and all shades in between.

In its relatively short existence as a ubiquitous means of communication we have seen it used by terrorists to lay their plans without regard to national borders on the one hand, and as the primary means of communication by the remarkable Jody Williams who, from her home in Vermont, was instrumental in achieving an accord to rid the world of the horror of landmines.

Tom Friedman of the *New York Times* in his book on globalization, *The Lexus and the Olive Tree* – a must read for any PR professional who is involved in multi-country communications strategy – describes Ms. Williams as a "super-empowered" individual, one of the growing number of Internet-savvy people who have mastered the technique of reaching and motivating thousands of people remotely to support a cause.

"Some of these Super-empowered individuals are quite angry, some of them quite wonderful – but all of them are now able to act directly on the world stage," wrote Friedman, several months before the world was stunned by the destruction of the World Trade Center in New York and the bombing of the Pentagon on September 11, 2001. "Osama bin Laden, a Saudi millionaire with his own global network declared war on the United States in the late 1990s, and the U.S. Air Force retaliated with a cruise missile attack on him (where he resided in Afghanistan) as though he were another nation-state. Think about that. The United States fired 75 cruise missiles, at $1 million apiece, at a person! That was a superpower against a Super-empowered angry man. Jody Williams won the Nobel Peace Prize in 1997 for her contribution to the international ban on landmines. She achieved that ban not only without much government help, but in the face of opposition from all the major powers. And what did she say was her secret weapon for organizing 1,000 different human rights and arms control groups on six continents? 'E-mail.'"

The Internet may also be an "equalizer" in adjusting the balance of power between small, proprietor-managed agencies and the global and national behemoths. As a tool, the Internet is so powerful that it can confer a communications advantage to a knowledgeable and technologically proficient individual or small firm over a more traditional and hidebound larger opponent. But the old rule of the fight game probably applies: A good big 'un will always beat a good little 'un.

The Internet's impact on news delivery

According to Mark White of Mainsail Interactive Services, few processes have been as dramatically altered by the Internet as the way the media delivers the news, and the way companies communicate with their stakeholders. He has charted the changes as below:

That was then	This is now
You had to own a printing press or a broadcast tower to be considered "the media."	Every Internet user has access to a global broadcast channel at no charge beyond local access fees.
Breaking news stories were reported exclusively by radio stations and 24-hour cable-TV news channels.	Employees, customers and competitors, and investors can access the most current news online.
Access to real-time newswire services was limited to journalists at large news organizations and an elite group of stockbrokers who could afford a proprietary newsfeed terminal.	Real-time newswire services are available to anyone with an Internet connection and a web browser.

That was then

Negative opinions about a company were limited to private one-to-one conversations via the telephone and perhaps around the infamous "water cooler." If a person wanted a larger audience, formal protest tactics such as lawsuits, letter-writing campaigns and strikes usually had to be deployed.

Press releases and media kits with corporate background information were distributed exclusively to working members of the media.

Press conferences were attended exclusively by the press. Likewise with analyst conferences for investment professionals.

If a journalist wanted to write a story about a company, he would usually contact the company's PR representatives first to receive background information and schedule an interview with a company spokesperson.

Newspaper and magazine archives were limited to physical copies of back issues in a library, microfilm, and expensive proprietary electronic retrieval systems.

With the exception of the "Letters To The Editor" page, media was a monologue from editors to their readers.

Public relations was primarily concerned with the delivery of favorable stories about clients in the media, currying favors with journalists in the hopes they would write a positive article about a client to supplement advertising and other marketing efforts.

This is now

Anyone can post opinions about a company and its products on countless online forums from traditional Internet newsgroups on USENET to investors' "clubs" to renegade sites that specifically encourage the airing of grievances.

Press releases and the contents of corporate media kits can be accessed by anyone from a company's website. In addition, press releases are listed next to "real" news stories (i.e., written by an objective third-party reporter) on many news sites.

Press and analyst conferences are available for listening and/or viewing through the Internet by anyone.

Reporters gather information about a company from online sources, including company websites, news archives and message forums, and write articles without ever contacting the company's PR representatives in advance.

Past articles and issues are often available online directly from the publisher for a slight fee to anyone who asks. In many cases, archival materials can be retrieved for free from various search engines.

Media is a three-way conversation among reporters, their subjects and their readers.

The media is just one of dozens of key audiences that posts opinions, comments and content about a company online, all of which must be monitored and managed by companies and their PR agencies.

"Despite these tectonic changes, many public relations departments and agencies continue to run their businesses the way they have since the dawn of the mass market in the 1950s," says Mark White. "The public relations service bundle of three years from now is going to look very different from today. The new mix of PR services will incorporate elements of management consulting, business intelligence, publishing, direct marketing and Internet strategy."

Nancy Ruscheinski, president of Edelman Chicago and an authority on interactive media, goes even further, stressing that public relations professionals must overcome the idea that an Internet component or strategy is an optional extra for PR programs. "Today an interactive component is an essential, integral component in every communications initiative, as automatic as printed press releases, video news releases and the other basic tools available to us. We must always remember that the Internet has not changed the basic precepts of marketing which are: The customer comes first; the customer wants great products at great prices, conveniently; the customer who is wronged will tell his friends and now, unlike in the past, he can broadcast his gripes to millions at a click."

Both White and Ruscheinski go on to point out some of the many new uses of the Internet within a holistic PR program:

- Enhancing and managing the "press room" section on corporate websites
- Disseminating corporate news directly to key audiences
- Providing online information to investors
- Developing viral marketing campaigns
- Forming partnerships and promotions
- Monitoring news and newsgroup forums in real time
- Deploying extranets to manage a company's PR and related marketing activities

The arrival of the commercially viable Internet presented four unique approaches to capturing its full potential: Advertising, Technology, Design and PR. Not surprisingly, these venerable sectors produced four unique types of firms to handle the task:

- Interactive Advertising Agency, typically the outgrowth of an advertising agency, with a focus on branding and advertising online as a means of delivering a message. Online advertising has proven itself ineffective, rendering the expensive branded website like a rudderless ship without a crew.

- Technology Focused Interactive Agencies: Focused primarily on e-commerce with a heavy advertising mix to drive traffic, these agencies have themselves floundered without the .com spending they grew up on.
- Design Houses: Many design agencies felt the Internet was their domain, and build many "pretty picture websites" that focused on an experience rather than content. Many early sites went this route only to discover how vital good content was to their success.
- Interactive PR: With so many ad dollars riding on the success of online ventures, PR was the silent below the radar approach from 1995 to 1997. However, PR started out with a distinct advantage, content. PR firms focused on getting the right messages to the right audiences, and successful PR promotions like the Blair Witch Project helped to validate the PR approach. With the sinking returns on online advertising, Interactive PR is now among the first considerations of people who are looking to build a lasting online presence.

The press room

Because the company website, which hosts the information source for the media, is in so many cases the responsibility of a department other than Public Relations, its effectiveness with the media is very poor. In many surveys, journalists criticize company information websites as being irrelevant, more concerned with fancy graphics than the basic information and illustrations that are being sought by working reporters.

So the first step for the most senior PR executive in the organization is to achieve control of the press room or online media center.

Once a PR professional gains control of the contents of his client's or company's online press room, he must address the components of the section. Although circumstances may dictate slight variations, every corporate press room should include the following:

- Press releases posted at the same time they are distributed on newswires
- A search engine covering all information in the press room (including the most current releases)
- High-resolution photographs of the company's products and senior executives
- High-resolution digital renditions of the company's brands and logos
- Executive biographies, including recent speeches and presentations

- Investor information such as analyst presentations, quarterly earnings releases, 10-K filings and annual reports. These can also be included in a separate investor relations section and linked to the online press room.
- Corporate history and related background materials (for example, information about the company's copyrights, registered trademarks and service marks and their proper use in print media)
- White papers and other public documents providing more details about a company's philosophies, products, services or approaches to a market
- Information about a company's civic and charitable activities
- The mailing address and general telephone number (not the toll-free customer service line) of the company's headquarters and overseas subsidiaries (not the regional sales offices)
- The contact information (name, telephone number, e-mail address) of a public relations representative for every country where the company does significant business

Disseminating corporate news

There are a variety of tactics a company can implement today to decrease further its reliance on traditional media placements and paper-based press materials. In each case they have a common component: They are distributed online:

1. **Opt-in press release distribution:** Visitors to an online press room should be able to provide a company with their e-mail address to receive a copy of the company's press releases at the same time they are distributed on the wire services. This allows journalists to elect to receive these e-mails without someone contacting them first to gain their permission. It also allows other interested parties to receive the information in real time directly from the company.
2. **Electronic press kits, newsletters, brochures, reminders** are now used to maintain relationships with the media in the same way that sales and marketing CRM (Customer Relationship Management) have long used direct response vehicles for existing customers and prospects.
3. **Webcasts:** The technology for "streaming" audio and video through the Internet improves every day. Costs of producing, storing and streaming these files are on the decline, and this will pave the way for broader uptake. We look forward to a day when full-motion video will be as common as MP3 music files on the web. Companies do not have to wait

for this to take advantage of online video today. Any corporate site can benefit from developing and implementing an online video strategy today, and this could be as simple as including the company's most current television advertisements in their online press room, instead of forcing journalists to go to third-party aggregators of this content.

Monitoring news and newsgroups

Every "public" company (i.e., corporations whose stock is traded by the public on an exchange) is the subject of several dozen online newsgroups, forums, bulletin boards, investment "clubs," chat rooms and other messaging services that allow anyone anonymously to post their opinions about any aspect of the company, including its products, its employees, its past, its future prospects and its overall viability as an investment.

There are similar message forums for industries like retailing and fashion that also cover "private" companies, as well as "sound off" boards run by magazines. There are websites for prospective employees where existing employees can post their opinions about what it's like to work for a company. Trade unions, suppliers and online exchanges also offer online messaging services for their customers and/or members.

More recently, there have been dozens of websites launched that track companies simply to make fun of their foibles by encouraging people to post outrageous rumors, not to mention "confidential" e-mails, memoranda and marketing plans. Some of these sites are among the most popular destinations on the Internet.

Every newspaper, magazine and television network has its own website, many of them staffed separately from their paper and broadcast equivalents, and many of them updated continuously versus once or twice a day.

There are also thousands of online-only news sources, many of which are run exclusively by individuals who answer to no one but themselves and perhaps their advertisers, if they even have any.

In some cases, these "unofficial" news sources (and who's to say what constitutes "official" media in an era where owning a printing press or a broadcast tower is no longer a criterion for entering the market?) have superseded the offline equivalents in terms of being the first to report exclusive stories of historical importance like President Bill Clinton's sexual affair with Monica Lewinsky.

Others don't "play by the rules" established in the offline world, such as sites where moviegoers who attend an advance screening of an unreleased movie can post a review months before the official premiere.

Love them or hate them, it is critical for a company's public relations agency to track and monitor each and every one of these messaging and online media sites in real time using a monitoring software application that gives account teams instant access from any web browser to the latest news articles and newsgroup postings.

The extranet

Extranets – an extended interactive website to all members of a public relations team in a company, at its various locations and its agencies and suppliers – is the best-practice method of facilitating multinational communications strategy and programming.

Public relations extranets include three core components:

1. A database of documents such as press release drafts, executive biographies and product spec sheets
2. A calendar of account activities
3. A contact list for all account team members

These features can be supplemented by:

- Real-time news feeds
- Real-time newsgroup monitoring results
- Links to media placement results
- Message boards, online conferencing and instant messaging applications
- Conference collaboration tools such as virtual whiteboards
- Scrolling message alerts
- Media lists
- Editorial calendars
- PR program measurement and account activity reports
- Links to relevant online resources, including media sites, industry associations and competitors
- Lists of approved outside vendors for specialized projects
- Private webcasts of client meetings and announcements

Extranets provide both the agency's account teams and their client contacts, with real-time access to everything, the need to successfully implement a public relations campaign, both traditional and interactive.

And the efficiencies can be tremendous. Instead of faxing versions of a press release for approval, or sending it as an attachment to an e-mail, clients can simply download the most current version from the extranet, then upload a revised or approved version as soon as it's ready. Team members can get everything they need to run an account while traveling or working at home. Every office has the same ability to access key documents without being connected through a cumbersome local area network. Directions to the company's various offices, today's media hits, product photographs – the extranet provides a level of functionality that would not have been possible five years ago.

Knowledge management

Smart software, combined with the Internet, enables knowledge management to take over the role of the person who exists in every organization – the keeper of the history, who also knows who can answer any question. What's more, a well thought out and constructed knowledge management system will be even better than that one person because it will be 24/7, more comprehensive, the result of *shared* input and available on a *shared* basis, and will live on when the older member of the organization departs, dies or begins to suffer from a failing memory.

A study by IMT Strategies and the US Council of PR Firms concluded that the PR industry is not leveraging Internet technology as effectively as other industries. Clients ranked the ability to adopt technology as more important than agencies. The case for knowledge management to be a primary element of the infrastructure of any agency or PR department is clear. Knowledge is surely the *only* stock-in-trade of the PR practitioner and should therefore be valued and nurtured as nothing else. Of great importance in any organization selling a single product in a single market, the importance of knowledge management is magnified by the matrix of multi-product, multinational corporations and the agencies that serve them.

There are many good definitions of knowledge management and it is too big and complicated a subject to deal with here, but for most PR purposes, I would like to suggest that knowledge management is the combination of shared *data* and *experience* organized into learnings that can be applied to planning and executing future programs.

Kay Bransford of Vocus, which specializes in developing knowledge management tools for PR practitioners, says:

"Using knowledge management enables your organization to understand:

- What you already know;
- How to create value from what you already know;
- How to respond to the information needs of your key publics and the media."

She points out that corporations have already adopted tools for knowledge management when it comes to dealing with their customers (CRM or Customer Relationship Management) as well as for attracting new clients (SFA or Sales Force Automation). These can be, and are being, adapted to Client Relationship Management and Media Relationship Management models for use by PR agencies and client organizations.

Most of the component fields of knowledge that need to be organized, catalogued and referenced are dealt with elsewhere in this book. There are two broad categories of knowledge: Proprietary and Public knowledge.

Proprietary knowledge management

Proprietary knowledge management encompasses the following:

Document Registry: This is vital for all global organizations with a "global voice" policy. It will contain all approved materials in one place – all press releases, key messages and programs, white papers, biographies, photographs, names of spokespeople and so on. The information must be easy to locate on an intranet or extranet as described earlier.

Transaction Repository: A place where every call to every media and influence contact is noted so that knowledge of what particular journalists are interested in – or not – can be shared among a wider community of colleagues.

Coverage Repository: This venue for historical reporting on the organization by media of importance to you can be a vital element of planning future media initiatives.

Case Studies: The reservoir of knowledge of any organization, but especially the PR agencies, lies in its case studies or past work knowledge gained through practical experience. It is vital these studies are carefully prepared and cross referenced to "pop up" when needed in credentials presentations and for planning future programs which can benefit from the learnings achieved.

Biographies: In addition to having the standard bios of key management and PR staff members, agencies and multinational corporations should install a database of staff experience and capabilities. In the event, for example, that you are called upon to find a person with previous experience in the petroleum industry, who could speak English, French and Arabic fluently and had no family ties that would prevent him from traveling at short notice, this bio-database should deliver the name or names of candidates.

Public knowledge management

Knowledge management does not begin and end with proprietary information and for most PR practitioners the huge body of knowledge available from public sources can be even more important. The range of information is far too wide to describe but will include previous coverage from Lexis/Nexis or other databases on specific organizations or topics; websites and chat groups devoted to specific topics; libraries; case study files of the IPRA, PRSA, IPR and other public relations societies; media databases and manuals, and Internet search engines.

Concludes Bransford of Vocus, "The knowledge management system must be available 24/7, just as we are. Now, organizations can adopt a knowledge management system with all the features that are needed without requiring a huge IT investment because of the growth of the Internet. The emergence of the application server providers who distribute the hardware and support load across thousands of users for a lower cost of ownership have been able to bring a robust system to the public relations community. All the user needs is an Internet connection and a browser."

Search engine optimization

No interactive effort will achieve anything like its full potential without a strong commitment to search engine optimization because, as Nancy Ruscheinski says, "You can't market to somebody who can't find you. Remember, 80 percent of Internet users access web content through a search engine or directory for their 280 million searches per day."

These are tips she gives for PR professionals to optimize search engine positioning:

- Smart site design and meta tag usage
- Proper submission to directories and engines
- Identify and accommodate popular search phrases
- Understand and utilize newer options like goto.com (bid for placement)
- Increase and improve quality of inbound links

Viral marketing

The all powerful "word-of-mouth" message sought by marketers is now in heavy use as "word-of-e-mail," according to Ruscheinski. "In viral marketing you get an exponentially multiplying impact for your message. You encourage people to tell their friends, refer their friends and to send a message or offer on to their friends and family." This has now spawned a large number of variants and is a true example of the interactive power of the net! The illustration overleaf shows how EIS deployed viral marketing for Acuvue contact lenses.

Online promotions & partnerships

Budweiser's "Whazzup" campaign translated from a TV advertising campaign to a viral marketing campaign through digitizing the commercial and sending it through e-mail, in turn creating a "craze" on the Internet and adding long-lasting arms and legs to the program.

Online promotions and partnerships leverage the power of the Internet to communicate a targeted message to your client's stakeholders, drive them to interact with their brand and develop a one-to-one ongoing relationship with them. Examples of online promotion include:

- Opt-in/permission e-mail marketing campaigns
- Online contests, sweepstakes and giveaways
- Search engine optimization campaigns (described earlier)

Establishing credibility has long been a core strategy of traditional public relations. Whether it is achieved through using a spokesperson, forming a partnership with an industry association or a third party endorsement, credibility instills a feeling of trust and assurance in the consumer about a brand. The Internet allows you to leverage a partnership to speak to a global audience and to introduce a highly qualified audience to your brand through content or editorial. The online environment also offers a new opportunity to communicate with Internet-formed grassroots communities through creating partnerships, or an affiliate network. Ways to use partnerships online to achieve PR goals are the following:

- Use a spokesperson in a chat or webcast online tour.
- Place content or editorial on a heavily trafficked site where you know your target market is already interacting.

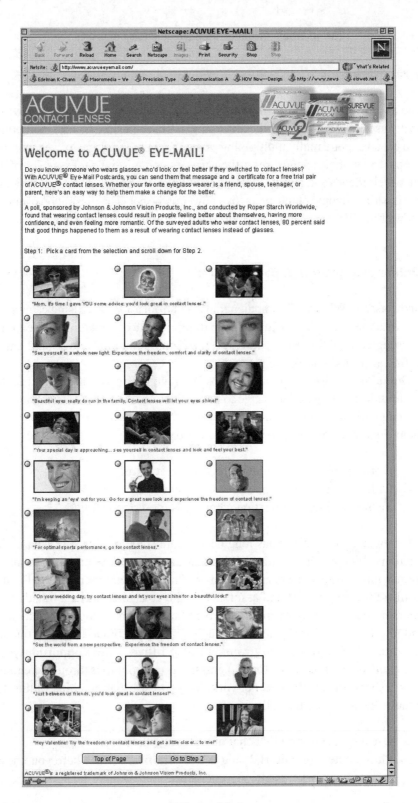

Chart 12.1

- Place a link to a reputable organization on your site to increase credibility.
- Trade links with grassroots-level sites. This will increase brand awareness among community-level sites of the Internet.

Communications management

In the all-important business of media relations it used to be said there are three key elements: contacts, a good list and a fine news sense.

Now contacts are known as connections or, more often, relationships. News sense, or the ability by instinct to know (or to package) a story that will grab an editor's attention, remains a vital quality. And the media list has now grown up into a database.

Here once more technology and the Internet have turbo-charged the ability of the PR practitioner to manage in a knowledgeable way all his dealings with the media, as well as all the other targets that he may wish to influence such as legislators, regulators, investors, industry and financial analysts, NGOs, etc. Communications management is the term coined by John Pearce of Media Map, a company that for 15 years has been developing database and automation systems, primarily to the larger agencies, by adapting the well-known elements of customer relationship management (CRM) to provide the PR practitioner with three important tools.

- Relationship Management – enhancing the creation and maintenance of each individual relationship in the PR universe, elevating the quality of relationships with key constituencies, the productivity with which staffs manage those relationships, and the service individuals receive.
- Distribution Management – efficient, integrated communications capabilities that ensure delivery of information via the medium preferred by each contact, with clear reporting on communications history and projects.
- Performance Management – integrated analytics and reporting that provide management with real time visibility into project status, campaign impact, qualitative assessments, and results history to manage present projects and enhance campaign planning and ROI.

In this new era, according to Pearce, the Communications Management system will be ubiquitous: Every manager, staff person, and client executive will have instant desktop and global laptop and wireless access to the system, integrating the work of the agency and the client across multiple geographies

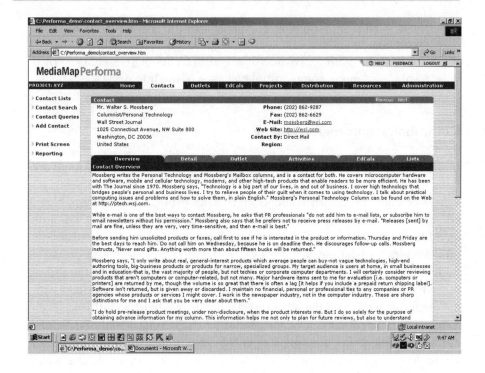

Chart 12.2

into powerful, effective teams. The system will support unified project management, with every team's activities logged and visible to account and agency management, and every new interaction coordinated worldwide. The system will be truly global, with integration of worldwide media databases that may be reliably outsourced, yet fully customizable, and including the widening range of non-media PR constituencies.

Financial reporting

It is important that any PR practitioner in a global or multinational corporation be fully conversant with the regulations covering financial disclosure in his own market as well as those of the US Securities and Exchange Commission (SEC) which makes the rules for Wall Street. Although most of the world's major corporations now need Wall Street as an important source of their capital, they are excluded from the most recent Fair Disclosure regulation of the SEC issued in 2000. However, the free market will favor those companies that play by the rules even if they are not obliged to do so.

This most recent Regulation FD (Fair Disclosure) provides that when an issuer, or person acting on its behalf, discloses material nonpublic information to certain enumerated persons (in general, securities market professionals and holders of the issuer's securities who may well trade on the basis of the information), it must make public disclosure of that information. The media is not included in the list of "certain enumerated persons." In short, everyone should receive information in the proper form at the same time and this is where use of the Internet is invaluable.

According to Mark White of Mainsail, "The biggest change wrought by Reg FD is the outright prohibition of invitation-only quarterly earnings teleconferences with a company's favorite Wall Street analysts. This has led to an explosion of Internet-enabled conferencing strategies that allow anyone with a browser at least to listen in, if not actively participate in these sessions by posing questions directly to senior management. Some companies also feel the same approach must now be used for press conferences."

CHAPTER 13

The Infrastructure of your Organization

Finding the right structure for a PR department is one of the hardest tasks facing the head of communications in a global corporation.

And when you think you have a superb plan with all your personnel needs identified and a really workable structure laid out on paper, you are still at the bottom of the mountain.

I learned this when I was asked to analyze the existing PR structures and resources and assess future needs at the Basel headquarters of Hoffman La Roche. At the end I was expected to prepare a plan and present it to the then chairman, Mr. Fritz Gerber.

In addition to the extraordinarily interesting professional challenges presented by undertaking this assignment for one of the world's most successful companies with a pronounced corporate culture, the arrangements made to enable me to conduct my work efficiently added an extra layer of interest.

The assignment called for my presence "on site" to conduct interviews with board members and senior management. I also had to observe the PR operations in action and conduct a communications audit of all materials produced. To do this, I was provided with the office of Dr. Adolf W. Jann, Mr. Gerber's predecessor as chairman. It was of a size and furnished in the manner that you might expect for one of Switzerland's leading companies, which at the time boasted the world record share price and produced the top selling drug, Valium. A single Roche share was worth close to US$100,000.

The windows gave onto a courtyard where a gleaming white Henry Moore sculpture sat resplendent on a manicured green lawn with perfect edges. This was testimony indeed to a long line of effective and financially rewarding medications produced by the company which spent more on its research and development than any other pharmaceutical company.

Working from the retired chairman's office immediately signaled to everyone within Roche that the work I was doing was of the highest importance. All doors were open and I was given full cooperation in my task.

It was, however, a somewhat eerie experience. To work from Dr. Jann's office was one thing. But it was exactly as he had left it. His pencils and pens on the desk. His books on the shelves. Various gifts and souvenirs on the occasional tables. Photos of his family on the desk and shelves. At first I felt an impostor, but as no one else, including the secretarial staff in this exclusive office area where the top directors worked, thought anything of it, I soon got used to it and it became my temporary "home."

On completion of my study, a meeting was arranged with Mr. Gerber, the chairman. He listened attentively, his sharp intellect somehow advertised in his eyes, as I described the structure I proposed Roche adopt to handle corporate communications in the future. My recommendations had carefully written job descriptions for each of the important positions and the whole plan was illustrated by the necessary organization chart (organigram, as it is known in most European countries), with a solitary box at the top of the Christmas tree for the Head of Corporate Communications.

Mr. Gerber peered at this intently and then asked a single question: "Who has this position?"

I replied by saying we needed to hire that person and then outlined the qualifications needed and the briefing that I had written for the executive search. It was a top job and needed a Renaissance man (or woman).

Mr. Gerber closed the meeting: "Let me meet that person when you have found him and I will tell you if the whole thing will work, or not."

Of course he was right. In a profession such as public relations, the human factor is all-important. A technically correct organizational structure is doomed if it has the wrong person at the pinnacle. But then, that is true of any organization, military unit or government department.

It is just as true that a superb leader of a major company's corporate communications needs a structured team if he is to accomplish anything worthwhile.

So assuming that Mr. Gerber – or your own CEO – thinks that he has the right leader for corporate communications, what kind of departmental organization structure is "best practice" and what size should it be? What kind of talents should the employees have? Where should they be located? What reporting lines are solid and what are "dotted line"?

There may be studies and reports on this but they cannot possibly be conclusive. In my experience the range of sizes and structures among various companies is so wide and disparate that they do not lead you to any kind of "norm."

Big vs. modest

At one end of the scale stands a company like AT&T before 1996, when a major staff reduction program got under way. The public relations department had over 800 employees, 8 with the title of vice president or higher, more than

25 with the title director and 600 or 630 with the title manager. The majority were based in the United States. One wag was heard to suggest that the media be notified of a new toll free (Freephone) number with which to get information from the company – 1–800 ATT PROS.

This number of people reflected a commitment to public relations by the company, which had started decades earlier when it was the cornerstone of the Bell Telephone System, of which the legendary Arthur Page was director of public relations from 1927 to 1946. Communications with its customers, the public, the communities it served and the lawmakers whose understanding and votes were needed to expand telephony were a top priority in the company. While 800 PR staffers might seem a huge number to some who are trying to manage with a very small department, it only represented one PR person for 100,000 customers, a ratio that is exceeded by many other companies. Moreover, AT&T had a philosophy rooted in its history as a public service utility, which demanded (by law, as well a simple business judgment) onerous obligations for disclosure, dialogue and public debate.

At the other end of the spectrum, there are a few companies like United Parcel Service which has twice as many employees as AT&T and half the revenues, and which manages its global public relations with a team of no more than 16 executives in-house, not including those involved in employee communications and public affairs. And no less than 10 years ago, before the 85-year-old company undertook its twin initiatives of modernization and globalization, it had fewer than half a dozen PR officers and no agency of record.

Both companies augment their department with the assistance of PR agencies.

There is little point in suggesting that the ideal size for a PR department is 408 people (the average of the total staffs of those two companies). That would be nonsense. But it is surprising to me how many people believe there is a model department that can be taken off the shelf and will fit any company with some minor alterations.

There are, however, some basic principles, a few alternatives and different combinations of resources.

The trick is to fit the structure to your own needs after you have analyzed them carefully. No one model is necessarily better than another. But it might be a better fit and therefore work better for you.

The functional model

The functional structure is probably the original model for major corporations, quite commonly in use in the 1950s–1970s and still to be found in quite a number of companies. This model (see chart 13.1) usually features a single executive who is responsible for all company communications, which he undertakes with the assistance of various functional departments. There might be a press officer whose sole duties are the production of press releases and contact with the media. Sometimes that assignment is kept in the hands of the senior officer and the press officer is only concerned with the production of the news material and its distribution.

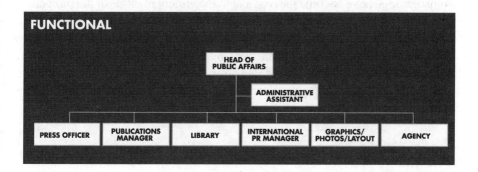

Chart 13.1

The arrangement is quite usual in Europe where the major companies have executives nominated to the position of "speaker or spokesman." The spokesman issues company statements and gives comments. In the unofficial links with the media, journalists know that only the "spokesman's" comments can be quoted as the company's official viewpoint, even though they may have gleaned information from others in the company. This arrangement can also be seen at work in various government institutions where the spokesman gives the daily briefing on important matters.

A second unit is a publications department, which is often under the management of a person with a journalistic background. Here are written and produced the various documents any company needs: employee magazines and newsletters, customer newsletters, the annual report, brochures etc.

Sometimes linked to the publications department, but often separate, is a graphics production unit which might maintain a studio of commercial graphic artists, photographers (with darkroom), film cameramen and videographers. There is the ability in such units to produce finished art and occasionally there is the addition of an in-house printing facility able to produce to a high standard and in some quantity.

A library, or archive, is also maintained to store the materials produced.

If the company operates internationally, there is usually an international PR officer charged with the task of working with the international media, usually through local press officers in the subsidiaries or their locally hired agencies.

An agency is invariably retained in such structures because a strong production capability is not always matched by a strong general or specialist counseling capability and the wider pool of skills among agency executives can be called upon as needed.

This functional model has become outdated as "headcount reduction" and "outsourcing" have become the magical management mantras of the moment. Moreover, with the high speed at which technology has changed the production processes of graphic design and artwork, printing and cinematography, most companies do not want to risk equipment investments which might be outdated the day they are installed. Most countries have now spawned a host of large and small organizations specialized in each of these production techniques and their services can be contracted at excellent prices.

The quadrant

It is the dream of a serious and ambitious public relations practitioner to be directly responsible for the management of what I describe as the Communications Quadrant.

The Communications Quadrant is shown in the illustration 13.2 which also indicates the function in which the communications representative is most usually based and his direct line reporting. In most corporations today, he will have a greater or lesser degree of input on all four sections, depending on the character and territoriality of other members of the executive board.

In some companies, all the communications executives in each quadrant report directly to the chief communications officer (CCO) or head of public relations and have a dotted line relationship with the managers of the staff departments concerned (chart 13.3).

In such a model the CCO reports directly to the CEO of the company and will almost certainly be a member of the executive committee or board of the company, along with the general counsel or chief legal officer, the chief financial officer, the head of marketing and the head of human resources.

This schematic is, however, quite rare in my experience. More common is a structure in which the most senior public relations professional reports to the CEO, and maintains a close relationship with him and in the decision-making processes of the management committee. But he will have only a very small staff reporting to him – and sometimes no staff at all beyond a personal assistant. The people in charge of each branch of communications report directly

THE COMMUNICATIONS QUADRANT

Chart 13.2

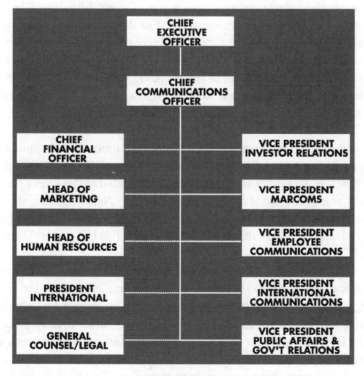

Chart 13.3

to the senior officer of each function. Thus, the vice president of investor relations is directly employed by the chief financial officer but will maintain a dotted line reporting relationship with the chief communications officer.

Study of 100 companies

A major benchmarking survey, conducted in 1997 by Edelman Public Relations Worldwide, the Medill School of Journalism and Opinion Research Corporation, sheds some light on how companies organize themselves to handle corporate communications. One hundred international companies participated. Here are some of the more interesting findings about reporting lines and infrastructure:

- Of the top communications officials 60 percent are at the vice president/vice chairman level. Nearly 2 in 10 hold the title of director, and 1 in 10 are senior vice presidents. The remaining 13 percent hold the following titles: manager (8 percent), corporate vice president (3 percent) and executive vice president (2 percent).
- The senior-most communicators report directly to the CEO at 54 percent of the companies surveyed. For those communicators who do not report directly to the CEO, 30 percent report to the vice president, senior vice president or vice chair level of the organization.
- Regardless of direct lines of reporting, 93 percent, nearly two-thirds of the most senior communicators, counsel with the CEO at least weekly and 15 percent counsel with the CEO on a daily basis.

Although survey respondents reported a variety of functional communications areas for which senior-most communicators are primarily responsible, the core public relations functions are much better represented at this senior level than are other areas such as advertising or marketing. Nearly one-third of these senior-most communicators have corporate communications as their primary functional responsibility, followed by public relations (16 percent) and public affairs (12 percent).

The range of specific functions which fall under the corporate communications umbrella is becoming more diverse. More than 4 in 10 report that corporate communications maintains final oversight for advertising, marketing and promotional activities. Surprisingly, more than 10 percent are also directly responsible for customer service at their respective organizations.

Nearly 9 in 10 respondents indicate the use of external communications agencies at corporate headquarters, with more than 7 in 10 also using external

CORPORATE COMMUNICATIONS RESPONSIBILITIES

Media Relations	99%
Crisis/Issues Management	93%
Employee Communications	88%
Corporate Identity/Image	83%
Financial Communications/Investor Relations	75%
Research & Measurement	75%
Community Relations/Corporate Philanthropy	74%
Advertising, Marketing & Promotions	43%
Government Affairs	35%
Customer Service	11%

Chart 13.4

agencies at the discretion of each business unit. Further, more than 5 in 10 also employ external communications agencies within their various geographic regions. Only 5 percent do not use outside communications agencies.

Overall, the annual operation budget (excluding salaries) for corporate communications activities was reported as follows:

GLOBAL CORPORATE COMMUNICATIONS BUDGET

[US$ equivalent]:	
Less than $1 million	25%
greater than $1 million, but less than $5 million	39%
greater than $5 million, but less than $10 million	11%
greater than $11 million, but less than $15 million	4%
greater than $20 million	15%

Chart 13.5

It is customary for most companies to draw a clear line between communications in the "home country" of operations and in international operations, with one person assigned to be responsible for management of communications in non-domestic markets.

This rule is true for most multinationals, whether the home base is in the UK, USA, Germany, Switzerland, Sweden, Netherlands or France.

It has yet to be seen if this will change as some multinationals aspire to grow into global corporations and the distinctions between domestic and foreign markets disappear.

Separate role for international PR

Meantime there are good practical reasons why the separate role of the international PR manager within corporations continues to exist:

- Most companies have a long history in their own communities and know their way around the local and national media, the influential groups important for the business, their political representatives and their customers. They are less certain of themselves in their overseas markets, which vary widely in almost every respect. An international PR manager who makes it his business to be knowledgeable about these markets and can manage a network of widely dispersed PR representatives is worth his weight in gold.
- As a rule, the chief communications officer at corporate HQ has to be intensely involved in certain aspects of his function that are of lesser importance overseas. Investor relations might be necessary in various markets where the company's stock is listed and traded but it remains essentially something that is conducted from HQ. It is still true that the large majority of shares of even the most global companies are owned by people in the "home" country. Similarly, human resources and regulatory affairs have a heightened importance in the home market of most companies, which means that unless there is a senior person responsible for the international component and an active advocate for action, the pressures of the home market can leave international communications as the Cinderella.
- While the home market pressures place its needs uppermost in the minds of top management in many countries, it is especially the case with many American corporations. This is not just tradition or a way of thinking, it is also a matter of size. The average major corporation in the USA (excluding public utilities which have traditionally served local communities) is likely to have 80 percent of its sales in its home market, a factor of its great population, wealth and appetite for consumption. For the Swiss or Dutch multinational, the motto "export or die" (or, more likely nowadays, "establish overseas subsidiaries to make and sell") is apt. In both cases the home market is likely to represent less than 10 percent of the potential. So the need for the smaller nations to achieve the right formula for overseas communications is that much greater.
- The qualifications of the international PR manager might be quite different from those of an executive who needs only to operate in the home market. Some of these qualities are described in chapter 1.

Briefly, he will need to be culturally aware, patient, open-minded and inquisitive about alien customs and government procedures, with the ability to work with people from a variety of nations.

■ At the same time, the international executive must never become detached from the "mother company" and totally concentrate on the non-domestic operations. One vital role is to act as a bridge to the PR staff overseas who need and rely on him to be their link to headquarters, the conduit of policies and news. Never underestimate how most employees who work a great distance from headquarters feel starved of information. Finally, he is the coach and inspiration who transmits that most indefinable but, arguably, most important element: the corporate culture.

PR aligns with main structure

The public relations organizational structure must be aligned with the main management structure of the business.

If there is a total devolution of authority to national operating units, the PR arrangements must reflect this. If the company manages through a highly disciplined network of regional control centers, which in turn manage the national operating units, then the PR department should provide a matching interface. If most authority is centralized at headquarters, PR will follow suit.

Given a general business trend in which companies break the world into geographic regions, it is now very common for PR departments to organize along the same lines. The organization of the world into trading blocs (e.g. the European Union, North American Free Trade Agreement, Association of South East Asian Nations) along with the wish to keep costs down by doing certain tasks at a regional level rather than many times over at national level, are just two of the factors driving this trend.

A typical regional structure is shown in chart 13.6.

In practice, the VP of international public relations usually maintains a close liaison with the regional PR directors and may well have been the most important person in their selection. For geographical and structural reasons in most companies, the direct reporting line is to the regional general manager, or his appointee; at the operational level, dual management exists. The same slightly blurred reporting lines exist between the regional PR director and the country PR manager (or agency), which is really in the front line of the action. In this case and almost every case where consumer products companies are concerned, the solid line is usually with the general manager of the operating subsidiary.

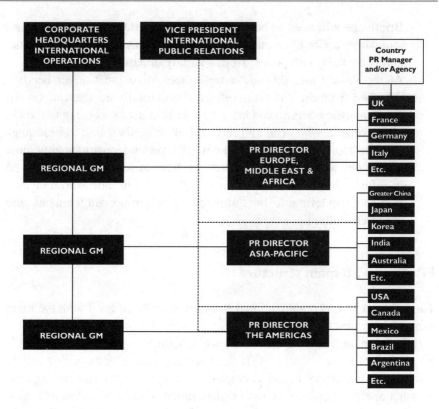

Chart 13.6

Agency support

The idea that companies make a choice between installing an in-house PR system or using a consultancy/agency is no longer valid.

The majority of companies nowadays combine external and internal resources. Of those responding to the Edelman/Medill/ORC benchmarking survey, 95 percent said they retained agencies to work in concert with internal staff.

Companies which started their international expansion early and had established a network of overseas subsidiaries began to recognize the importance of public relations in the early 1960s, some time after they had established a system to handle their international advertising needs. This was one reason why, in the case of the major American corporations, public relations usually started as a service outgrowth from their (American-owned) advertising agencies. The advertising agencies served clients whose creative work – the advertisements themselves – was identical in every market around the world, save for a change of language. Tampax was one such company, and the policy seems to have worked. The negative side was that the ad agency's subsidiaries in the various markets had nothing to do other than to place the order for ad space and deliver the artwork which had been prepared in New York.

Many of the ad agency networks that are now huge worldwide operations thus built their networks on the commissions earned from their home-based clients, going into local markets to serve their needs.

The pattern established by the Americans in the sixties was later emulated by the Europeans (Saatchi & Saatchi), starting with their stable of loyal British clients, and the Japanese (Dentsu), with their marquee brand names. Each of the ad agency networks spawned or bought a PR agency to fill out the service offering to their clients.

However, until recently, advertising agencies have not shown themselves to have been successful as managers of PR operations.

In other cases an enormous degree of autonomy was conferred on the local subsidiary, which selected its own advertising – and PR – agency or exercised total control over the work of the corporate agency branch in the local country.

In some cases the independence was so extreme that brand and corporate identities of certain companies grew far apart and lost strength.

Over the years six basic agency relationship structures have become the most commonly used.

The worldwide agency of record

For many clients – not to mention agencies – the ideal relationship they seek to achieve is one in which there is a single agency retained. The agency has to provide an identical match of skills at the corporate head office and in each of the worldwide markets in which the client company operates.

In the mature commercial world that now exists, companies seeking to make such an arrangement will almost certainly have a great deal of tidying up to do, dismantling myriad individual agency relationships that have grown up over the years.

The advantages sought by the clients that want to go this route are:

- Size, which will bring a high level of commitment by the agency, access to its top talent and a readiness on the part of the agency to invest in areas of importance to the client, but that otherwise might not have been a priority.
- Exclusivity. A financially sizable multi-faceted relationship will provide the client with leverage to assure the agency is not available in any place to serve the client's competitors.

- Efficient contact procedures. If the agency provides a limited number of points of contact and undertakes to manage the day-to-day aspects of the programs, the client has relieved himself of a huge amount of work.
- Budget control and centralized billing. If the system works well, administrative time for the client and his staff working through bills from a large number of different agencies, all presented in different formats, will be avoided.
- Staff management. When things go wrong, as they undoubtedly will from time to time, or when a member of the agency staff is not performing adequately, the problem can be raised centrally, saving the client the unpleasant task of seeking to make a personnel change with a local agency manager.

Although such a global agency-of-record relationship might seem like nirvana for the chief corporate communications officer of a global enterprise, it is also fraught with problems of implementation.

- Gaps on the map and in PR specialties. There are few agencies that can offer clients matching global coverage in all their markets although a single handful, my own among them, are represented in the principal business centers of the world. If the geographic spread is adequate, the expertise in specialist PR skills – Public Affairs, Investor Relations, Marketing Communications – might have some blank spots. Even if all these factors show up well on the first screening, it will be the greatest good luck if the agency is completely free from potential conflicts. The client might also find that he is not equally impressed with the agency's capabilities or creativity in all markets or specialties.
- Inadequate strategic competence and coordination. Although the agency might demonstrate to the client sufficient dots on the map and experts in all the specialist fields of importance, the "chemistry" and added-value judgment provided by the top client service manager may be considered lacking; there might be real difficulties in getting the agency groups to work effectively as a team – among themselves and with the client.

If for any of these reasons it seems undesirable for client or agency to establish a global relationship, then a number of alternatives are available, and in today's marketplace for PR they are in the majority.

Strategy and core program development

It is now quite usual in the pharmaceutical and technology sectors for global companies to engage the services of a PR agency to develop core programs for the world launch or roll-out of new products.

The work product is a detailed plan (not unlike an architect's blueprint for a new building). The client and its retained agencies in various markets, or agencies hired for the specific project, implement the plan with adaptation in markets around the world. The selection of the local agencies is the responsibility of the local subsidiary or affiliate of the client. The local office of the agency, if it has the necessary skills, is usually on the selection short list. In such cases, full responsibility for the management and coordination of the program is firmly in the hands of the client company. It can mean that many agencies which are highly competitive with each other are required to work in harmony.

Agencies with regional responsibilities

Some clients are now forging agency relationships based on regional responsibilities. They feel that, although it might be impossible to find a single agency that can serve their needs worldwide, they can make exclusive arrangements region by region, with perhaps one agency responsible for strategic development and core programs.

For example, the giant Korean chaebol (conglomerate) Samsung has gone this route. Its corporate PR agency of record in Japan is Hakuhodo, in Europe Golin Harris and in the other regions of the Americas and South East Asia the agency is Edelman Worldwide.

The piebald network

There are many instances of clients that are very nearly able to establish a full worldwide network in partnership with an agency and a compromise is reached in which a minority of network offices are drawn from independent local firms or the local branch of a multinational agency. There can be any number of reasons for this, including the following. An otherwise strong international agency might have a few weak spots in markets of importance to the client; it is mutually agreed that, if the agency cannot strengthen its operation, the client is best served by seeking alternative counsel and assistance. It might be that the global agency has no representation in a market; or the client company has an excellent historical relationship with a local agency which it wishes to continue. In such circumstances, I believe that most reputable global agencies welcome the addition of the "non-family" agencies into the network and soon operate quite well as a team.

The cherry-picked network

Some senior international PR practitioners favor the so-called "cherry picking" method of agency selection to form an international network. In fashion in the 1950s and 1960s, this ideal-sounding way of selecting the best candidate agency in each market and forming a superb network is much harder now, and is fraught with landmines.

First, it places a huge burden of time, responsibility and administration on the client's most senior communications professional, in an era of drastically reduced PR department manpower. Few now have the chance to tour the world in leisurely fashion, interviewing candidate firms.

Second, the chances are strong that a well-established local firm will be eliminated through conflict.

Fine local firms are also candidates for acquisition, and many client companies which have "cherry picked" a network with great success find that it is short-lived; a local agency is often bought or merged with another, which changes the relationship and might even end it if the merger partner serves a rival client.

The agency implant

There is one other option to be considered when structuring a public relations department and network, and that is an agency implant or executive on loan.

This was a service model pioneered by Carl Byoir in the years immediately following the end of World War II and was hugely successful, propelling his agency into becoming the largest in America. Instead of serving clients from staff largely based in the agency premises and working on more than one client engagement at a time, Byoir assigned executives to clients on a full-time basis and situated them at the clients' offices. The arrangement almost guaranteed that Byoir came out with a profit and that the client received a specified level of service. The implant system is gaining in favor once again, but for different reasons. In the strange world of corporate logic, a budget for an agency might be tight but funds might be found to support a contracted executive who cannot be hired as an employee, with agency profit margin built in.

The loaned executive is also an ideal solution for engagements which are known in advance to be short, and adding to the permanent staff would make no sense.

Other instances in which implants are useful are when a member of the permanent staff leaves and it will take time to find a replacement; or when a staffer must take a leave of absence for health reasons. In such cases, the agency might be able to assign an executive fully experienced in that client's program, who could step into the breach and fill the position on a temporary basis.

CHAPTER 14

The Public Relations Agency

The public relations consultancy business (or counseling, as it is known in the USA) is one of the fastest-growing businesses. There is every prospect that this growth will continue.

Just consider: the world's ten biggest PR firms in 1990 recorded fee income of $910 million, according to O'Dwyer's Directory of PR Firms. Ten years later the top ten fee income had risen to $2.508 billion, as reported by the Council of PR Firms and published in *PR Week*.

"The astonishing growth of the PR business over the last decade has not been confined to the US and UK," says Stephen Farish, managing director of *PR Week*. "Similar growth rates have been achieved in major markets like France and Germany, and also in developing markets like Asia and Latin America, albeit from a lower base."

"The fact that *PR Week* now has editions in the UK, USA, Germany and Asia is another sign of how the PR industry has become a global phenomenon in recent years. We see that growth continuing and consolidating in the years ahead, even though the heady increases of 2000 may not be repeated."

A massive consolidation of the largest PR agencies took place as the twentieth century came to a close and continued at the beginning of the twenty-first. Larger agencies continued to acquire smaller ones as the principal agency networks sought to flesh out their service to clients geographically and by specialty practice. To this a phenomenon new to the world of public relations – but which had been seen in the world of advertising for many years – was added: A series of acquisitions that has created the formation of three global super-groups, each comprising several agency networks or brands. Omnicom agencies combined to record $810 million, Interpublic $708 million and WPP $844 million in fees for the year 2000, in the Council's rankings. These new groupings have made bedfellows of previously fierce competitors such as Hill & Knowlton and Burson-Marsteller, now both owned by WPP, the British-based communications conglomerate.

Chart 14.2 shows the principal brands in each of these new super-groups.

WORLDWIDE TOP 10 FEE INCOME		
RANK	FIRM NAME	WORLDWIDE 2000
1	Fleishman Hillard	$ 342,840,620
2	Weber Shandwick Worldwide	334,960,755
3	Hill & Knowlton	306,264,000
4	Burson-Marsteller	303,860,000
5	Incepta (Citigate)	243,938,000
6	Edelman Public Relations Worldwide	238,044,792
7	Porter Novelli International	208,157,000
8	BSMG Worldwide	192,194,536
9	Ogilvy Public Relations Worldwide	169,453,900
10	Ketchum	168,247,000
TOTAL OF TOP 10 FIRMS		$2,507,960,603

Source: Council of PR Firms/PR Week

Chart 14.1

PRINCIPAL COMMUNICATIONS GROUPS 2000			
	WPP	OMNICOM	IPG
TOTAL REVENUE	$55.6 Billion	$6.1 Billion	$5.63 Billion
Public Relations Fee Revenue	$844 Million	$810 Million	$708 Million
Principal Current or Heritage Agencies	Hill & Knowlton	Fleishman Hillard	Weber Shandwick
	Ogilvy	Porter Novelli	Golin Harris
	Burson-Marsteller	Gavin Anderson	BSMG
	Cohn & Wolfe	Ketchum	Carmichael Lynch Spong
	Carl Byoir	Brodeur	Imada Wong
	Robinson, Lerer & Montgomery	Cone	
		Clark & Weinstock	

Source: Council of PR Firms/PR Week

Chart 14.2

For the most part, the well-known agency network brands that have gone to form these groups have continued much as before, each with a clear identity. The benefits of common ownership are to be found more in the back office, strategy management and investment in growth than in the more obvious client-facing work. But they are increasingly working together in subtle ways to overcome client conflict problems and to create client service teams drawn from different agency brands. An example of this is the virtual team that won a sizable global assignment when IBM decided to have a major realignment and reduction in the number of PR agencies it used. Ketchum led a team composed of members of sister agencies in Omnicom, Fleishman Hillard and Brodeur to achieve a success it might have been unable to manage alone.

It will be interesting to see if this trend may lead to a more formal reorganization of the PR units within Omnicom and WPP in the way that has happened within Interpublic under the leadership of PR czar, Larry Weber.

Weber is an entrepreneur who by 1997 had built fees in his tech specialist firm up to $61 million, entering the world's top ten for the first time, according to O'Dwyer. He sold out to Interpublic, a laggard in public relations compared with rivals Omnicom and WPP, and quickly moved to acquire Shandwick, which had global reach but had lost its way. Following a series of subsequent acquisitions, the most important being BSMG, he has reorganized the brands with a series of internal mergers leading to the first PR agency brand, Weber Shandwick, with annual fees of over $500,000,000 on the day it started trading.

Why this sudden surge of interest in public relations on the part of advertising agencies? Even in the buoyant economy of the nineties, it was clear that traditional advertising was not growing as fast as other communications and marketing techniques. Direct marketing, public relations and interactive marketing were not only more relevant to meeting the needs of clients but offered greater opportunity for both growth and profit. PR was no longer simply commando support for the heavy guns of advertising, it was now an important offering and business in its own right. Soon, it became apparent to the major communications conglomerates – as happened at Interpublic – that they would be at a severe competitive disadvantage without a high-quality PR component to their business. They would get poor ratings not only from clients but from investors and the financial community as well.

To understand today's universe of agencies it is useful to track its evolution.

History

The description "consultancy" or "agency," depending on the country concerned, was applied to the firms, individuals, partnerships and companies that established themselves in practice in the early years following the Second World War. At that stage the larger part of the services offered to clients consisted of practical implementation of public relations tactics and there was less emphasis on the analysis of problems and the supply of advice alone, than is the case nowadays. Because several of the early post-war practitioners had a background in journalism – although by no means all of them – the element of consulting and advice grew out of their special knowledge of the working of the media, the correct way to present a story for publication and a feeling for the way in which the public might react to publicity in the media.

A few individuals stand out as major formative figures in the establishment of the public relations consulting and agency profession on an international basis. Marion Harper, the creator of Interpublic, based on the international network of McCann Erickson advertising agencies, was an important figure. McCann at one time had what I believe was the largest international PR operation, which operated under the name Infoplan. Its principal offices were in the USA, UK, Germany and France. (A sister company, Marplan, was a force in the world of international market research.)

Tim Traverse-Healy built Infoplan into the powerhouse of its time, an early pioneer in multinational programs for its clients, mostly in the field of fast-moving consumer goods. Now Professor Traverse-Healy, and teaching at universities in England, Scotland and Ireland, he formed his own consulting company after leaving Infoplan.

The earliest international pioneer among then independent agencies was John Hill of Hill & Knowlton. Hill came from Cleveland, a comparatively small city but one which has been the birthplace of other remarkable world-class professional service firms – Ernst & Young, the accountants and management consultants, and the Jones Day law firm.

Hill was a reporter on the *Cleveland Plain Dealer* before crossing the line into PR and establishing the partnership with Knowlton. Hill's client, the Iron and Steel Institute, persuaded him to relocate to New York during the big steel industry strike in 1934. The story is told that, at the time, Hill was eager neither to move nor to undertake the assignment. So when the Institute pressed him hard, he named an outrageously high fee which he was certain they would refuse.

They accepted. Hill relocated. The new New York-based firm, which was to become the industry leader for many years, was born. And John Hill established a pricing policy which ensured he and his associates were paid top dollar. But Knowlton remained in Cleveland and played no significant further role in the growth and success of the firm.

Hill & Knowlton entered Europe in the early 1960s but made a major impact internationally when they acquired Eric White and Associates in 1970, thus gaining a ready-made and strongly established network in the Asia-Pacific region. Eric White, the founder, was an Australian who in a few years established one of the world's most potent networks, including a strong operation in London.

Hill & Knowlton was quickly followed as a firm with international ambitions by Burson-Marsteller and Daniel J. Edelman, Inc., each of which established operations in London in the 1960s.

Harold Burson (the PR half of the partnership; Marsteller was an advertising man) was born in Memphis, Tennessee, and established his firm in New York. Dan Edelman was a New Yorker who established his firm in Chicago. Both had studied journalism and served during World War II in the US Army's psychological warfare section, perhaps the perfect grounding for the profession both were to enter after the war.

Burson's early strength was its work for industrial companies which were attracted by the combination of media relations, trade press advertising and printed brochures the firm supplied. Edelman, on the other hand, was the acknowledged leader in public relations for consumer products and gained fame in the USA as the creator of the media tour – a PR technique in which a company spokesperson visited key markets, performed store openings, did radio and newspaper interviews and, most important of all, participated in a talk show on local television.

Now both companies offer their clients a complete range of specialist PR services from offices in most key centers around the world.

Another giant of international PR who had his career shaped during the war was France's Jacques Coup de Frejac. While he always gives recognition to the leadership of the USA in most PR techniques, he opened the minds of many people in France, elsewhere in Europe and beyond, to the importance of communications. Perhaps more important, he played a major role in encouraging clients in the USA and UK to understand the French market and the European movement. De Frejac was the name given to Jacques Coup when he joined the French Resistance. He was only 18 years old when he served as aide de camp to General de Gaulle in the early years of World War II.

In the 1980s Hill & Knowlton, Burson-Marsteller and Edelman were joined by a new – and differently constructed competitor – Shandwick. The newcomer was different in two obvious ways. First, it was founded in Britain, by Peter Gummer. Second, it was a publicly held company, its shares listed on the London stock exchange. The big three American multinationals were privately held (until Burson-Marsteller was bought by Young & Rubicam and Hill & Knowlton by J. Walter Thompson). Subsequently, both firms became linked under the ownership of WPP, following the merger frenzy of 1999/2000.

Peter Gummer (now Lord Chadlington) used a strong UK base of operations built from a number of autonomous units practicing financial and investor relations, public affairs and consumer PR, and the availability of finance from Shandwick's status as a public company, to launch a major buying spree of 35 agencies in the USA, Europe and the Far East.

A combination of Shandwick "paper" and cash enabled Gummer to achieve an international presence in a fraction of the time it had taken others to assemble their networks.

Shandwick owed its strength in the Asia-Pacific region to the vision and industry of another of the titans of international public relations – Taiji Kohara. The Japanese PR doyen was to his region what John Hill, Dan Edelman and Harold Burson were to the USA, Tim Traverse-Healy and Jacques Coup de Frejac to Europe and Eric White to Australia.

Having started his own company in Tokyo in 1968, Kohara went on to establish International Public Relations (IPR), an immensely strong network of offices in 43 countries stretching from Japan to Australia, which Shandwick acquired in 1988 for a price estimated to be $45 million.

The majority of PR budgets in the early years were within the control of the marketing departments of business organizations. Given that they were generally allotted as a tiny percentage of the advertising budgets, it was natural that these public relations or publicity programs were entrusted to the advertising agency. It was, after all, staffed with skilled communicators who were seen as being able to do the job required. Moreover, because they controlled the larger advertising budget, it was often assumed, if not said aloud, that they exercised considerable leverage over the media, and this would ensure the desired level of editorial publicity.

The advertising agencies took on staff as the demand for public relations services increased and established special departments. In due course, these grew into separate subsidiary companies engaged exclusively in public relations. The proper fees and costs could now be established for the services which had grown too great to be given free to large advertisers. Because they were in close contact with client organizations, and they had resources of finance and ancillary services of design, production and printing, the public relations divisions, or subsidiary companies of the large advertising agencies, established themselves as the largest "agencies" in the USA and Western Europe.

While these developments were taking place, a number of independent public relations agencies were launched and were gaining in reputation. Some specialized in a specific branch, others were generalist. They had a great strength-building challenge, outside their skills as publicists: They had to survive on what they could earn by providing public relations advice and services. They had to become viable businesses, charging realistic fees covering all their costs and leaving profits for investment. Unless they managed this, they would cease to exist.

Many not only managed to exist – they flourished, and took over the leadership from the advertising agency offshoots. But the advertising agencies were not to be outdone, and ultimately once again achieved a dominant ownership position in the field of public relations. In the early 1980s, three large, international PR agencies were acquired by advertising agencies anxious to re-establish themselves in public relations. Further acquisitions of major PR firms have taken place in the second half of the 1990s. Now, eight of the world's largest PR companies are owned by advertising agencies; another, Incepta PLC, is a publicly traded company on the London Stock Exchange; and Edelman Public Relations Worldwide is independent and privately owned by the Edelman family and senior executives of the company.

The description "public relations agency" today is suitable, but still less than accurate, for the majority of firms. While there are a number of people practicing as consultants only (they do not engage in the practical implementation of the advice and strategies they recommend), the majority of public relations companies are both consultants and agents. This is the reason why, together with the original ad agency public relations divisions, the public relations agency is usually referred to as "the agency."

For the majority of agencies, there are two clearly defined roles:

1. The provision of expert and objective advice to clients based on a knowledge of the mechanisms that will affect the opinion of key publics, allied to a good knowledge of those clients' organizations, their industries and markets. In this, the consultant will draw on his and his firm's experience gained from previous assignments of a similar nature.
2. To act as the public relations agent of the client, assuming responsibility for executing agreed-upon programs on the client's behalf. This might involve, for example, the establishment of an information office for the client, the provision of public relations personnel, the production of various printed and videotaped materials, the execution of events, and the conduct of media relations and publicity efforts.

Often one agency will fulfill both roles, with the senior staff (partners or directors) providing the consulting or counseling service and then involving other executive staff in the agency function. It is not unusual, however, for a client organization to retain the services of more than one agency to meet its needs for advice on the one hand – often specialist in nature – and executional services on the other.

Types of agency

A large proportion of modern agencies could describe themselves as "full service," in that they have staffs with a blend of experience that enables them to offer both consulting and agency services across the different "specialties" within public relations – for example, media relations, technical communications, government relations, employee communications, international communications and marketing support. Even if the full range of highly qualified specialist advice is not available within the agency, the "full service" firm will, in most instances, be able to bring the necessary qualified person into its team as a part-time adviser.

The 1970s saw the rapid development of a number of strictly specialist agencies. The description "specialist" can be applied in a number of ways.

There are agencies which specialize in particular branches of industry; examples are firms which operate exclusively in the field of health and medicine, or those which confine themselves to clients involved in travel, tourism and related activities, and yet more which concentrate on fashion, beauty, household products and food.

More generally, however, specialization means that the firm restricts itself to one of the sub-specializations or "practices" of public relations, such a financial communications, government relations, and employee and community relations. Chapter 7 deals more fully with specialized fields of public relations.

Public relations agency structures

Although some of the largest PR agencies are now owned by ad agencies or communications conglomerates, most continue to operate as autonomous units. And the majority of public relations agencies are privately owned, limited companies. It is perhaps surprising that, with aspirations to professional status, this form of corporate structure for public relations firms should be the norm, rather than the partnership structure to be found in the accounting and legal professions. Whether public, ad agency-owned, or private, most public relations companies have some method of profit-sharing to enable at least the senior staff to participate in the success of the enterprise.

Because the origins of many public relations companies are linked with advertising agencies, it is common, but an error, to compare structures and costs between these two branches of communications. Public relations agencies are closer, in many ways, to management consultants, accounting and law firms. They charge fees related to the time spent on client work. Although most agencies charge an additional commission on production costs, this mainly reflects the administrative costs of overseeing production and is not the principal source of income.

There are two main kinds of operational structure within public relations agencies as related to client service. The following examples relate to typical full-service rather than specialist agencies.

The first, and less usual nowadays, is the functional structure. This has an obvious relation to the usual advertising agency structure. Primary consultants and program supervisors are usually called account directors or supervisors. Their job is to advise clients, develop the strategy, budget and method of operation for the programs, and then mobilize the resources of the agency and its subcontractors.

In a functionally structured agency, the staff are specialists in one or another aspect of public relations and invariably work on all the agency's clients, under the supervision of the account director. Take for example a program with extensive demands for a wide range of actions, including an intensive press relations campaign, a strong effort with local radio stations, a briefing for elected officials and an audio-visual presentation for general use. The account director will brief the head of the agency's press office, the specialist whose sole task is working with radio and TV, the public affairs specialist and an executive from the audio-visual and film section.

In my view, while the merits of the functional system are clear, the disadvantages only become obvious in practice. Too many people are involved, those responsible for the actual execution do not have close enough contact with the client and, in general, the time of the account director and the functional executives is spread across too wide a range of projects for sufficient commitment and attention to be given to each. Another problem is that the person aspiring to a broad career in public relations can easily get trapped in a single functional department.

The more usual structure now is that of the account group, in which the account director and one or more executives are responsible for a group of clients whose interests are in some way related.

Many agencies form their account groups by public relations specialty (rather than functional specialty). They will have, for example, account groups for clients whose needs are in investor relations, and others for government relations, technical and industrial public relations, consumer marketing public relations, and so on. The heads of these groups might have started as specialists but they will have been trained and have developed over time as competent all-around consultants and executives. Alternatively, they may have started as all-rounders but then developed a specialist skill. In such an agency, the top management will have discussed the client's needs fully with him.

If the work is largely, say, public affairs, the client will be served by the government relations group. The head of this group will offer consulting services and will also undertake or supervise directly much of the day-to-day work of the program. If the client is large and the program involves intensive activity in, say, government relations, investor relations and marketing public relations, the work will be divided into three programs undertaken by three different groups, with a management coordinator appointed to oversee the total quality of service to the client. Such account groups are, in effect, mini-agencies, and in many cases are managed as profit centers. They provide an opportunity to learn teamwork and offer training for senior management positions.

Public relations consultancy costs

Agencies are in business to make a profit for shareholders and a good living for their staff, as well as to offer service to clients. In general, they seek to make an overall profit from income of between 10 and 20 percent before tax from the fees they charge clients. Dividends to shareholders and profit-sharing to staff are paid from this profit. The balance goes to finance the growth of the agency and provide it with the necessary reserves to ensure stability. Thus an agency with an income of $10,000,000 per annum might expect to make a pre-tax profit of $1,500,000. A part of that – say, $500,000 – might be allocated for profit-sharing or an annual bonus. A prudent board might also have invested say $250,000 in new equipment as the likely profit became known. Of the remaining balance of $750,000, close to 40 percent ($300,000) will go toward taxes, leaving $450,000 to cover dividends and cash to be retained in the business. This will be needed to finance cash flow and growth.

To achieve that profit, however, requires good management and adherence to a pricing policy.

Staff salaries are the largest single cost of an agency. Surveys of members of the Public Relations Consultants Association (PRCA) have shown that in nearly all agencies staff salaries are around 50 percent of income. So our "sample" $10,000,000 agency will have an annual salary bill of $5,000,000.

The second largest single cost (usually about 10 percent) is rent. Then come all the other costs, such as telephone, travel, entertaining, hiring and training, which should not amount to more than another 25 percent if 15 percent profit is to be made.

When an agency discusses its costs openly with clients, it seldom has difficulties in getting fees appropriate to the assignment.

Following are the main fee systems in operation.

Fixed fee. This is negotiated annually with the client, based on historical knowledge of the volume of work and time involved, or is estimated based on agency experience with similar programs. The fee is usually paid monthly.

Retainer fee and hourly or *per diem* **charges**. In this system, clients pay a very modest retainer fee, which means they can draw on the agency's services when needed, but the retainer does not automatically "buy" any service and it is payable even if no work is done. When service is needed, an agreed-upon hourly rate is charged to the client. This might be broken down by the hours put in by specific individuals, for example one rate for a senior consultant, another for a junior staff member, and shown as such to the client on the invoice. It is also quite usual for a uniform "team" time rate to be established, which reflects the average of the combined time of senior consultants, executives and support staff. In certain countries, hourly rates are established and recommended by national public relations institutes.

Minimum fee and hourly charges. This approach is often confused with the retainer system because of similarities, but there are significant differences. The minimum fee is invariably more substantial than the retainer. It reflects the fact that the agency has calculated that it is likely to spend a given amount of time each month working for the client and has assigned the staff to do so. The hourly charge comes into operation when the basic time has been used up. Thus, when clients pay a minimum fee of $10,000 per month for, say, 50 hours work at $200 per hour, and the actual time expended in the month is 60 hours, the bill for that month will be $12,000. In a month when only 40 hours work is done, the minimum fee of $10,000 is still payable. Sometimes there is a quarterly "equalization" system built in, to reflect the ups and downs that are inevitable.

It is normal for agencies to charge subcontract, production and out-of-pocket costs, in addition to the professional fee.

Working with the client

In most respects, the working day and practical duties of public relations agency executives are similar to those of their equivalents in the public relations departments of their clients. The likelihood is that the agency people will find themselves working in close cooperation with a public relations professional or at least an experienced communicator within the client organization.

Until the mid-1960s, it was normal for clients embarking on public relations programs to make a decision either to retain an external agency or to employ a public relations executive internally. Now it is relatively common for the larger, forward-looking organizations to have established internal public relations departments and for these to retain the services of agencies in addition.

In the case of well-staffed client PR departments, the prime need is for expert, objective external PR consultants. In other cases where the internal staff is small but there is going to be extra work over a defined period, it makes sense to retain specific agency services.

Qualities of good PR consultants

Over and above the qualities needed by *all* public relations practitioners, the following are those required of agency executives:

- Observe the successes and failures of techniques employed for other clients and bring this knowledge and experience to bear for the benefit of clients you are currently serving.
- Achieve mastery and knowledge of the subcontracting services available to the agency that will benefit clients.
- Use the resources and expertise of other professionals within the agency when faced with a complex problem.
- Sharpen your creative edge by maintaining regular contact with other professionals in the firm.
- Maintain strong powers of analysis, presentation and creativity, because an agency has to sell its services in competition with other agencies. In short, consultants have to win the right to practice public relations.
- Understand budgeting and business management, vital elements for a career in a PR organization.
- Keep abreast of media developments, new communications techniques and the current mood of public opinion on a variety of issues, if your advice is to be valued as smart, objective and reliable.
- Manage your own time expertly, allocating it appropriately among client contact, program execution, monitoring results, reporting to the client and maintaining direct contact with the media and other publics. Though difficult, the right time blend must be achieved because the client pays for a combination of expertise and time.

CHAPTER 15

Research

Business executives underpin planning with research. No new product is launched without extensive market research. New plant siting requires researching community attitudes.

Entering new markets is never done without pre-testing potential benefits and downsides. The effective PR executive must be in step with the business research phenomenon and he must use research to test the effectiveness of his own work product, the messages he wants to communicate and the channels to be used.

An aspiring international public relations executive needs to master research in all its forms.

He must know the different research specialties and when to use them. He must know how to develop questionnaires; structure simple research projects; and the strengths and weaknesses of the specialist research organizations for the occasions when a project must be subcontracted. He must learn where research already exists and can be bought at a reasonable price so that he can avoid wasting money.

Furthermore, he must understand the value of quantitative vs. qualitative research, statistically projective vs. anecdotal research, focus groups vs. phone surveys, literature searches and market research, demographics and psychographics.

Above all, he must be able to interpret the findings produced by all kinds of research projects so that the data can be effectively used at the outset in the development of public relations programs and to make adjustments during their implementation.

That research has become critical to public relations is reflected in the criteria set by major PR awards competitions around the world. Virtually all require a research section which sets out the scope of the challenge or opportunity facing the organization. The last section of an entry, devoted to the results and evaluation of the program that has been entered, is expected to link back to the initial research findings, demonstrating what has been achieved. No program, however creative the central idea or brilliant the execution, is likely to walk off with the prize if the research section is weak.

The attention that is now paid to research is an important sign of the "growing up" of public relations. PR is all too often criticized (I am sorry to say, with good reason) by others in other business specialties for being too "instinctive" or "seat of the pants." PR practitioners in the past have been unable to hold a strong position in debates on policy, direction or creative content of communications programs because their ideas and interventions were not grounded in the research and analysis that appeared to be the hallmark of others, especially those from management consultancies, marketing and advertising agencies.

PR people were also less prepared to be accountable by any concrete form of measurement and evaluation. This had the effect of devaluing the perception of the contribution PR could make as a component in any integrated communications project.

Another factor has militated against widespread use of research for PR programming – cost. The cost of undertaking a reliable, thorough research study to establish the effect of a PR program can be prohibitive. In some instances, research cost is greater than the cost of the PR effort itself. As a consequence, until recently research was seldom undertaken. That has gradually changed as the size of PR programs has grown, along with the costs of PR advice and program implementation. Because good upfront research sets up the need for a PR program, the executives proposing the PR budget will not get approvals unless they provide adequate research underpinning and measurement of results, and the research cost is at an acceptable ratio to the basic PR costs.

Historically, an inability to prove the tremendous cost:benefit ratio of public relations in relation to other communications techniques left the PR manager with a tiny slice of the marketing communications pie and, sometimes, no slice at all – especially compared to the large allotments for advertising.

If a basic knowledge of research is important for every PR practitioner, there are additional compelling reasons for competency on the part of those engaged in international communications.

While research can add to specific knowledge in single-country work, it might be possible – in a small and homogenous country – for a practitioner to have enough accumulated knowledge of the population, trends, geographical differences and other data to construct a program that will be generally on target.

But, on a worldwide basis, where you will be expected to make decisions about programs being undertaken in countries of which you have no first-hand knowledge and which you may not even have visited, a research-based foundation for your programs is essential.

Research then is vital both as a tool that will enable you to assess the situation you face as you start your PR activities as well as a form of measurement at periodic intervals to check whether your progress is satisfactory. Where can help be found?

There is a variety of resources available to the PR practitioners covering many specialist fields of research. There is almost certain to be research already available or new studies that may be commissioned that will be relevant to you in the huge range of activities covered under the heading of PR.

This chapter does not attempt to be a primer on research for the PR executive. There are other books and courses available for anyone wanting to study the subject at length. I hope to provide a helpful guide for the person who needs to know where to go for data and would like to know of money-saving short cuts, if they exist.

(Note: Research is also covered briefly in chapter 3, on Corporate Reputation Management, and in chapter 8, Issues Identification and Management.)

Check existing sources

It is quite likely that some of the data you need already exists. It is just a matter of finding out where, and if it is available to you.

It will be very much like looking for a suit.

Clearly, your best choice would be to go along to the finest tailor, get measured up, choose your cloth and have the garment cut and stitched to fit you perfectly. This carries a high price, appropriate for the degree of skill, personal attention and customization it is given.

But excellent, serviceable and high-quality suits can be found ready-to-wear. In many cases you can mix and match trousers and jackets, or find "not quite finished suits" which can be altered to be almost like a bespoke article. Research products exist that are identical to the custom-tailored, near-ready and ready-to-wear suits.

Ultimately, you can also find a second-hand suit which might be ideal. You might not like such a suit in your wardrobe; you would not worry quite so much were you to find some piece of research which tells you what you need to know but has been paid for by someone else.

The first place to look is at home.

Large companies are the repositories of huge amounts of data. Most of it has been acquired over the years by various departments and seldom is it concentrated in one place. It is not uncommon for different divisions to be questioning the same people – even for different departments in a division to do so – without being aware that the other is doing so. Data is accumulated by one brand that is not necessarily shared with other brands. At time of writing, many companies are appointing Chief Knowledge Officers, one of whose responsibilities will be the assembly and arrangement of this information in easily accessible form to approved users. Meantime, your first step must be to question the person responsible in the central research department archive (if such exists). Step two is to contact other company PR and marketing people to establish what recent studies they have undertaken. They will likely have an Aladdin's cave of information about the market trends, your company's or brand's position in the market, its qualities and comparisons with competitors.

What you find may enable you to proceed without commissioning additional research because you will be able to piggy-back on these studies. And even if you decide you need additional data, the available information will help you focus your new studies more accurately and thus save time and money.

Make sure you contact the chief financial officer. You will find he also has a storehouse of information, starting with reports of analysts from financial institutions. It is their job to know more about your company than you know yourself and to rate it against its competitors, and they have the resources to find out. In their periodic reports, you get superb appraisals of your industry and insights into your own company. And it all comes FREE.

The CFO might also consult you, if you are responsible for investor relations, for other data that might be of great importance to him. Most public companies want to know the names of the people who own their shares. While this data is of limited use in tranquil times, if a merger or hostile bid is likely, it becomes exceptionally important that the company be able to reach out to shareholders whose holdings are in the names of nominees. Then it is useful to know who is behind the nominees so that you can reach them with the specifically targeted information that you know will help them to make the right decision – as you see it. There are a number of companies that do this work on the international stock exchanges, among them: Corporate Investor Communications, Inc., Carson Group, Technimetrics, D.F. King & Co. and First Chicago Trust Company.

Historical data from continuous studies

Check out the major research companies for the historical data that is available from the studies that they may have been conducting continuously over several years.

You may be surprised to find that your company or brand has been included for comparison purposes in the regular panel audits that ACNielsen conducts in shops and the home, or in a variety of research projects routinely undertaken by Gallup, ORC, MORI, Harris Polls and others. This will give you a head start in establishing your current position. All you need to do is to join the study – and pay up – to establish how your PR work is changing the company or brand perception.

One such study of special importance to public relations practitioners is undertaken periodically by Yankelovich in the USA. It surveys a large number of journalists and editors from all forms of general and specialist media on a number of topics. Useful enough in itself to PR executives, the study allows subscribers to ask specific questions and include their own trade media. The survey can help you ascertain how strong the relationship is between the company and its key media, and find out what techniques are working well and which are not. It also rates the company's media relations performance against its main competitors.

Societies, ruling bodies and other organizations

You may be called upon to become an instant expert in some special population sector. For example, someone might propose that a PR program be undertaken that involves anglers or hobby fishermen, or perhaps mountain bikers.

The best sources – and the least costly – are always the ruling bodies or societies that serve these interest groups. The society or association will usually send you at no charge beyond postage a wealth of material containing demographic and psychographic information about its members. This will quickly help you establish just how useful a group it will be to your company. More often than not, nowadays, the information from these societies is also available from the websites they maintain.

In the major PR field of healthcare communications, a prime source of data can be the patient support groups that exist in most countries and are very well organized. Examples are patient associations for people suffering from kidney ailments, heart conditions, cancer, MS, diabetes, AIDS and other illnesses. In addition to being a source of information, these groups can be excellent partners in communications initiatives, offering a direct and highly targeted channel to a group of people of specific interest to you.

A secondary source is the journals serving these interest groups.

Country information

Those practicing PR on an international scale will often want to gain objective information about a specific country to match with the information being presented by the company representatives there.

The first port of call should be to the local embassy or consulate general of that country, which will usually provide you with a great deal of useful information about the country. From this you can build up your own picture, perhaps in advance of a visit. The second should be the Foreign Office or Department of Trade (Export) of your own country's government. You will find that they usually have a wealth of knowledge about overseas markets and will also give you their opinion on such important matters as the political stability of the country and even some do's and don't's of doing business there. Remember, you have paid for this through your taxes, so you have a right to the help from your own public servants. Mostly, they are glad to oblige.

You should complement this by requesting the most recent study undertaken of that country by the Economist Intelligence Unit, which will be available at a cost of around $200. Or collect the most recent advertising-supported "special report" or supplement on that country published by *The Economist*, the *Wall Street Journal*, the *Financial Times* or another reputable and serious journal.

Some of the very best country-by-country business profiles are published by the world-renowned consulting firm Ernst & Young in a series of books intended to be very informative to prospective investors or those doing business there.

Caravans

Caravans are regular researches undertaken weekly or monthly by many specialist research organizations under contract to major corporations. These track product purchases, opinions and voting intentions. The skill of the research organization goes into selecting small panels on a so-called random basis (that is anything but random), which will reflect the demographics of the population as a whole. As a PR executive you should master the interpretation of results gleaned from these caravan studies.

In addition, you should also exploit the opportunity presented by the fact that the research company undertaking the study almost certainly has covered its cost and is making a profit before you even sign up. For a relatively small cost, you should be able to negotiate up to five additional questions relevant to you. This achieves a limited custom-tailored research which might well have been out of reach if you were the sole sponsor of the study.

PR people who are knowledgeable and alert know that research data is one of the magical routes to winning coverage in the media, which has an insatiable appetite for information about what people think or do. So in addition to using caravan research as an economical way of finding out data of real importance to the construction of a PR program and its key messages, use additional questions in caravans to generate data that will be appetizing to the media and can be linked to the product, corporation or theme for which you want to achieve publicity.

Focus groups

Focus-group testing is probably the research format of most importance to public relations practitioners. The information one can gain is highly qualitative and detailed.

Beyond learning how people feel about a certain product, person or concept, the skilled researcher can establish the strength of feeling, and the ease with which that opinion might be altered and how that might be done. Focus groups, because they involve people for several hours – for which they get paid a fee – are also able to establish the acceptability of alternative product offerings and ideas.

This method is routinely used by politicians and political parties to check how the public might react to various initiatives.

Most important for people in the public relations field, focus groups are the testing ground for ideas and messages, the grist to the mill of all who practice communications.

All focus groups can be useful when interpreted with skill and intelligence. But the methods sheltering under this uniform description can range widely. You might have a fairly simple gathering of a group of people who are a representative sample, in a conference room at your company or agency or research firm, or even in an hotel room rented for the purpose. At the other end of the range, you have the use of custom-built research centers fitted with microphoned rooms behind one-way mirrors and "voting" buttons through which the panelists can give instant responses to questions put by a focus-group facilitator. There is great value for the PR practitioner to attend the more sophisticatedly-organized focus groups. Attendance offers a marked heightening of understanding of human reactions to the issues raised, as compared with a later reading of the written results.

A well-run focus-group study is a superb navigational tool for the PR practitioner aspiring to chart the course for a successful communications program. It can establish your exact position on the map at the starting point. It will tell you the course you must set to reach your destination. It will suggest course corrections. It will also tell you the blind alleys and the way that is fraught with dangers and obstacles. And, if used periodically, it will tell you your progress and chart your new position. Finally, it will tell you when you have reached your destination.

When British Airways (BA) decided it wanted to acquire a substantial shareholding in US Air to establish a strategic alliance that would benefit both airlines, a coalition headquartered in the USA was immediately established to fight the plan. The influence of American Airlines, United Airlines, Delta and Federal Express was formidable and their publicity machine was quickly mobilized to tell the story of the damage that would be caused, along with the threat to security, employment and the American economy.

BA realized that they had a fight on their hands. They were going to get no points or thanks for stepping in and offering a new lease on life to an airline that appeared to have no future. American law prevented the acquisition of any US carrier by a foreign entity and there was a gray area around even minority holdings if they could be shown to transfer effective control of the airline into foreign hands. So the opposition coalition challenged even BA's intention to take a minority interest, suggesting it was the thin end of the wedge, and, in any case, the investment promised by BA would give it *de facto* control, exercised from behind the curtain.

BA knew it would have to assemble an influential group of allies if the US government watchdog organizations were not to be steamrolled by the opposition group.

It listed all the benefits that would emerge from the strategic alliance if it were to be approved. These included benefits to flyers such as a single ticket, baggage transfers and neat connections to destinations worldwide from all points served by US Air in the USA; increased tourism opportunity for customers flying in from Europe; a certain future for US Air instead of the possibility of its failure financially; a prospect of continuing prosperity and good airline service for the many towns and cities in the Northeast of the USA; and, finally, the safety of the many jobs that were at risk.

At the outset it was hard to know which of these arguments, and others, would prove the most compelling.

But soon there was no contest. Focus-group testing in several of US Air's regional centers came to one conclusion. There was only one issue at stake. Jobs.

And jobs, jobs, jobs.

The message was clear. Passenger benefits, increased inward tourism and all other good results of the strategic alliance would play second fiddle to the constant theme of jobs. The BA–US Air alliance would assure the jobs of people in the many communities served by US Air. Not only would this resonate in those places and with their local political leaders, it was also the key issue for decision makers in Washington, D.C.

Jobs became the theme of the campaign, which succeeded in its goals, with BA taking a significant minority shareholding in US Air.

In the years that have gone by since that achievement, US Air has returned to respectable profits and even changed its name. But BA has raised it sights and has established a new strategic alliance with the much larger American Airlines, so as to be a stronger force in the new competitive arena where it is imperative to be a global airline power to assure a successful future.

Copy and ad testing

Focus groups are used regularly by advertisers to test alternative copy and creative concepts but very few PR creative ideas are subjected to similar, rigorous, routine trials. If and when PR creative testing becomes more common, many unsuccessful campaigns will be eliminated before they cause embarrassment and a waste of time and money.

Clip count and analysis

While the ultimate result of the work of the PR practitioner can only be established through awareness and opinion research conducted with the target groups he is seeking to influence, resources are not always available to undertake studies of the necessary scale and frequency. Moreover, changing of awareness and opinions is most often the result of several factors – perhaps a combination of advertising, direct mail, word of mouth and editorial coverage. All organizations should try to establish the relative impact of each of these techniques so that the investment and weight of effort can be adjusted as necessary.

For this purpose PR executives must measure the output of their work.

Some assumptions can be made: If the number of communications that take place – whether in the form of speaking engagements, newsletters or videos distributed, interviews conducted, articles published, and TV and radio broadcasts aired – is at a high level, then the awareness of your company or product will be correspondingly high.

And, if the content of these communications is broadly positive, then listeners, readers and viewers will most likely react positively to that information.

There is a variety of services in the world's larger markets that offer media analysis in varying degrees of sophistication. Most of the clippings services, which in years past merely clipped and sent in packets of cuttings on a weekly basis, now offer enhanced analysis. On request and the payment of an additional fee, they will provide a classification of the content of each press report. The most basic of these services will tell you if the report is negative, neutral or positive, and the information is presented in easy-to-look-at graphic format, useful for presentation purposes to wider audiences.

Analysis will also document how, over a period of time, it is possible to establish an improving trend (from negative toward positive coverage) or the opposite. This allows the PR director to take appropriate action.

Airtours improves PR effectiveness with integrated research

Public relations flies blind without an understanding of reputation's underlying structure, as Airtours, the UK-based global holiday travel company, found out. Although Airtours had become the largest company of its kind in the world, it was considered a regional, entrepreneurial upstart to the well-established Thomson Travel and JMC/Thomas Cook.

The group's rapid growth created significant operational challenges for the company, often resulting in bad publicity and litigation, and proving easy targets for televised consumer watchdog programs. Little time was paid to reputation issues, until its business started to suffer.

Against complaints on accommodation, staffing and customer services, the company's positive stories went unreported or had little effect. The company turned to Echo Research, a global reputation evaluation company with offices in New York, London, Brussels, Paris, Stockholm and Kuala Lumpur, to assess both its reputation and the effectiveness of its public relations program.

Needed was a way to quantify the situation, identify sources of positive and negative coverage and use the research to make strategic operational and public relations decisions. To get the full picture of the architecture of Airtours' reputation, Echo conducted an integrated research effort that included:

- Analysis of how the media were reporting Airtours, including identifying specific journalists who were covering the company and its industry and the positive/negative orientation of their articles.
- Market research techniques that involved about 1,000 consumer interviews to understand attitudes on various issues, including complaint handling, which the media analysis showed was a lightning rod for negative stories.
- More than 40 journalists, including travel editors, were interviewed on their opinions of Airtours and its competitors.

The findings were then integrated to provide a clear and detailed picture of Airtours' reputation and the factors on which it was based.

Airtours' problems were confirmed. According to Jacqui Walford, a senior vice president of Echo and head of the New York office, proactive media contact was limited and unsolicited media coverage dominated, thus exposing consumers to negative stories. And Airtours ran a poor third to its two primary competitors, Thomson and Cook, in the eyes of journalists.

In its initial study, Echo recommended a series of public relations strategies that Airtours adopted: Spokespeople were identified and trained, the in-house public relations team was increased, relationships with travel editors were developed through one-on-one contact, media with a record of consistently negative reporting (e.g. BBC Watchdog) were given special attention and opportunities for favorable coverage were created.

Spontaneous plaudits - 1999 and 2000

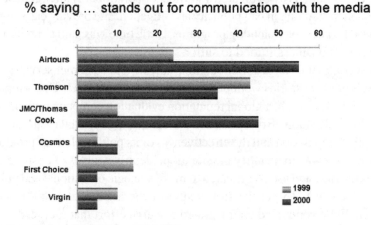

% saying ... stands out for communication with the media

Base: 20 Journalists, Summer 1999 & 2000

Copyright : Echo Research

Chart 15.1

A repeated integrated reputation evaluation a year later discovered:

- The media considers Airtours the best communicator in its industry, improving from 25 percent to 54 percent, and surpassing Thomson (at 35 percent) and Cook (at 43 percent).

- Airtours' rating for market knowledge improved from 15 percent to 55 percent.
- Its rating for quality of information jumped from 20 percent to 55 percent.
- Accuracy of information improved from 10 percent to 50 percent.
- Crisis management improved from 10 percent to 25 percent.

The implementation of a more focused PR strategy successfully improved relationships with key journalists. "Airtours have been getting in touch in a more substantial way," said Paul Gogarty of the *Daily Telegraph*. "Press releases have got better and there are more of them," added Eric Jackson of the *Manchester Evening News*.

Improvements in 2000

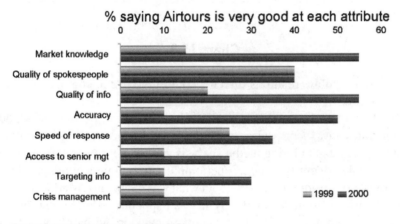

% saying Airtours is very good at each attribute

Base: 20 Journalists, Summer 1999 & 2000

Chart 15.2

The company's image became more in line with the image it sought to present – customer focused, good value and family friendly. June Smith, from *Chat* magazine, was among those to endorse the efforts made by the company: "Airtours is working hard, listening and taking it on the chin. They are a good example to others."

As the *Sunday Times'* Mark Stretton said, "Airtours has overtaken Thomson Travel to become Britain's leading tour operator. It has successfully evolved from a one-shop operation to a global giant." This was an ideal "report card"

Current perception

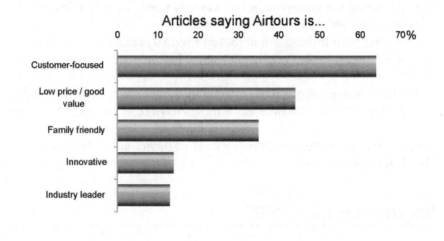

Copyright : Echo Research

Chart 15.3

that Airtours' public relations director could give to the company's senior management.

The Airtours turnaround in media relations in the period 1999/2000 demonstrates how successful research can inform effective decision making. By integrating and tailoring media analysis and market research techniques, Echo was able to identify strategic operational and communications problems. Media analysis informed Airtours about what was happening. Market research enabled Airtours to understand why it was happening. Combining the two gave the company a unique insight into its own reputation and that of competitors, facilitating decisions which helped the company wrest control of the media agenda, promote an image in keeping with its strategic aim, and outperform competitors.

Sandra Macleod, Echo's CEO, concludes: "The definition of evaluation should be a wide one. The profile of the whole company from the perspective of every stakeholder, internal and external, should be our target. Only that way will we really have our radar trained on every aspect of our business, ready to catch every opportunity and every threat, from wherever these may come."

Continuous interactive image tracking

Some international companies are now installing interactive brand awareness tracking studies in major markets. These provide real-time information.

They involve setting up panels of individuals equipped with the electronic response terminals. They record awareness and opinions of a company or brands at regular intervals. By matching the increase or decrease in awareness, it is possible to identify the impact of various promotional events, conferences, advertising, special offers or PR initiatives.

These methods of monitoring public reactions are important enough on a day-by-day basis. But they increase in value in times of crisis or when there is a major burst of negative media coverage. The day-by-day responses can provide the skilled PR operative with a vital navigational aid. The data can be used to determine whether to adopt a low-key containment policy or whether to become proactive. What's more, those strategies can be varied from region to region, as this kind of research can pinpoint where an event has caused a major furor and where it has passed unnoticed.

Index